From Bangkok to Bali in 30 Minutes

From **Bangkok**

to **Bali** in 30 Minutes

175 Fast and Easy Recipes with
the Lush, Tropical Flavors
of Southeast Asia

Theresa Volpe Laursen
and **Byron Laursen**

The Harvard Common Press
Boston, Massachusetts

To Melodie and Sally,
for bringing all their gifts
to the table

THE HARVARD COMMON PRESS
535 ALBANY STREET
BOSTON, MASSACHUSETTS 02118
WWW.HARVARDCOMMONPRESS.COM

Printed in the United States of America
Printed on acid-free paper

Library of Congress Cataloging-in-Publication Data

Laursen, Theresa Volpe.
  From Bangkok to Bali in 30 minutes : 175 fast and easy recipes with the lush, tropical flavors of Southeast Asia / Theresa Volpe Laursen and Byron Laursen.
      p. cm.
Includes index.
  ISBN 1-55832-234-5 (hardcover : alk. paper) — ISBN 1-55832-235-3 (pbk. : alk. paper)
1. Cookery, Southeast Asian. I. Laursen, Byron. II. Title.
  TX724.5.S68L38 2003
  641.5959—dc21   2003001806

Special bulk-order discounts are available on this and other Harvard Common Press books. Companies and organizations may purchase books for premiums or resale, or may arrange a custom edition, by contacting the Marketing Director at the address above.

10 9 8 7 6 5 4 3 2 1

BOOK DESIGN BY DEBORAH KERNER/DANCING BEARS DESIGN
ILLUSTRATIONS BY RICHARD WAXBERG
COVER PHOTOGRAPH BY E.K. WALLER

Contents

Acknowledgments

Deborah Krasner is both an exceptional agent and a true friend. Her belief in us was steadfast. She loved our ideas from the very first. Her keen intelligence, integrity, and enthusiasm were extremely welcome sources of support—from concept to completion. She even laughs at our jokes, a real plus.

Thanks to our editor, Pam Hoenig, who immediately saw the potential in a cookbook unlike any that had been published before. Our publisher, Bruce Shaw, confidently backed Pam's vision with his own approval and commitment.

Valerie Cimino, managing editor, Virginia Downes, production manager, and Jodi Marchowsky, production editor, successfully oversaw a demanding production schedule, making sure that the many ingredients of this book blended smoothly. Sunshine Erickson and Dana Garczewski, our main contacts in the marketing and sales department, did a tremendous, thoroughly detailed job on behalf of this book, always with high enthusiasm and good cheer. Skye Stewart, publicist for The Harvard Common Press, did everything imaginable to make the larger world aware of the book you're now reading.

Deborah Kops provided a most meticulous, yet artistic, copyedit. Designer Deborah Kerner and illustrator Richard Waxberg seamlessly combined their talents to make this an especially inviting, beautiful book.

Jaye Myrick's inspired coaching helped shape an environment for us where creativity could flourish. We're also grateful to Anita Fore for her support and counsel.

Hula sister and great friend E. K. Waller, who applied her artistic vision, spirit, and vitality to our first cookbook, once again opened the resources of her terrific Los Angeles studio—and those of her keen eye and superb photography. Assisting her, always with a terrific sense of creative play, steady hands, and artful vision, was food stylist par excellence Wendy Blasdell of Edible Style.

Finally, we offer warm thanks to our helpful friends Carol Souvin at free hand and Tara Riceberg at Tesoro for providing stellar tableware to highlight our cover photograph.

China

India

BURMA

LAOS

Bay of Bengal

THAILAND

VIETNAM

CAMBODIA

South China Sea

Southeast Asia

MALAYSIA

SINGAPORE

MALAYSIA

Indian Ocean

I N D O N E S I A

(BORNEO)

(JAVA)

(BALI)

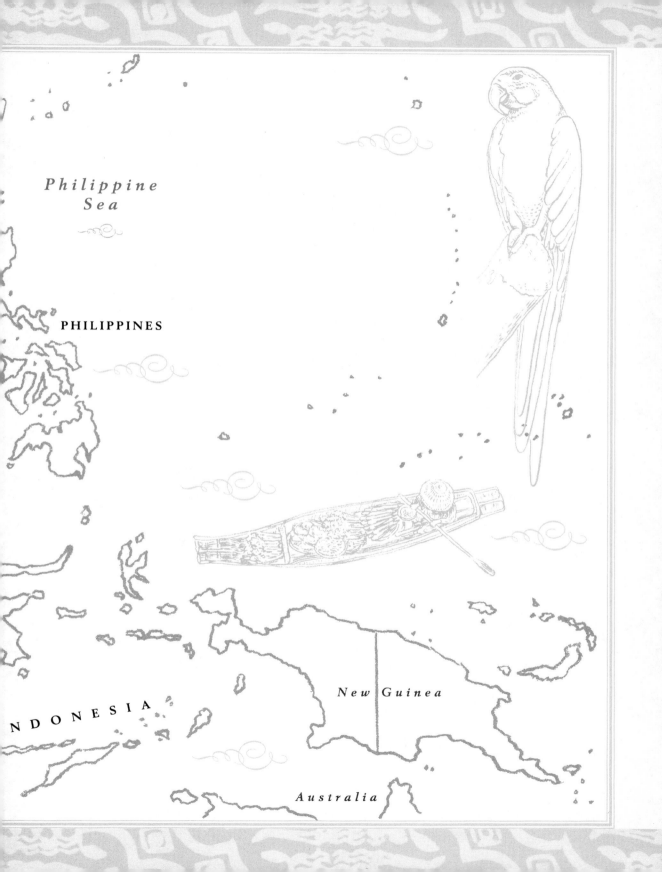

Philippine
Sea

PHILIPPINES

INDONESIA

New Guinea

Australia

A *Life* of *Flavor*

When I traveled to the Asian tropics in the late 1970s, very few Americans then knew that these nations were the homelands of some of the world's most fascinating, flavorful, and healthful cuisines. I went there partly to satisfy a sense of adventure, but mostly as someone who had sampled some of the fantastic flavors of the region and wanted to experience much more.

I was then living in Los Angeles and working in the film industry, and was both lucky and adventurous enough to eat frequently in the city's first Thai restaurants. In those days, Los Angeles was receiving the first waves of what would become a terrific post–Vietnam War influx of Thai and other Southeast Asian immigrants. (By the mid-1980s, Los Angeles had more Thai people than any city in the world, except Bangkok, while one of its suburbs drew so many immigrants from Vietnam that street signs in Vietnamese were put up everywhere.)

My love of food, and of travel, grew organically from my family background. My grandparents ventured from Ischia, a sister island to Capri, off the coast of Naples, to become island-dwelling Americans in a resort town near the southern tip of New Jersey. When I was little, their house was often packed with more aunts, uncles, and cousins than I could count, all of them enjoying wonderful Italian dishes from my grandmother's kitchen and laughing out loud at the familiar jokes and stories they told one another in Neapolitan dialect. I couldn't understand a word, yet I also couldn't help laughing along with them. Their spirit was so contagious and the shared delight in food was so heartening.

My grandfather Nicolo built a thriving business as a contractor, but also devoted a great deal of time and patience to gardening a plot of land he had purchased next door to his home. It was big enough to hold another house, and he proudly made it produce miracles. Everyone in the family was wonderfully surprised when, in the early 1950s, he gave that plot of land to my mother, Rose, and her sister, Theresa.

They had told him that they dreamed of establishing the town's first Italian restaurant. His garden plot was sacrificed to make their dream come true. They were both hard workers and Nicolo believed in them. He also believed that good food could evoke something powerful in people's hearts, a recognition of shared humanity, and that our town could use some of that kind of medicine. Italian-Americans of his generation were made sharply aware of the dominant culture's discrimination and disdain. Back then people called the Italian-American section of town Macaroni Street, and it was not said with affection.

"Feed the people," my grandfather told his daughters. "It's harder for them to hate you when they love your food."

Their restaurant, called Voltaco's, thrived. It was the town's first restaurant outside the norm of diners and restaurants serving Yankee-style overcooked deep-fried seafood, and it was happily embraced. It still thrives today, proudly proclaiming, "Serving the Shore Since '54!"

I identified strongly with my family's culinary heritage, but I was different from those who built their lives around the restaurant. Maybe I inherited more of the New World–seeking gene than the rest of them. This was especially obvious during and after my university days in Washington, D.C., because I had discovered there, very suddenly, almost every kind of ethnic restaurant that could be found within United States borders.

I loved those flavors. I craved them again and again. To the best of my ability, with the best cookbooks I could then find, I brought them to my family. On some occasions, my mother would take a curious and puzzled look over my shoulder in the kitchen and then ask me "Where did you come from?"

By the time I arrived in Los Angeles in 1972, Thai restaurants were multiplying all over the vast city, ubiquitous as taco stands. I was twenty-two, eager for any and all culinary adventures L.A. had to offer, and went happily and hungrily from one flavorful infatuation to the next. Then I discovered the Siam Restaurant on Hollywood Boulevard, and the thunderbolt struck. *Phat Thai*, fiery shrimp salad, stir-fried morning glory greens, jasmine rice . . . you never forget your first true love. It changed my life.

Babes in Thailand

Some years later, on a trek in northern Thailand, a girlfriend and I set off with a guide in his long-tailed riverboat to visit remote hill tribes. As we came around a wide bend in the river, we first saw the beautiful *nagas*, long dragon-like serpents in statue form defining the sides of a stairway that led from the riverbank into the jungle and up a muddy hill, cresting at an ornate temple that came into our view.

As we came ashore, I gradually became aware that the Thai lyrics filling the air were sung to a melody I knew very well: "I'm in love! I'm all shook up!" Elvis was reverberating in the Thai jungle.

People were selling lotus flowers to carry up to the temple as offerings. Once my floral offering had been accepted, someone smiled and gave me a ribbon printed with Thai script. I didn't learn what it said until a few years later, on one of my first dates with Byron, several months before we became partners both in marriage and in writing books.

Our Hollywood Romance

It was one of our first dates, and Byron and I had just given a waitress our dinner orders in Sompun, a sweet Thai restaurant located where the eastern edge of Hollywood blends into the district called Silverlake. I asked our waitress to read the imprinted ribbon I had saved from my Thai travels. She took it in her hands, studied the first few characters, and began to blush like a schoolgirl. After some hesitation, she told me that it was my fortune, and it said I would soon meet the one who was meant for me. And I suddenly heard that Thai Elvis singing again.

We come from very different backgrounds. In his family, bunny-ear pancakes on Sunday mornings were a consolation prize for eating fish sticks every Friday night. But Byron is a naturally gifted cook, with a wonderful, unruly, and adventurous palate. More than twenty years later, I still love to watch him in the kitchen, all six-foot-four of him, busily pacing, chopping, tearing, and tasting, his face radiating pleasure with himself and the dishes he is creating.

The Flavors Develop

Unhappy with the lack of Thai cookbooks on the market—the poorly translated ones from Thai originals only made the cuisine more unintelligible—we resolved to create the book we longed to have. And so, my dream of working in the kitchen of a Thai cook came true. Only it was my own kitchen, and the chef was from L.A.'s acclaimed Siamese Princess. Every week for several years, he came to our house to cook. Our combined efforts resulted in *True Thai: The Modern Art of Thai Cooking*. From the outset, our new familiarity with ingredients such as fish sauce, cilantro roots, and palm sugar led me to punctuate everyday Western dishes with the hot-sweet-sour-salty-pungent flavors of Southeast Asia. It was so much fun, and ultimately became a chapter in *True Thai* called Cooking with a Thai Accent. With a firm foundation of tradition, respect, and love, it is wonderful to innovate freely in directions dictated by personal taste and delight.

We approached the recipes in this new book with the same joyful spirit. It is how we hope your journey with us through Thailand, Vietnam, Laos, Cambodia, Burma, Indonesia, Malaysia, and the Philippines, will progress—from traditional Thai curries to Insalata Siam (page 123), from Vietnamese-Style Hot-and-Sour Shrimp Soup with Pineapple (page 115) to Philly-Style Vietnamese Hoagies (pages 186 and 203), and Malay Chilli Shrimp (page 211) to Malay Tiger (page 42) cocktails.

It Happened One Night

From *Bangkok to Bali in 30 Minutes* was conceived at a promotional appearance for our first cookbook. It was a pre-holiday evening, in a suburb along Philadelphia's Main Line. A young but somewhat harried-looking matron rushed up to our table. "I'll buy your book," she said, "if you can show me three easy recipes I can make for a dinner party tomorrow, without any fancy ingredients, that my kids will like too."

We instantly replied, "Coconut Rice, Bangkok-Style Barbecued Chicken, Sweet-and-Spicy Dipping Sauce." Sold!

This "Three Easy Pieces" experience got us thinking. Thai and other Southeast Asian cuisines had grown infinitely more popular since the days when we launched our cookbook odyssey. Our Main Line dinner party hostess represented what must be many thousands of home cooks who would love to have first-hand creative experience with the lively flavors they've tasted in their travels and in Southeast Asian restaurants, but who wanted to get that experience quickly and easily.

From *Bangkok to Bali in 30 Minutes* is our response. We've set out to offer a great selection of simple-to-prepare recipes that deliver the fresh, seductive flavors of tropical Asia. It will not only take you from Bangkok to Bali, but also to Saigon, Singapore, Vientiane, Phnom Penh, Manila, and many other stops in one of the most diverse and amazing corners of this blue-green planet. Thirty minutes is our benchmark. Even when a dish requires extra time—to marinate or roast, for example—the active time for the cook is kept to a minimum. And you'll find tips on making and freezing, say, a double batch of Thai Red Curry Paste (page 292), which you can use later to make Spicy Peanut Sauce (page 88), Chilli-Buttered Corn on the Cob (page 254), Charred Beef in Red Curry with Green Peppercorns (page 187), and other complexly flavored dishes at a moment's notice.

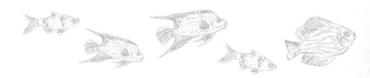

Style and Spirit

From Bangkok to Bali, through the Spice Islands of Malayasia and the ornate temple ruins of Angkor Wat, these exotic tropical Asian locales evoke not only the intriguing flavors of green coconuts, curries, and satés, and the delicious arrays of tropical fruits, but also a delicious lifestyle: tropical breezes, swaying palms, vivid colors under a hot sun, a sweet languor inspired by nature's abundance.

From Bangkok to Bali's recipes will take you there. And, if you'd like to make the experience even more sensuous, the following suggestions will bring the style and spirit of tropical Asia into your home.

Add a few Asian herbs, such as licorice-scented Thai basil, lemon, or holy basil to your herb garden. Vietnamese coriander has a special character, too, a cross between mint and cilantro. These herbs thrive in the same sun and soil conditions as their American cousins. Leafy spears of fresh lemon grass, which can take over a corner of the garden, grow equally well in a large pot on a sunny patio.

For your table linens, use a mix of bright, tropical colors—hot pinks, lemons, limes, and inky purples. Banana leaves (found in the frozen food sections of Asian and Latin markets) make beautifully rustic place mats or can be used as a colorful accent beneath the food on your serving platters.

While no special equipment is required for these recipes, a granite mortar and pestle will look handsome on your counter and will also bring home the authentic sounds of a tropical Asian kitchen while bringing out the deepest essences of every ingredient in your spice mixtures. When not in use, the mortar can be heaped with bright red chillies for a simple, colorful centerpiece.

We love large, traditional woks, the ones with fat, round bottoms. But flat-bottom woks are terrific too and they stay balanced on your stove top. Heavy, deep-sided skillets and grill pans are just as useful. But remember, with cooking equipment, bigger is better. A stone mortar should be at least 6 inches in diameter, a wok, 14 inches. Otherwise, it's like cooking spaghetti in too little water or trying to toss a salad in a tiny bowl. Give yourself room to pound, toss, and stir-fry with ease.

Thai people express a whole philosophy with a single word—*sanuk*. When something is *sanuk*, it's fun, lighthearted, and rewarding every step of the way. In Laos, the common greeting is not "How are you?" but "Have you eaten?" In asking the question, they're really asking, "Are you well?" because to eat well is to *be* well. And in Bali, the God of Fire, as embodied by each home's cook stove, is honored every morning with a small offering of rice.

As these examples show, the tropical Asian approach to hospitality is centered on ritual expressions of gratitude and generosity. To embrace this tropical Asian spirit, it's important to use the best and freshest ingredients, but even more vital, to offer a welcoming smile in a friendly, relaxing atmosphere. Whether you're enjoying a simple snack with the children or hosting a multicourse dinner party, savor each moment—from shopping to presentation—and serve your food with a happy heart and generous spirit. Then all will be *sanuk*, richly enjoyable and deeply flavorful. It has been a wonderful experience to share this chapter in a life of flavor with you, and I wish you many memorable culinary adventures.

With love and spices,
THERESA VOLPE LAURSEN

The *Tropical Asian Pantry*

Southeast Asian cooking is a great art form, but there's really less mystery to it than you might expect. After all, millions of native cooks make these beautiful dishes, and make them quite handily, every day.

Whatever mystery you may find will quickly begin to vanish, just as soon as you gain familiarity with some of the key ingredients described in this chapter. These include various fruits—some used both in their ripe state and when they are still green—and an intriguing variety of noodles ranging from very wide to very thin, along with lively fresh herbs and many spices, spice blends, and chilli pastes.

Of course, you don't need to go out and buy all of these ingredients before you begin. It wouldn't make sense: some are used frequently, some rarely. There are a few items, though, that can be considered staples. You will notice that in general these cuisines use an abundance of onions, garlic, shallots, peppercorns, and a few other items you probably already keep in your kitchen. Beyond these, we always keep the following on hand: jasmine rice, palm sugar, fish sauce, coconut milk, *sri racha* hot sauce, light soy sauce, sweet dark soy sauce, pure chilli powder, and liquid tamarind concentrate.

Other items you may want to simply grow for yourself, such as cilantro, which appears in all the cuisines outlined in this book. If you grow your own, you'll have the added advantage of being able to harvest the roots, which many green grocers discard, but which Southeast Asian cooks prize. Thai basil (*horapha*) and lemon grass are also good candidates for your home garden, even if that garden is limited to a sunny window box.

Begin your exploration by choosing a recipe that you'd like to try. If there are any ingredients that you aren't sure about, look them up in the pages of this chapter. Bit by bit, you'll develop a sure hand with these, the bold colors that make this culinary art form so vivid.

Anchovy Paste

Tropical Asian cooks make frequent use of a pungent, fermented product known as dried shrimp paste. It's terrific for building a strong base of flavor for curry pastes and sauces, but shrimp paste requires special handling, and a whole container ought to be used fairly soon once it has been opened. You can get much the same flavor, without those difficulties, by using anchovy paste, which comes in convenient, toothpaste-like tubes. Look for it in well-stocked supermarkets and specialty stores.

Baby Corn

Sometimes available fresh, but most often water-packed in a can, baby corn are tiny whole ears of corn prized for their sweetness and crunchiness. Most supermarkets and Asian groceries stock them. You will find them in stir-fries and mixed vegetable dishes, especially in Thailand, Indonesia, and Malaysia.

Basil

Botanists believe that basil may have originated in either Thailand or India. In addition to the Mediterranean type (usually called sweet or Italian basil) most commonly found in the West, there are many more delightfully different varieties found in Asia, especially Thailand and Vietnam. There are three main varieties of Asian basil, all of which are used in Thai cooking.

Thai Sweet Basil: Simply called Thai basil in the United States, this variety is known as *bai horapha* in Thailand and *rau hung* in Vietnam. It is perhaps the best known and most loved of the Asian basils. It's a beautiful plant with dark green leaves set off by deep purple stems and plump clusters of purple flowers. Its rich licorice fragrance and flavor are absolutely addictive. Fresh Thai basil can be found in Asian markets and upscale supermarkets. The plants are often available in well-stocked nurseries (see Sources for listings of seed catalogs, too). The best substitute for Thai basil is a full-flavored variety such as purple or opal basil. You can use Italian basil for its fresh, sweet taste, but you will miss out on the heady scent and vivid anise flavor that *horapha* imparts.

Holy or Sacred Basil (*Kaprao*): This pungent variety has a clove-like taste. It is often used in stir-fries because, unlike most varieties of basil, it intensifies in flavor with a little cooking.

Lemon Basil (*Manglak*): A variety with a clean, lemon-lime taste and scent, lemon basil is usually chopped and sprinkled over dishes as a garnish. Its citrusy flavor is especially welcome on fish and other seafood dishes.

While we encourage you to add holy basil and lemon basil to your herb garden (see Sources for listings of seed catalogs) and favorite recipes, Thai basil is our choice for all the recipes in the book calling for Asian basil.

Chilli Pastes

Chinese Chilli-Garlic Sauce: This Szechuan staple gives you a powerful dose of flavor and heat, as both its crimson color and its raw, fermented aroma suggest it will do. It is used throughout Southeast Asia, showing how pervasive Chinese influence is in the region. Many supermarkets carry the Lee Kum Kee brand, or look for the Lan Chi brand in Asian markets; see Sources for mail order.

Sambal Oelek: This vivid red Indonesian paste is made of ground fresh chillies with a little salt and occasionally vinegar, combining lots of heat with a bit of sour tang. It is a simple hot sauce, used to flavor everything from soups to salad dressings. If you don't have fresh chilli peppers, just add *sambal oelek* to taste. The Huy Fong Foods brand (look for the red rooster on the label), in 8-ounce plastic jars, is a staple in most Asian markets and well-stocked supermarkets; see Sources for mail order. You can always substitute Tabasco sauce.

Thai Roasted Chilli Paste: Known in its homeland as *nam phrik pao*, this paste is often labeled "Chilli Paste in Soybean Oil." It is a key ingredient in Thai soups and Asian salad dressings. Be aware, though, that there are many types of chilli pastes. To be sure you're getting Thai roasted chilli paste, check to see that tamarind (or, alternatively, "citrus fruit") is listed as an ingredient. *Nam phrik pao* can be found in Thai and Asian markets. The Maesri brand from Thailand comes in 16-ounce jars and is quite good; see Sources for mail order.

Chilli Peppers, Dried

Dried red chillies are a staple ingredient for making the great curry pastes of Thailand and other Southeast Asian countries. Combining two or more varieties creates a layering of taste and heat for richness and depth of flavor. Almost all of the chilli peppers listed below can be found in specialty stores and Latin markets; also check the Sources section.

California Chilli Pepper: Long and mild, this pepper dries to a rich, deep shade of red.

Chile de Arbol: The name of this pepper translates as "tree chilli" in Spanish. Short, thin, and potent, it can be effectively blended in curry pastes with larger, milder varieties.

Guajillo Chilli Pepper: The Guajillo look like its California and New Mexico cousins, but it is a lighter shade of red and has slightly more heat.

Japanese Chilli Pepper: A thin, short variety with plenty of heat, this pepper closely resembles chile de arbol. Like the arbol, it is great for combining with dried large, mild chillies to raise the temperature of a curry paste.

New Mexico Chilli Pepper: Similar in size and color to the California chilli pepper, the New Mexico has more heat and an earthier flavor.

Pure Chilli Powder: Made from finely ground dried red chilli peppers, pure chilli powder is hotter than the "chilli powder" found in supermarkets, which contains other spices as well. For the recipes in this book, use a hot chilli powder without additives (check the label to be sure). Powder from New Mexico chilli peppers has beautiful color and good heat. *Prik pon*, the Thai variety found in Thai markets, is usually past its prime. Instead, buy a fresh, bright chilli powder. We like hot or extra-hot varieties from The Chile Shop in New Mexico; see Sources. Fine quality pure chilli powder can also be found in well-stocked supermarkets. You can also substitute red pepper flakes.

Chilli Peppers, Fresh

Fresh chilli peppers are the New World's greatest gift to tropical Asian cuisine. Before Portuguese traders introduced the chilli pepper, Southeast Asian cooks relied on black pepper and ginger to add heat to a dish. Many kinds of chilli peppers are used in the region. Fortunately, two that are easy to find in American, Asian, and Latin markets—serranos and small Thai chilli peppers—happen to be perfect for most Southeast Asian dishes. Jalapeños are not recommended as they are hot, but comparatively bland, and throw off the taste of spicy Asian dishes. If the right chillies aren't available, it is better to use a little *sambal oelek* instead. Timid

American cooks often take the time to remove the seeds from chillies, but Asian cooks never do. Not only do they want all the heat the chilli can deliver, they also figure that any part of the plant that has the power to create new life is likely to be good for you medicinally.

By the way, do not drink water if you get too fired up with chilli heat. You'll get two seconds of relief, followed by more searing heat. Beer or wine will lessen the burn, and they both go so well with the food. Milk or yogurt will help tame the fire, too, or plain rice or bread, or simply a few grains of salt.

Serrano Chillies: These are short—about two inches long—hot, plump, and green. Though serranos are typically associated with South-of-the-Border cuisines, they have a robust flavor that is perfect for tropical Asian cooking as well. Many Thai who have come to the United States have developed a fondness for using serranos. They are now grown in Thailand, too. You'll find fresh serranos in Latin and Asian markets and well-stocked supermarkets.

Small Thai Chillies: Called *phrik khee nu* or Thai bird chillies, these prove the rule that the tinier the pepper, the greater the impact. Slender, 1 to 1¹/₂ inches in length, and red or green in color, they deliver plenty of flavor with their considerable heat. We like to use them in any dish that calls for a definite zing. Look for *phrik khee nu* in well-stocked supermarkets, specialty markets, and Asian markets.

Chinese Five-Spice Powder

Usually used to flavor roast meat dishes in Vietnam and Singapore, this is a mixture of finely ground star anise, cinnamon, fennel seeds, and Szechuan peppercorns. It can be found in Asian markets and well-stocked supermarkets; see Sources for mail order.

Cilantro

Also known as Chinese parsley or fresh coriander, this is the most popular herb in the world. It can bring out the flavors of a delicate dish and moderate the flavors of one that is quite rich. Cilantro looks similar to Italian parsley, with its broad green leaves. Its unique flavor carries notes of both grass and citrus. The leaves are used for garnishing and flavoring, but the roots and stems have the most concentrated flavor. They are best used in spice pastes, stir-fries, and salad dressing. Unfortunately, many greengrocers discard the roots. We grow our own cilantro from seed, resowing every few weeks because the plant's growth cycle is quite short. If you grow your own cilantro, you'll always have the freshest possible, and you'll be able to use the roots as well. Harvest a bunch at a time: trim off the roots, wash the herb, and dry it thoroughly, and store in a freezer bag; it will keep two to three months stored that way.

Coconut

Coconut Milk and Its Cream (Canned, Unsweetened): Coconut milk, which contains cream, is a key ingredient in most tropical Asian curries and quite a few soups as well. Creamy and rich, it is extracted from freshly grated coconut meat steeped in hot water. Some people like to make their own, but it's far more convenient to buy a quality brand of canned coconut milk. Just be sure you don't buy the sweetened kind, which is sold in liquor stores for use in mixed drinks, or the low-fat kind, which tastes awful. We like the Thai brands of canned coconut milk best. If you do not shake the can before opening, you will find the thick cream at the top. Once opened, canned coconut milk is highly perishable and should be stored in the refrigerator for no more than two or three days. We love the 19-ounce cans of the Mae Ploy brand for their generous amount of rich coconut cream. Also look for the 14-ounce cans of Chaokah and Chef's Choice. Asian markets have the best selection and lowest prices but even your local supermarket is likely to carry one or two brands. If not, ask them to carry it.

Coconut Palm Vinegar: This native Filipino vinegar, made from coconut sap, is less acidic than rice vinegar or plain white distilled vinegar. It's highly prized for its tang and bright fragrance in such classic Filipino dishes as *adobo* and *kinilau*, which is similar to ceviche. Look for it in Asian markets or see Sources for mail order; if you can't find it, dilute five parts regular distilled white vinegar with three parts water, or as specified in a given recipe.

Dried Shredded Coconut (Unsweetened): The dried shredded coconut you'll find in your supermarket's baking section is heavily sugared, and won't work for tropical Asian cooking. Unsweetened dried shredded coconut is naturally rich and sweet, and takes well to light toasting. It is added to sweet dishes, rice, curries, and salads. It is readily available in most health food stores and specialty stores, and well-stocked supermarkets; see Sources for mail order.

Fish Sauce

The ancient Romans made a sauce just like the kind used throughout tropical Asia: a fermented concoction of salt-packed fresh fish or shellfish. Fish sauce usually comes in a tall bottle and will last indefinitely without refrigeration. It is a thin, translucent, salty brown liquid, pungent in aroma, yet milder in flavor than soy sauce. It preserves the rich protein and vitamin content of the fish, and is a vital part of the everyday diet of Southeast Asians. Fish sauce has been used for at least 1,000 years in the cuisines of Thailand, Vietnam, Laos, Cambodia, and Indonesia. Burma and the Philippines also have a long history with fish sauce. Malaysia is the only Southeast Asian country that seems to prefer light Chinese-style soy sauce instead.

Cooking tames the pungency of fish sauce, leaving a subtle flavor that unifies all the others in the dish. The highest quality only costs a few pennies more; buy it. Avoid brands that include sugar, as some of the newer Vietnamese imports do. We like the Thai (*nam pla*) and Vietnamese (*nuoc mam*) varieties best. While there is no substitute for fish sauce, you can now find it in well-stocked supermarkets as well as Asian markets and specialty food stores.

Garlic

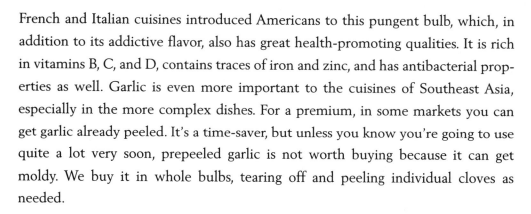

French and Italian cuisines introduced Americans to this pungent bulb, which, in addition to its addictive flavor, also has great health-promoting qualities. It is rich in vitamins B, C, and D, contains traces of iron and zinc, and has antibacterial properties as well. Garlic is even more important to the cuisines of Southeast Asia, especially in the more complex dishes. For a premium, in some markets you can get garlic already peeled. It's a time-saver, but unless you know you're going to use quite a lot very soon, prepeeled garlic is not worth buying because it can get moldy. We buy it in whole bulbs, tearing off and peeling individual cloves as needed.

Pickled Garlic: Garlic makes a surprisingly crisp, piquant, highly satisfying pickle—very popular in Thailand for use in soups, salads, and noodle dishes. Look for it in well-stocked Asian markets and specialty food stores.

Ginger

Siamese ginger is grown and used extensively throughout Southeast Asia, but in America, common ginger is much easier to find and can be substituted for it. Buy firm, fresh gingerroot with smooth, shiny skin. It should feel heavy enough to indicate there's still moisture inside. Gingerroot lasts up to two weeks in the refrigerator.

Baby Ginger: As spring turns to summer, harvest begins in the ginger fields of Hawaii. These roots, picked early in the season, are so tender that their skins are pinkish and translucent. This is ginger at its best: juicy, peppery, highly fragrant.

Pester your grocer to stock it. Because it is more perishable, much of the baby ginger crop is pickled and sold in Asian markets.

Siamese Ginger: Also called *galanga*, this variety of ginger has a lemony note and is a bit more peppery and aromatic than common ginger. Fresh Siamese ginger is bulbous and somewhat woody, with a yellow cast and pinkish knobs and sprouts. It is used primarily to flavor soup broths and curry pastes, and it is also steeped in hot water to make ginger tea. Both fresh and frozen Siamese ginger can be found in Asian markets. The dried form, called Laos powder, has more intense heat and is not recommended.

Pungent, Hot, and Healthy

For centuries, cooks throughout Southeast Asia have thought of good food as good medicine. Now medical science confirms it: The love of fresh, raw foods, pungently spiced, is a great strategy for long-term health.

Garlic, for example, lowers blood pressure while it fights bacterial infections. It also may help prevent emphysema or damage to the lungs from bronchitis. Garlic and onions also work much like aspirin, suppressing prostaglandins—chemicals that cause pain and inflammation. That may explain why ancient Egyptians worshipped garlic.

Ginger, like garlic, thins the blood and thus brings down blood pressure. It also reduces seasickness, which is why people living in boats in Hong Kong regularly chew pieces of raw ginger. Ginger also works to prevent cancer, as do shallots, pineapples, eggplants, and cabbage, along with many other fruits and vegetables. This may be why vegetarians have less cancer, stroke, and heart disease than meat eaters.

Bananas, meanwhile, may strengthen surface cells of the stomach lining, helping to prevent ulcers.

Lemon juice and lime juice, besides creating low-fat salad dressings, deliver lots of vitamin C.

Oyster mushrooms may strengthen the immune system, while shiitake mushrooms are a strong antiviral agent. Both may also help prevent arthritis and multiple sclerosis.

Chilli peppers speed up your metabolism, helping you burn calories even while sitting still. And the burning sensation they induce signals your brain to release natural pain blockers called endorphins.

Chilli peppers are also mucokinetic, which means they thin the fluids in your body, allowing your system to cleanse itself more easily. That's why a strong dose of chilli heat may put tears in your eyes, or give you a runny nose. This greatly benefits your lungs, where fluids that sit stagnant can cause disease. In a study of chilli-loving Latino men living in Los Angeles, the majority—including many who smoked cigarettes—had remarkably healthy lungs.

Kaffir Lime

The kaffir lime is a citrus tree native to Southeast Asia. Its fruits have bumpy, deep green skins and extraordinary fragrance. Southeast Asian cooks use only the fruit's peel and zest and the leaves of the tree. The juice is used in medicines and cosmetics. Fresh U.S.-grown kaffir limes can be found in Southeast Asian markets in most big cities.

Kaffir Lime Leaves: The fragrant oils in the leaves of the kaffir lime are released by simmering them in soups or slicing the fresh leaves into ultrafine matchsticks, which can be sprinkled over soups, curries, and salads. You can substitute the peel or the zest of the common lime. Fresh, U.S.-grown kaffir lime leaves can be found in Southeast Asian markets in most big cities. Asian markets everywhere should have packages of kaffir lime leaves in their freezer section; see Sources for mail-order kaffir lime trees and freshly cut leaves.

Lemon Grass

This easy-to-grow, aromatic tropical grass is about two feet tall, with long spear-shaped leaves. It imparts a smooth, bright, nonacidic lemon flavor and fragrance to spice pastes, soups, and salads. The stalks are sheathed with tough outer layers that you peel away to reach the tender inner stem, which is usually only slightly thicker than a pencil. Lemon grass can be steeped in water to make tea, sliced ultra-fine for salads, pounded into curry pastes, or sliced and simmered in soups. Fresh lemon grass is readily available in Asian markets and upscale supermarkets. The dried form lacks the sweet perfume and flavor of fresh lemon grass. You can substitute the peel, or zest, of fresh lemon; see Sources for freshly cut stalks and plants.

Mango

This is the world's second most popular fruit, outsold only by the banana. Mangoes offer a pleasurable spectrum of honeyed and peach-like flavors. Southeast Asians have cultivated them for at least 5,000 years, and they have a vast number of varieties to enjoy. At the peak of ripeness, mangoes are eaten out of hand for a snack, sliced into salads, intricately carved into edible art, or pressed into the most sublime iced juice. Ripe mangoes are also used in ice creams, blender drinks, and chutneys. Choose mangoes that are fairly firm with some yellow-orange color and a red or crimson blush. There should be some sweet perfume from the stem end, no matter how faint. The best varieties are often found in Indian groceries. Since Western markets most often carry greenish fruit, keep them a few days at room temperature, until they become more tender and aromatic.

Green Mango: Before the blush shows on their skin, before the sugars develop in their flesh, mangoes are firm and have a green skin with tart, pale gold flesh. They taste something like a Granny Smith apple and can be used in refreshing salads, dips, and pickles. If the recipe calls for green mangoes, check any Asian market or just select the greenest ones from your local supermarket and use them immediately.

Noodles

The Chinese influence on the cuisines of tropical Asia is nowhere more obvious than in the wide variety of noodle dishes prepared every day and the many kinds of noodles used. All of the noodles listed below can be found in Asian markets and well-stocked supermarkets.

Bean Thread Vermicelli: Because these white noodles turn transparent and gelatinous as you cook them, they're also called cellophane noodles, glass noodles, and silver noodles. Made from flour derived from mung beans, or bean sprouts as they are called in America, these noodles have little or no taste, but handily absorb the flavors of whatever dish they're in. They are sold dried, packaged in bundles of 1.7 and 3.5 ounces.

Chinese Egg Noodles: Dried and fresh egg noodles come in both thin and wide varieties. They are usually used in pan-fried and stir-fried dishes. You can substitute an Italian pasta such as fettuccine for the flat egg noodles.

Rice Noodles (Fresh): Fresh rice flour noodles are thick and wonderfully soft and chewy. You will find them in plastic envelopes, either in a sheet form that has been folded, or cut into wide strips. Already pliant, they have been steamed and don't need to be soaked—just rinse them briefly in warm water to wash off their protective oil coating and make the noodles easy to separate before cooking. They are usually tumbled into the sauce as one of the final steps of a stir-fry.

Rice Sticks: These dried rice noodles are opaque and brittle and made from rice flour. Unlike wheat flour noodles, rice sticks are never boiled. They just need a bit of presoaking—never more than 30 minutes. Rice stick noodles come in various widths. Rice vermicelli, called *pancit bihon* in the Philippines, is string-like, even thinner than angel hair pasta, and is used primarily in soups, salads, and stir-fries. Medium rice sticks are all-purpose noodles. *Chantaboon* is the Thai name for the ¼-inch-wide rice stick noodles used in *phat Thai*, quite possibly that nation's favorite dish, a stir-fry with shrimp and/or bits of pork and chicken, and a host of extras, such as ribbons of omelet and salted radish, tumbled with crushed peanuts in a savory tamarind sauce.

Palm Sugar

Often added to curries and stir-fries, this tropical sugar is derived from the sap of the palmyra palm. It is a coarse, golden-toned sugar and imparts a light hint of caramel. Sold in round, hard disks or as a paste in cans or small plastic jars, it is somewhat paste-like in warm weather, but hardens into a cake when cold. The disks can be easily grated on a cheese or box grater for measuring. Once you've tried this flavorful sugar in a cup of tea, you'll want to keep it around at all times. Avoid the heavier, dark brown variety. Palm sugar is available in most Asian markets and some specialty stores; see Sources for mail order. If you can't get palm sugar, light brown sugar can be substituted.

Papaya

Shaped somewhat like a little football, a papaya is a very healthful and tasty tropical fruit with tender, fragrant flesh just beneath the peel. American markets usually stock Hawaii-grown papayas, which weigh about one pound, but other varieties can be much larger. Choose papayas that yield only slightly to the touch, with more yellow than green showing on the skin. The thin skin is peeled away and the black seeds are often discarded, although Thai cooks sometimes use them in salad dressings for their earthy, peppery flavor.

Green Papaya: Just like a green mango, a green papaya is light in natural sugars and makes a terrific salad ingredient when julienned. Those unfamiliar with green papayas are often startled at the pristine white seeds and flesh revealed when an unripe papaya is cut in half. But that's exactly what you should see. The seeds are discarded, the flesh peeled and sliced. With their moist, firm flesh and bland taste—much like that of a jicama—green papayas are treated like a vegetable rather than a fruit. They can be cooked, as in our recipe for Braised Chicken with Green Papaya (page 202). Green papayas can be found in Asian markets or up-scale supermarkets.

Peppercorns

Black peppercorns are the dried berries of the pepper vine. White peppercorns are black peppercorns with their black husks removed. Before Europeans brought the chilli peppers to Southeast Asian, pepper was the dominant heat-provoking spice. It's still quite important.

Green Peppercorns in Brine: In tropical Asia, people gather soft, immature peppercorns from the vines. The closest equivalent in this country are green peppercorns packed in brine. Green peppercorns are especially good in curries. Canned and bottled green peppercorns are found in Asian markets and well-stocked supermarkets.

Rice

Rice, of course, is a defining element in any Asian cuisine. Tropical Asian countries, especially Thailand, are beautifully suited to rice cultivation—thanks to mountains that collect rainfall and empty it onto plains, which can be flooded to create rice paddies.

Jasmine Rice: The favorite rice in Thailand, and well regarded throughout the Asian tropics, jasmine rice carries a light floral scent and a subtle nut-like flavor. Long-grained and white, it has a slight translucence. We buy our jasmine rice in 3-, 10-, or 25-pound bags at Asian markets, where you'll find the highest quality at the lowest prices. Many well-stocked supermarkets and specialty stores also carry jasmine rice.

Sticky Rice: This variety, which is most common in mountainous regions, has a high gluten content, so it sticks to itself handily—making it perfect for finger-style eating, dipping into curries and sauces, and popping the food into your mouth. It is shorter grained than jasmine rice and more opaque. Look for sticky rice in Asian markets and well-stocked supermarkets.

Rice Vinegar

Although fresh lime juice and tamarind sauce are more often used by Southeast Asian cooks when they want to add a sour flavor, rice vinegar shows up in dipping sauces and salad dressings, where a more delicate balance of sour-hot-salty-sweet is desired. Rice vinegar is made from fermented rice. The Japanese rice vinegar found in most supermarkets is fine to use in Southeast Asian recipes. Be aware that seasoned rice vinegar has sugar added. Unless otherwise requested, use plain rice vinegar.

Saigon Cinnamon

We are fortunate that high quality cinnamon, hand harvested in the mountains of Vietnam, is now being exported to the United States. In the past, Vietnamese cinnamon was thought to be inferior. That's because only the poorest grades reached America. Spice enthusiasts rank the newly exported premium Vietnamese cinnamon as the world's best. With a higher oil content than most, this cinnamon is sweeter, brighter, warmer, and more aromatic than the hot, musky Chinese and Indonesian types most frequently found on our supermarket shelves. Vann's Spices was one of the first to import this premium grade, calling it Saigon cinnamon, after the port of Saigon, from which it is shipped. McCormick's soon followed, also calling theirs Saigon cinnamon. It has become a best-seller for their upscale line, called McCormick's Gourmet Collection. Like Vann's, they package this premium cinnamon in glass bottles. Both companies have a store locator service on their

Web sites and via their 800 numbers (see Sources for these and other purveyors). Or ask your supermarket to stock Saigon cinnamon. You can substitute regular cinnamon.

Sesame Oil

Plain sesame oil, made from raw sesame seeds, is sometimes used for cooking, especially for stir-fries in Indonesia and in some other Southeast Asian countries. You can find good quality cold-pressed sesame oil in health food stores.

Toasted Sesame Oil: Made from toasted sesame seeds, toasted sesame oil has a rich, golden color and wonderfully nutty taste and aroma. Unlike plain sesame oil, it is not used as a cooking oil. It serves as a condiment, drizzled over stir-fried noodles in Indonesia, for example, or blended into East-West salad dressings. You'll find toasted sesame oil in well-stocked supermarkets, health food and specialty stores, and Asian markets.

Shallots

The shallot, not used much by American cooks, is a smaller, milder, subtler cousin of the onion. Supermarkets and gourmet stores often charge high prices for shallots, but in Asian markets they're always plentiful and inexpensive.

Shrimp Chips

With their subtle, seafood-y undertaste, these puffy and crisp deep-fried wafers of shrimp and tapioca are delicious as snack chips, or as an accompaniment for salads and dips. They are known as *krupuks* in Indonesia and Malaysia, where they are most common. The Vietnamese, who call them *banh phonz tom*, love them for scooping up their tangy, herb-laden salads. You can fry dehydrated wafers for maximum freshness (see page 285), or buy them already prepared and bagged like potato chips. The dried wafers and prepared chips are available in Asian markets. Some specialty stores and well-stocked supermarkets also carry the chips.

Shrimp Paste

This key flavoring agent in Southeast Asian cooking is made from tiny, sun-dried shrimp, which are mixed with salt and ground to a thick, soft paste. You can find it in any Asian market. The Thai brands are usually best.

Shrimp paste delivers a pungent aroma and a salty, assertive taste. It is used, therefore, only in small amounts. Most cooks roast their shrimp paste first, to enhance the aroma and smooth out the raw taste. Traditionally, this would be done in a banana leaf. Modern cooks simply seal the paste in a double thickness of aluminum foil and roast it in a dry skillet over medium heat for a few minutes, turning the packet over once or twice, until the fragrance develops.

We often substitute anchovy paste. It's readily available in supermarkets and comes in convenient, toothpaste-like tubes. Use an equal amount of anchovy paste for the shrimp paste listed in any given recipe.

Soy Sauce

Soy sauce was first used in China over 3,000 years ago, and the Japanese began making it about 400 years later. Soy sauce remains little changed from the thin, salty liquid of that time, except that today it is completely filtered and free of any bits of the fermented soybeans used to produce it. There are two main types: dark and light. Plain dark soy sauce is rather thick, with a deeper flavor, although it is less salty than light soy. The Japanese tamari is an example of plain dark soy sauce. Southeast Asian cooks, however, prefer a sweet dark soy sauce. Both light soy and sweet dark soy sauces are manufactured throughout Southeast Asia.

Kecap Manis: Ketchup, that favorite American condiment, derives its name from *kecap manis*, an Indonesian-style sweet dark soy sauce. This fragrant blend of light soy sauce, palm sugar, garlic, star anise, and Siamese ginger is used as both an ingredient for cooking and a table condiment. Like sweet dark soy sauce, which makes a fine substitute for it, *kecap manis* is not very salty. It has a thicker consistency than light soy sauce. You can substitute a mixture of one part light soy sauce to three parts pure maple syrup. You'll find *kecap manis* in Asian markets; see Sources for mail order.

Light Soy Sauce: Light, or thin, soy sauce is a Chinese-style soy sauce made from soybeans roasted with wheat, yeast, and salt. It is the most readily available type and is usually labeled simply "soy sauce." Kikkoman brand is found in most supermarkets (don't confuse light soy sauce with the company's "lite" soy, however, which is low in sodium). We also like the San J and Eden brands, found in health food stores. When shopping in Asian markets, look for Pearl River Bridge Golden Label Superior Soy Sauce.

Sweet Dark Soy Sauce: This is slightly thicker soy sauce, with molasses or caramel added to create a rich, sweet flavor that's very useful in sauces and marinades. Sometimes you will find sweet dark soy sauce simply labeled "sweet sauce." You can substitute *kecap manis* or use a mixture of one part light soy sauce to three parts pure maple syrup. Sweet dark soy sauce can be found in Asian markets; see Sources for mail order.

Thai Mushroom Soy Sauce: This is a pale, thin soy sauce with mushroom essence added to create a great flavor enhancer. It adds subtle depth and dimension to any broth or mild-flavored sauce. You can substitute light soy sauce, but you won't have quite as interesting a flavor. Never confuse Thai mushroom soy with the Chinese brands, such as Pearl River Bridge, which are much heavier and sweeter, in the manner of sweet dark soy sauce. We like the Thai brand called Healthy Boy sold in Asian markets; see Sources for mail order.

Spring Roll Wrappers

These supremely thin and delicate crepes are made of flour and water. You will find them, both square and round, in the freezer section, in packages of 10 or 25. Defrost them in the refrigerator before opening. They are easier to separate if you trim the edges slightly. Any that you don't use can go into a zipper-top plastic bag or other freezer container, to be refrigerated for up to a week or refrozen for up to a month. Most Asian markets and well-stocked supermarkets carry spring roll wrappers.

Sri Racha Hot Sauce

Originally, *sri racha* referred only to a certain spicy, garlicky, rich, smooth Thai chilli sauce produced in the seaside village for which it is named. Its popularity as an all-purpose hot sauce has grown so much that it is now produced in other Southeast Asian countries, and in the States as well. We use it on noodles and stir-fries, seafood soups, grilled and roasted meats, even scrambled eggs—anyplace where its flavor-rich heat might work magic. It's easy to whip up a batch of your own (see page 81). Our favorite brand of prepared *sri racha* is Grand Mountain, from Thailand, sold in Asian markets and by hot sauce purveyors, but it is easier to find the Vietnamese-American brand from Huy Fonz Foods (look for the rooster on the label) in well-stocked supermarkets.

Star Anise

One of the components of five-spice powder, star anise is the elongated, eight-pointed, star-shaped pod of a small evergreen tree. As its name suggests, it is prized for its licorice flavor. Star anise appears in cuisines with a strong Chinese influence. The Vietnamese add it to soups and sweet syrups. It is used in spice pastes in Singapore, where the Chinese-Malay fusion cuisine called *nonya*-style cooking is a specialty. You'll find star anise in Asian markets and well-stocked supermarkets; see Sources for mail order.

Star Fruit

Also called carambola, the star fruit originated in India. It grows throughout Southeast Asia and is now cultivated in Hawaii and Florida as well. The ripe fruit is used in fruit salads, where it is admired for its sweet-tart taste and crisp texture. When ripe, star fruit is glossy yellow on the outside, and is shaped like a tiny, elongated orb with five ribs running its length. A cross section cut looks like a five-pointed star. The ribs should look juicy, not shriveled. Unless you want a pronounced sour tang, let your star fruit ripen at room temperature until it is completely yellow. Star fruit does not need to be peeled. If you wish, you can flick out the occasional seed with the point of a knife. Look for star fruit in well-stocked supermarkets and Asian markets.

Tamarind

The tamarind tree is native to Africa, but now grows in some Southeast Asian countries, too. It produces a long pod, from whose pulp a dusky, sweet-sour flavor (sometimes compared to the taste of raisins) can be extracted. Although tamarind may be new to you by its name, you've probably noticed it as one of the defining flavors in Worcestershire sauce. All over Southeast Asia, where tart, sour flavors are key components of the cuisines, tamarind sauce is used to lend its fine, sharp, uniquely sweet-tart flavor to everything from soup stocks and saucy stir-fries to marinades, salad dressings, and refreshing iced beverages.

Liquid Tamarind Concentrate: Although you can buy whole tamarind pods and pressed blocks of tamarind pulp for making the smooth, thick sauce, the easiest form to work with is a liquid concentrate, packed in small plastic jars. We like the P. Pra Teep Thong brand from Thailand. Look for liquid tamarind concentrate in Asian markets or specialty stores; see Sources for mail order.

Tempeh

These white, chewy cakes made from boiled and lightly fermented soybeans are often used in Indonesia and Malaysia as a meatless source of protein. Of all soy-based products, tempeh comes the closest to resembling meat and is nearly as adaptable as tofu. It can be made into veggie burgers, croutons, and kebabs, and included in stews, salads, curries, and in chili. A four-ounce serving may contain as much as 21 grams of protein. Tempeh probably originated in Java about 1,000 years ago. It looks somewhat like brie cheese, including its downy rind of edible mold, but it needs to be cooked before it's eaten. You will find it in eight-ounce, vacuum-sealed packages. Once opened, tempeh will keep two to three days in the refrigerator. You can find tempeh in well-stocked supermarkets and Asian markets and health food stores. Two good brands to try are White Wave 5-Grain Tempeh and Lightlife 3-Grain Tempeh.

Thai Coffee and Tea

Thai people love to see how they can make basic flavors more complex, and this desire to experiment has brought about many interestingly spiced blends of tea and coffee. Thai coffee combines roasted corn, sesame, and spices with roasted coffee beans. Thai tea is based on a native red-leaf tea laced with sweet spices such as star anise and cinnamon. Thai coffee and tea can be purchased in Thai and other well-stocked Asian markets; see Sources for mail order.

Vietnamese Coriander

Called *rau rom* by the Vietnamese, this leafy green herb is native to Southeast Asia. It is especially loved as an accent to noodle soups and salads in the southerly regions of Vietnam, setting their cuisine apart from the more Chinese-influenced cookery of the north. In Malaysia, and especially Singapore, where it is called *daun laksa*, Vietnamese coriander is showered over bowls of noodle curry. *Rau rom* is often referred to as Vietnamese mint, but it is not in the same family. It has a clean lemon-and-cilantro-like flavor and fragrance, with a peppery aftertaste. The leaves are glossy and pointed, with stems joined by slightly bent "knots" or "knees," hence its genus name, *Polygonum*, or "many knees," and its English name, knotweed. Look for it in Vietnamese markets; see Sources for mail-order seeds and seedlings. You can substitute fresh cilantro or mint.

Vietnamese Rice Papers

Known as *banh trang* in their homeland, these are uniquely Vietnamese wrappers for spring rolls, salad rolls, and spring rolls. They are fragile and translucent sheets of rice flour, salt, and water, and really are as thin as the most delicate paper. The mixture is pressed and cut into circles, and the damp circles are then sun-dried on bamboo mats, which produce their characteristic crosshatch pattern. The rice papers keep indefinitely in their dry state. Soak them in warm water for 15 to 30 seconds before filling them. When served fresh they are called salad rolls or summer rolls. When deep-fried, they are called spring rolls. Rice papers are sold in Asian markets; see Sources for mail order.

Yard-Long Beans

Also known as Chinese long beans, these are not really green beans at all but rather the immature pods of black-eyed peas. They look like green beans on steroids, though, being typically a between a foot and one-and-a-half feet in length. They are milder in flavor than green beans, with a crunchier texture, and they cook well in sauces and stir-fries. You will find them sold in bundles or loose knots in Asian groceries. Buy thin, flexible beans. The ends of the beans are usually black, which is fine, but reject beans with dark, discolored areas.

Beverages

FILIPINO-STYLE HOT CHOCOLATE

GINGER COFFEE

VIETNAMESE-STYLE ICED COFFEE

JASMINE ICED TEA

LANG-SON CHAI

THAI ICED TEA

TAMARIND COOLER

RANGOON ROSE COOLER

GINGER FIZZ

BANGKOK-TO-BALI LIMEADE

VIETNAMESE-STYLE FRUIT SMOOTHIE

MY THAI MAI TAI

LYCHEE BELLINIS

MALAY TIGER

MO' BETTA MOJITO

The heat and humidity of the tropics

inspire all who live there to search out delicious ways of satisfying their thirst. In fact, it's just about an obsession. As soon as refrigerators started to become affordable for Southeast Asians, they used them first and foremost for stashing cool drinks.

That tropical dedication to finding perfect thirst quenchers has inspired our selections for this chapter, including some fascinating cocktails and vibrant fruit elixirs, along with smoothly spiced coffees and teas, both hot and cold.

One thing a visitor to Southeast Asia soon discovers is that its people enthusiastically adopt taste combinations from practically every new culture they encounter. We've created some singular cocktails in that spirit. Some of them impart tropical Asian flavors to popular cocktails you may already know—such as the My Thai Mai Tai (page 37), the Mo' Betta Mojito (page 43), and the Lychee Bellinis (page 39)—and an intriguing new combination we call the Malay Tiger (page 42).

Wine can also be beautifully paired with Southeast Asian dishes, but it is very expensive throughout the region. That's why we've emphasized the cocktail end of the spectrum. If you prefer wine or beer to distilled spirits, experiment confidently to discover your favorite combinations. White wines with higher acidity, such as Sauvignon Blanc, Fumé Blanc, Pinot Blanc, Viognier, and Gewürztraminer, usually can balance even the most spicy and assertive flavors. Full-flavored beers and ales will usually be the most satisfying choice in their category. In fact, there are some wonderful beers from Southeast Asia in American markets, like Singha, a Thai product. The locally produced whiskeys and other forms of liquor, though

very popular in their native lands, tend to be too raw for American tastes.

Nonalcoholic drinks are the real essentials, though. With all the thirst the tropics create, they are true liquid assets. There are more juice-filled fruits and refreshing herbs than you can possibly imagine, as well as several varieties of tea and coffee, all growing abundantly. That being the case, you may be astonished to find this parade of beverage recipes begins with hot chocolate. But one taste of the satisfyingly rich Filipino version—which the people of that multi-island nation love to pair with sweet cakes and sunny conversation—will make it your choice for chilly North American days.

Cool drinks are well represented here, of course, including Bangkok-to-Bali Limeade (page 36) and a homemade Ginger Fizz (page 35) that will make you forget commercially bottled ginger ale ever existed. In this chapter you'll also find Thai Iced Tea (page 32), the creamy, vanilla-scented elixir that delights almost anyone who ever experiences its taste, and Vietnamese-Style Iced Coffee (page 28), a dense, dark-roasted brew barely tamed with sweetened condensed milk.

Filipino-Style Hot Chocolate

Made rich, dark, and smooth, the New World flavor of chocolate is the drink of choice for *merienda*, the Filipino tradition of serving coconut cakes and sweet breads for a lavish late morning or afternoon treat. This tropical version of hot chocolate is also wonderful in place of American-style cocoa on a chilly evening. Use best quality semisweet chocolate, such as Ghirardelli's, which has more depth and earthiness because the cacao beans are roasted. Evaporated milk, a staple of the tropics, imparts rich taste and satiny texture.

4 ounces best quality semisweet chocolate, cut into 1/4-inch pieces
1/2 cup water
1 cup evaporated milk
1 tablespoon plus 2 teaspoons sugar
Pinch of salt
Two 3-inch-long cinnamon sticks (optional)

1. Place the chocolate and water in a medium-size saucepan over low heat, and stir until the chocolate has melted.
2. Gradually whisk in the evaporated milk, then the sugar and salt, and continue whisking until blended. Add the cinnamon sticks, if desired, and bring the mixture to a simmer.
3. Remove the cinnamon sticks and pour the hot chocolate into small bowls or mugs. Serve immediately.

Ginger Coffee

The islands of Java, Sumatra, Bali, and Sulawesi grow some of the world's boldest and most intense coffees. Starbucks calls these earthy, full-bodied coffees "the heavyweights of the coffee world."

Indonesians love their coffee very sweet and infused with ginger. Our ginger syrup–infused coffee creates a moderately sweet brew, allowing the robust coffee flavor to come through with an inviting ginger warmth. Be sure to brew a rich, full-bodied coffee, preferably made from Indonesian beans. This recipe can be multiplied to make as many cups as you like.

1¹/₂ to 2 teaspoons Ginger Syrup (page 296), to your taste
1 cup freshly brewed coffee

Stir the ginger syrup into the cup of hot coffee and serve.

Vietnamese-Style Iced Coffee

The Vietnamese brew their coffee to a strength that makes the average American cupful seem like Ovaltine. During the period of French colonial rule, they developed a taste for a traditional French dark roast. But, as tropical heat would dictate, they love their coffee over ice, sweetened with condensed milk.

In traditional Vietnamese style, coffee comes to the table with an individual metal drip filter over each cup. The coffee drips through slowly, thickly, into a pool of sweetened condensed milk in the ice-filled glass below. These drip filters are an inexpensive find in Asian markets, but you can get a similar brew in a couple of alternative ways. We like to use a French press–style coffeemaker. It produces a rich, thick consistency, which is most appropriate for dark-roasted coffees. And because the coffee cools quickly in the process, this type of coffeemaker is particularly good for making iced coffee. Stove-top espresso makers are inexpensive and also very effective, producing coffee with more body than a drip coffeemaker does, though not as concentrated as that produced by the more expensive electric pump-style espresso makers.

If you're using an espresso maker, make one double espresso for each glass, then sweeten and serve as for the French press method, which follows.

$1/2$ cup coarsely ground French roast coffee (espresso grind)

2 cups boiling water

$1/2$ cup sweetened condensed milk, or more to taste

1. Put the ground coffee in the carafe of a French press. Add the boiling water and allow to steep for 4 minutes. Stir, then slowly press down the plunger until the grounds are trapped at the bottom of the carafe. If you feel resistance as you press down the plunger, ease it back up a little to release the vacuum; then you can push it down easily.
2. Put 2 tablespoons of sweetened condensed milk in each of four 8-ounce glasses. Fill the glasses two thirds full with ice cubes. Divide the coffee among the glasses and serve with iced-tea spoons for swirling the milk into the coffee.

Jasmine Iced Tea

Serves 6

Although the people of Southeast Asia are not quite as devoted tea drinkers as the Chinese or Japanese, a simple green tea or jasmine flower–infused green tea is often served with meals in restaurants throughout tropical Asia. It is said to have a calming effect. There are several grades of jasmine tea available from specialty tea sellers, such as Rishi Tea. The types of Jasmine tea include Jasmine Pearl and Jasmine Silver Needle (see Sources), all made by adding jasmine blossoms from the Fujian province of China to tender shoots of green tea. We make our jasmine tea with honey to bring out its flowery perfume.

²/₃ cup loose jasmine tea leaves

7 cups water

¹/₄ cup honey

1. Place the tea leaves in a clean saucepan and set aside. Heat the water in a kettle or pot just until it begins to simmer. Do not let it come to a boil. Remove the water from the heat and immediately pour over the tea leaves in the saucepan. Let steep for 2 to 3 minutes, then strain into a pitcher. Stir in the honey and let cool to room temperature. (You can also place the tea leaves in a teapot or a strainer insert and place in the pot. When the tea has steeped, remove the insert or strain the tea, stir in the honey, and let the tea cool before serving.)

2. Serve cold in tall glasses with plenty of ice.

Lang-Son Chai

Serves 2 to 4

Sweet spiced Indian tea, or chai, has become popular all over North America. Everyone loves its creamy consistency, spicy flavor, and deep fragrance. Our recipe adds yet another irresistible flavor, the bright licorice note of star anise from Vietnam, where it is primarily used for soups and stews and in some sweet syrups for fruit cocktails. Besides its wonderful flavor, star anise is believed to sweeten the breath and aid digestion.

To give our version of chai even more of a Southeast Asian identity, we added coconut milk and palm sugar. We call it Lang-Son Chai, after the province in northern Vietnam where star anise is grown.

2 black peppercorns or $^1/_8$ teaspoon freshly ground black pepper

4 cloves

5 cardamom pods

1 star anise

3 cups water

$^1/_4$ teaspoon ground ginger

$^1/_4$ teaspoon ground Saigon or regular cinnamon

$^1/_2$ cup canned unsweetened coconut milk

$^1/_2$ cup 2 percent milk

2 tablespoons plus 1 teaspoon palm sugar or light brown sugar

2 tablespoons loose black tea leaves, such as orange pekoe

1. Lightly crush the peppercorns, cloves, cardamom, and star anise together in a mortar or spice mill. Do not pulverize.

2. Transfer the crushed spices to a small saucepan. Add the water, ginger, cinnamon, and ground black pepper (if you haven't used peppercorns). Bring the mixture to boil over medium heat. Remove the pan from the heat, cover, and let steep for 5 minutes.

3. Stir in the coconut milk, 2 percent milk, and sugar and return to a boil. Remove the pan from the heat and add the tea. Cover and let steep for 3 minutes.

4. Stir the chai, then strain it into a teapot or small pitcher. Adjust the sweetness to your taste. Serve hot or cold.

Thai Iced Tea

Native Thai tea is spiced with star anise, cinnamon, and vanilla. Labeled "Thai tea" or sometimes "cha Thai" in Asian markets, it's a drink that is practically a dessert in a glass.

This sweet, rich tea is brewed until the flavors are bright and clear, then mixed with sugar syrup and served in tall, ice-filled glasses. Evaporated milk, used by necessity in tropical Asia, offers an exceptionally creamy indulgence that's unique to Thai iced tea. You could also use half-and-half. There is no substitute for the cha Thai, however, so if you don't have access to an Asian market, you may need to order it by mail. It's well worth the extra effort.

4 cups water
$^3/_4$ cup Thai tea
Sugar Syrup (page 296)
$^3/_4$ to $1^1/_2$ cups evaporated milk or half-and-half

1. Bring the water to a rolling boil in a large saucepan. Add the tea and remove the pan from the heat. Stir gently to submerge all the leaves and let steep for about 5 minutes. The liquid should be bright orange and have a clear, strong taste. As with most teas, if it's brewed too long, it can become bitter, so taste every few minutes.
2. Carefully pour the tea through a coffee filter or fine-mesh strainer into a large pitcher, being careful not to splash the richly colored brew (it can make quite a stain).
3. Starting with 1 cup, add the sugar syrup to taste and stir to blend. Let cool to room temperature, cover, and refrigerate until serving time.
4. To serve, fill tall glasses with crushed ice or ice cubes. Pour in the tea until each glass is about three quarters full, then float 3 or 4 tablespoons of evaporated milk in each glass. Serve with iced-tea spoons to swirl the milk into the tea.

Tamarind Cooler

*T*his is a popular Indonesian refresher, sold in bottles or made at home, where the Indonesian cook has a varied arsenal of fruit-based syrups for making cool drinks. Since tamarind is used in cuisines all over Southeast Asia, it's a wonder that other countries in the region don't seem to have a version of this drink. Its sweet-tart flavor is lively and refreshing, and pairs especially well with spicy dishes.

TAMARIND COOLER SYRUP:

1 cup sugar

1 cup water

$1/4$ cup plus 2 tablespoons liquid tamarind concentrate

Big pinch of salt

TO FINISH:

$1^1/3$ cups cold water

1. To make the syrup, combine the sugar and water in a small saucepan and bring to a boil over high heat. Reduce the heat to medium-low and gently simmer, stirring a few times, until the sugar dissolves and the liquid thickens, about 5 minutes. Add the tamarind concentrate and salt and gently simmer for 2 minutes more. Remove the pan from the heat and let the syrup cool to room temperature. When the tamarind syrup is cool, refrigerate it until serving time.

2. When you're ready to serve, fill a pitcher with the cold water and add the tamarind syrup. Stir until blended and pour into 4 ice-filled glasses.

Rangoon Rose Cooler

*I*ndian rosewater-flavored drinks and desserts, such as *gulab jamin*, may have inspired the Burmese love of rosewater-flavored beverages such as this one, although Indonesians love them, too. In Burma, they press fruit-flavored gelatin through a sieve to make squiggly shapes for this drink. We think this rose cooler is great with cubes of black cherry Jell-O or little handfuls of dried tart red cherries, but this creamy, sweet elixir is also heavenly when served simply over ice, with nothing else added.

1 cup Rose Syrup (page 297)
1 cup canned unsweetened coconut milk
$1/2$ cup water
One 3-ounce box black cherry Jell-O (optional)
1 to 2 tablespoons dried red cherries, to your taste (optional)

1. Place the rose syrup, coconut milk, and water in a medium mixing bowl or 1-quart measuring cup, and stir until blended. Cover and refrigerate until serving time.
2. If making Jell-O cubes, follow the package instructions and chill the mixture in an 8-inch-square baking pan. When the Jell-O is firmly set, cut it into $1/2$-inch cubes.
3. To serve, divide the cold rose syrup and coconut milk mixture between 2 to 4 tall, clear glasses. Top each serving with some of the cherry Jell-O cubes, or sprinkle with some dried red cherries, if desired. (Reserve any leftover Jell-O cubes for another use.) Provide iced-tea spoons to eat the Jell-O cubes or cherries.

Ginger Fizz

This lively drink is really a homemade ginger ale, but with a fresher, more piquant flavor than the best ones you can find at the market. All you need is some ginger syrup and seltzer water, plus a wedge of lime and/or sprigs of mint, if you like.

Seltzer is sodium free and doesn't impinge on the great natural flavor of the ginger. Club soda can also be used, and the results will be quite good. Sparkling water is a distant third choice; the mineral content seems to mute the ginger flavor.

We like our ginger fizzes served straight up, but you can also use tall highball glasses and add ice cubes after spooning in the ginger syrup.

One 1-liter bottle seltzer water, chilled
1 cup Ginger Syrup (page 296)
1 lime (optional), cut into 4 wedges
Sprigs fresh mint (optional)

1. Pour cold seltzer water into four 8-ounce glasses, filling each about two thirds full. Spoon ¼ cup ginger syrup into each glass. (If you spoon the syrup slowly down the sides of the glasses, it will form an attractive layer at the bottom.)

2. Serve with an iced-tea spoon for stirring and a wedge of lime or sprig of mint, if desired.

Bangkok-to-Bali Limeade

*A*ll across Southeast Asia, people love their limeade made strong and lively. The way to achieve this peak flavor is first to create a concentrate by steeping lime rinds and sugar in boiling water, and then mix it with the fresh juice. The essential oils from the lime rinds give it a vibrant depth of flavor. In Thailand, they add a pinch of salt for a more piquant experience. If you'd like to try it Thai-style, simply stir a half-teaspoon of salt into the pitcher.

12 limes
3/4 cup sugar
2 1/4 cups boiling water

1. Roll the limes on a cutting board, pressing down firmly with the palm of your hand to help release their juices. Cut the limes in half and squeeze the juice into a large pitcher. Set aside. Put the lime rinds in a large heat-proof bowl or a clean 2-quart saucepan.
2. Add the sugar to the rinds, then pour in the boiling water. Let the mixture steep just long enough to produce a strong, lively flavor, 10 to 12 minutes.
3. Strain the concentrate into the pitcher of lime juice. Before discarding the rinds, squeeze each one into the pitcher to release all the liquid. Stir the limeade once or twice, then fill the pitcher about two thirds full with ice cubes. Chill in the refrigerator until serving time.
4. To serve, add ice cubes to each tall glass and pour in the chilled limeade.

Vietnamese-Style Fruit Smoothie

Serves 2

*D*epending on the flavor combinations you choose, these smoothies could be served alone or with a light meal. Almost any favorite fruit will blend deliciously with the sweetened condensed milk: mangoes, papayas, even avocados, or combinations, such as strawberry-banana. We like ours made with mango, with a little crushed cardamom seed added for a pan-Asian touch.

4 cups ice cubes

1 large ripe mango, peeled, flesh cut away from the stone, and cut into chunks

1/2 cup sweetened condensed milk

1/8 teaspoon ground cardamom (optional)

Sugar, if needed, to taste

1. Wrap the ice cubes in a clean cloth and crush with a pestle, hammer, or rolling pin. Put the ice and remaining ingredients, except the sugar, in a blender or food processor. Process until smooth, stopping occasionally to scrape down the sides of the blender or work bowl.

2. Add sugar, if needed, and serve cold.

My Thai Mai Tai

Serves 2

*T*here are almost as many recipes for mai tais as there are people who enjoy them. The tropical sweet-and-sour tang of tamarind distinguishes this one, lending an intriguing undertone. Some mai tais are made with equal parts pineapple and citrus juices. Ours is slanted toward the sweetness of pineapple juice in order to balance the tamarind. Feel free to play with the proportions and make My Thai Mai Tai your own.

1 cup pineapple juice
1/2 cup fresh orange juice
1/4 cup light rum
2 tablespoons Cointreau or Triple Sec
2 tablespoons liquid tamarind concentrate
1/4 cup dark rum

1. Combine all the ingredients, except the dark rum, in a cocktail shaker or a pitcher. Shake well and pour into two 16-ounce highball glasses half filled with crushed ice. (To make a quick job of crushing ice, wrap some cubes in a clean cloth and crush with a pestle or rolling pin.)

2. Float 2 tablespoons of dark rum on each drink and serve immediately.

Tamarind Cubes

LIQUID TAMARIND CONCENTRATE TYPICALLY COMES IN 16-OUNCE JARS. ONCE OPENED, THE CONCENTRATE LOSES ITS FLAVOR RATHER QUICKLY—EVEN IF REFRIGERATED. YET MOST RECIPES ONLY CALL FOR A SMALL AMOUNT. HERE'S WHAT WE DO: POUR THE LIQUID TAMARIND CONCENTRATE INTO THE COMPARTMENTS OF A STANDARD ICE CUBE TRAY. WHEN FROZEN, TRANSFER THE TAMARIND CUBES TO A FREEZER BAG AND USE AS NEEDED. EACH CUBE WILL YIELD APPROXIMATELY 2 TABLESPOONS.

Lychee Bellinis

T his is like the classic Italian Bellini, the effervescent cocktail made with champagne and peach nectar, freshly reinvented with a tropical look and taste. Pink champagne, sometimes labeled *brut rosé*, and pureed lychees create a lovely sight—the palest petal-pink color with a sweet tropical perfume, which you can accentuate with a plump, champagne-soaked whole lychee at the bottom of the flute. A bottle of pink sparkling wine is a delightful and less expensive alternative to champagne.

One 20-ounce can lychees in heavy syrup, chilled
1 bottle pink champagne or other pink sparkling wine, chilled

1. Drain the lychees, reserving 1 cup of their syrup. Set aside 8 lychees. Put the remaining lychees and the reserved syrup in a blender. Process until liquid and smooth.
2. Transfer the lychee mixture to a pretty serving pitcher. Slowly pour in the champagne.
3. Drop 1 reserved lychee into each of 8 champagne flutes. Stir the pitcher of Bellinis gently, if necessary, to blend the nectar with the champagne, then pour into the flutes and serve.

Jackfruits and Rambutans, Lychees and Durians, and Other Tropical Exotics

In open-air markets from Bangkok to Bali, the array of tropical fruits is a Day-Glo astonishment of shapes, colors, and fragrances. Heaps of soft and spiky red rambutans sit alongside baskets of pink-shelled lychees, whose delicate perfume wafts across the stalls till it hits that fetid, bottom-of-the-bay-at-low-tide musk from the notorious durian—six- to ten-pound bombs of foul-smelling fruit with a decidedly sweet and lovely flavor. The bounty also includes dozens of varieties of mango and papaya, soft, custard-like cherimoya, tangy star fruit, piquant guavas, mangosteen, and jackfruit.

Many hotels, airports, and car rental agencies in the Asian tropics post signs showing a durian fruit silhouetted behind a red circle and a diagonal bar, meaning "Keep those stinkpots out of here." The fruit, which has a thick, green, spiky shell, is usually eaten raw. And the stench, some say, is like a ration of decomposing meat held in an overripe sweat sock.

We once bought durian that was already sliced, packaged in plastic, and frozen. Unfortunately, although we were spared the fruit's pungent aromas, its flavors got lost somewhere along the way.

The pomelo is the world's largest citrus fruit and the grandparent of today's grapefruit. It looks like a grapefruit that took a handful of growth hormone, but the difference in size is mostly due to the pomelo's incredibly thick pith between the rind and the fruit. Pomelos are milder in flavor than grapefruits, but the membrane between the segments is tougher. Their skins may be yellow or yellow-green. To choose a good pomelo, pick it up and notice the weight. It should feel somewhat heavy, indicating plenty of moisture inside. The dry ones are very disappointing, the juicy ones heavenly. When you get your pomelo home, make two cuts in the rind in the shape of an X and begin prying off sections of the thick peel to uncover the segments of fruit underneath.

Rambutan gets its name from the Malaysian word for *hairy*, because its red skin is covered with soft, curvy, green-and-red spines that resemble hairs. The fruit is small and delicate, somewhat like a very plump and flavorful pale grape. Canned peeled rambutan is quite nice, though less distinctive in flavor than the fresh item. When buying fresh rambutan, look for a rich red hue. A dark skin tells you the fruit is overripe. Rambutans keep well in the refrigerator and reasonably well at room temperature.

Cherimoya, now grown in southern California, is a multiflavored miracle. You will detect a bit of honey, a hint of banana, a slice of peach, and a mouthful of apple, all in a creamy-textured fruit that separates easily from its large seeds as you eat it. The cherimoya is roundish but irregular in shape, generally bigger than a large apple. The thin rind is a pale green, with small depressions in the surface that almost look as if they were made with a rounded chisel. A cousin fruit, the soursop, is about twice as large, with short, soft spines on the outside. When fully ripe, it becomes brownish and the flavor is like that of a cherimoya, but slightly sharper. In Latin American countries it is called *guanabana*.

Guavas originated in South America, but are very popular throughout Southeast Asia, where they now thrive. They are shiny and yellow, shaped somewhat like a small, rounded, but irregular pear with a few shallow pits on the surface. If you cut a guava in half, you'll see a circle of tasty flesh surrounding a center where the little seeds appear to be suspended in jelly. Often, the seeds are soft enough to be eaten with the rest of the fruit (excluding the peel, of course). Filipino cooks like to add guavas to fish- and meat-based stews, but most people prefer them raw. The flavor is slightly sharp, indicating the high vitamin C content guavas possess, but extremely pleasant.

Mangosteens have leathery, purple skin on their small, round forms, but they are pearl white and delicious inside. They grow abundantly in Southeast Asia. You will rarely find mangosteens in American markets, even those that cater to Asians. They don't travel well and are quite expensive. If you do happen to find one, make sure it is firm. The skin is so rich in tannins that it is used for tanning leather hides. Cut it completely away before eating the flesh, which is segmented and has a small seed or two per segment.

Jackfruit, a botanical cousin of the fig, is the biggest fruit on the planet. It can be fully a yard long and half a yard in width. In fact, it looks quite a bit like another of its relatives, the breadfruit, with its hard, greenish skin coated liberally in warty bumps. It's important to pick a jackfruit with a pleasing, sweet aroma. Lacking that, they can be rather flavorless. Jackfruit is also available canned.

The lychee grows in southern China and is strongly associated with Chinese cuisine, but it is also a favorite throughout Southeast Asia. It has been cultivated for over a thousand years. Underneath a tough brown skin that peels away effortlessly, it has a subtle flavor reminiscent of the Muscadine grape or the scuppernong, which is common in the American South. Canned lychees are readily available, but they don't compare well to the fresh item. Farmers in some of our warmer states are growing lychees now, making them fairly abundant in season, and not at all expensive.

Malay Tiger

*H*ave you ever heard a tiger purr? Here's a smooth but potent East-West cocktail that just might do the trick. The botanical essences in premium gin combine wonderfully with fresh lime and ginger syrup. We serve our Malay Tigers straight up, in martini glasses.

¹/₂ cup premium quality gin, such as Tanqueray Ten
¹/₂ cup fresh lime juice
¹/₄ cup Ginger Syrup (page 296)
2 cups ice cubes

1. Combine the gin, lime juice, and ginger syrup in a cocktail shaker or a pitcher. Add the ice cubes, cover, and shake or stir well.
2. Strain into 2 martini glasses and serve.

Mo' Betta Mojito

*T*he mojito, which means "little wet one" in Spanish, originated in Cuba in the late nineteenth century, when rum-making became an industry. Infused with fresh mint and lime juice and supremely easy to make, mojitos quickly became an island-wide hit. Wealthy landowners drank them with ice and soda, and this is how we serve the cocktail today.

But the mojito's combination of mint and citrus–spiked rum could just as well have been created in Southeast Asia, and it makes a great prelude to any tropical meal.

We've taken mojitos a flavorful step further by replacing the soda water with coconut water. Shake a ripe, heavy coconut and you'll hear the slosh of coconut water, the slightly opaque liquid inside. Once only available on tropical beaches around the world, coconut water is now sold in cans in supermarkets and Latin groceries.

1 small bunch fresh mint
Juice of 1 lime, plus 2 lime wedges for garnish
1/2 cup white rum
4 teaspoons sugar
One 11.8-ounce can Goya brand coconut water

1. Pick enough mint leaves off their stems to make 2 small handfuls, about 1/4 cup. Tear the mint leaves in half. Reserve a few whole mint sprigs for garnish.
2. Divide the torn mint leaves and lime juice between 2 tall cocktail glasses. Gently muddle (crush with a pestle or wooden spoon) the mint with the lime juice. Add 1/4 cup rum and 2 teaspoons sugar to each glass. Stir well, or cover and shake. Add some crushed ice or ice cubes, and top off each glass with the coconut water.
3. Garnish each drink with 1 lime wedge and sprigs of mint and serve.

Appetizers

SPICY STIR-FRIED CASHEWS

GREEN MANGO AND PROSCIUTTO

EGGPLANT FANS

AVOCADO SAMBAL DIP

CILANTRO PESTO AND SHRIMP DIP

CALIFORNIA SUMMER ROLLS

VIETNAMESE-STYLE SUMMER ROLLS WITH
SHRIMP AND MANGO

FRIED SPRING ROLLS FILIPINO STYLE

CRISPY PEPPERCORN SHRIMP

BANGKOK-TO-BALI SHRIMP COCKTAIL

BANGKOK-TO-BALI BEER-BATTERED SHRIMP

CAMBODIAN STEAMED MUSSELS WITH
PINEAPPLE AND THAI BASIL

FILIPINO-STYLE CEVICHE WITH SALMON AND
GREEN MANGO

STIR-FRIED PORK, SHRIMP, AND COCONUT IN
LETTUCE LEAVES WITH CRUSHED PEANUTS

MINCED PORK AND PINEAPPLE TIDBITS WITH
RED CHILLI AND CILANTRO

About half of this chapter is devoted to

traditional Southeast Asian appetizers. These recipes have the rich complexity of flavor and texture you expect from tropical Asian cuisine, yet are wonderfully quick to fix. Spicy Stir-Fried Cashews (page 47) is a classic dish throughout the Asian tropics, as is Crispy Peppercorn Shrimp (page 60). Saté is too irresistible to be limited to just one recipe, so we've given you two. It originated on the Malay peninsula, but now is also closely associated with Thailand and other neighboring countries as well. Other traditional dishes come from the cuisines of specific countries, like Fried Spring Rolls Filipino Style (page 58) and Minced Pork and Pineapple Tidbits with Red Chilli and Cilantro (page 69), which is a Thai favorite.

Culinary improvisation and adaptation are honored through-out Southeast Asia, and we want you to see how easily you can bring these new flavors you're learning into your own personal cooking style. So the other recipes in this chapter are cross-cultural personal favorites. Sometimes your ideas may be based on adding Asian touches to a Western dish, just as we did in Green Mango and Prosciutto (page 48)—which we happen to like even better than melon and prosciutto, the Italian dish that inspired it. Bangkok-to-Bali Shrimp Cocktail (page 62) may become your favorite version of an American classic.

Sometimes the inspiration ricochets from one culture to another, then back again. For example, Indonesians love avocados, but use them as a fruit—in smoothies or in fruit salads. We took the notion of using mashed avocados in a dip, like guacamole, but with Indonesian influences. The result is a flavorful Avocado *Sambal* Dip (page 50). Then we reimagined the California roll, the West Coast–style sushi made with crab and avocado, as a traditional Vietnamese salad roll to create California Summer Rolls (page 54).

Besides introducing you to some remarkably delicious starters for your family and guests, we hope these recipes will encourage you to create your own favorite dishes with the flavors of Southeast Asia.

Spicy Stir-Fried Cashews

This irresistible Thai-style snack tastes great with Bangkok-to-Bali Limeade (page 36) or a cold Thai beer. We like our cashews spicy, but you can adjust the heat level to your own liking. This recipe comes together quickly, so have all the ingredients ready by your stove. It's best to present the stir-fried nuts in a serving dish instead of a bowl so all the nuts will be dotted with spices.

1 tablespoon peanut or vegetable oil

1/2 pound raw cashews

1 tablespoon finely chopped garlic

2 teaspoons finely chopped small Thai chillies or crushed red pepper to taste

1 teaspoon sugar

1 teaspoon salt

1. Heat a wok or large skillet over medium-low heat until hot, add the oil, and rotate the pan a bit to coat it evenly. When the oil is hot, add the cashews, garlic, and chillies and stir-fry until the nuts are browned, about 2 minutes. Add the sugar and salt and mix well.
2. Transfer the nuts to a platter or shallow serving dish and serve warm.

Green Mango and Prosciutto

Serves 4 to 6

*P*rosciutto, a highly savory type of ham from Italy, is typically served with slices of honeydew or cantaloupe. We think it makes a much more alluring duet with green mango.

The green mangoes usually eaten in the tropics are rather too tart for American tastes, so this is one time when you might prefer to shop in a conventional supermarket instead of an Asian store. You want mangoes that have been delivered recently. They should be firm, with a blush beginning to spread across their mostly green skins. The fruit within will be pale, its color about half of the intensity of a fully ripe fruit, with a little bit of sweet juiciness, but enough crispness so it will hold its shape when cut.

2 large green mangoes
16 paper-thin slices prosciutto
White pepper to taste

1. Peel the mangoes. Hold each one on edge lengthwise and slice down each of the "fat" sides, avoiding the stone and creating two cheek-shaped sections from each mango. Then cut a wedge from each end of the fruit. Slice each "cheek" section into 3 wedges, giving you 8 wedges total.

2. Wrap each wedge in a slice of prosciutto. Arrange them on a serving platter, sprinkle with white pepper, and serve.

Eggplant Fans

*H*ere's a dish that's as beautiful as it is delicious. We use the slender Japanese eggplant, which is the perfect size for this recipe. Each eggplant is sliced into an inviting fan shape and fried until crisp in a coating flavored with chilli powder and hints of fragrant coriander. Make one eggplant fan per person.

1 recipe Bangkok-to-Bali Beer Batter (page 288)
4 Japanese eggplants
Peanut or vegetable oil for frying
Coarse salt to taste

1. Mix a batch of Bangkok-to-Bali Beer Batter in a shallow mixing bowl or pie plate and set aside.
2. Cut the bulb end of each eggplant into parallel slices about $1/4$ inch wide, leaving all the slices connected to the stem end. Gently fan the slices as evenly as possible, so that each can be well coated with batter.
3. Pour about $1/2$ inch of oil into a large skillet, preferably cast iron, and heat over medium-high heat to about 360 degrees F. (To test the oil temperature, dip a wooden spoon into the hot oil; the oil should bubble and sizzle around the bowl of the spoon.) Dip the eggplant fans into the batter one at a time and set them down flat into the hot oil. Fry them in batches, depending on the size of your skillet. Cook until one side is crisp, 4 to 5 minutes, then turn and cook until the other side is also crisp, about 3 minutes more. The fans should be golden brown and cooked through. Transfer the fried eggplant fans to a baking sheet lined with paper towels, or a paper bag, to drain.
4. Arrange the fans on a large serving platter, with the stems meeting in the center and the fan slices facing out, like spokes in a wheel. Sprinkle with salt and serve immediately.

Avocado Sambal Dip

*Y*ou may want to call this guacamole, but the recipe is actually inspired by a *sambal* known as *dabo dabo lelang*—an Indonesian blend of lime, chillies, onion, and fresh basil. There are many types of *sambals*, and all of them are based on fiery hot chillies (see page 92). Here the licorice-edged flavor and fragrance of Thai basil are great accents for the mellow richness of the avocado. Once you've had a taste, you may want to pair Thai basil with avocados all the time, in sandwiches and salads, too.

1 medium-size ripe, but not soft, tomato, seeded and cut into $1/4$-inch dice

$1/4$ cup diced ($1/4$ inch) red onion

1 teaspoon minced small Thai or serrano chillies

$1/4$ cup fresh lime juice (about 3 limes), plus the rinds

1 teaspoon salt

3 large ripe, but not soft, Hass avocados

Salt and freshly ground black pepper to taste

1 tablespoon torn fresh Thai, sweet, or purple basil leaves

Homemade Shrimp Chips (page 285), or one 2.5-ounce bag shrimp chips, corn chips,

    or other snack chips

1. Combine the tomato, onion, chillies, lime juice, and salt in a small mixing bowl. Stir in the lime rinds. Let the mixture stand at room temperature for 15 minutes to develop the flavors.

2. Cut the avocados in half and remove the pits. Scoop out the flesh with a soup spoon, drop it into a large mixing bowl, and mash with a fork.

3. When the *sambal* mixture has marinated, remove the lime rinds, squeezing out any juice before discarding them. Transfer the *sambal* mixture to the bowl of mashed avocadoes and mix well. Season with salt and black pepper and top with the fresh basil.

4. Serve at room temperature with chips on the side.

Cilantro Pesto and Shrimp Dip

Serves 4 to 6

T he Thai people love *lon*, their traditional cooked dipping sauces, which they make with chicken or fish, yellow bean sauce, and coconut milk. We've devised one using tofu, fresh shrimp, and a favorite Thai spice paste that Westerners might call cilantro pesto.

In Thailand, *lon* is served with *khao tang*, crispy cakes made from sun-dried sticky rice. They're wonderful, but unfortunately are seldom found in America's Asian groceries, so feel free to pair this dipping sauce with your favorite chips or with mini–rice cakes.

$1/2$ teaspoon black peppercorns

1 tablespoon plus 1 teaspoon chopped garlic

3 tablespoons chopped fresh cilantro, including the stems, plus a few sprigs
   for garnish

2 ounces soft (silken) tofu, drained and finely chopped

1 pound medium-size shrimp, peeled, deveined if desired, and cut into $1/2$-inch dice

1 tablespoon peanut or vegetable oil

1 cup canned unsweetened coconut milk

1 teaspoon palm sugar or light brown sugar

1 teaspoon Asian fish sauce

Pure chilli powder to taste

Snack chips or mini–rice cakes

1. Using a mortar and pestle or a spice grinder, crush or grind the peppercorns until coarsely ground. Combine the crushed pepper, chopped garlic, and cilantro in a mini–food processor and grind the mixture into a fairly smooth paste. Transfer the spice paste to a small bowl and set aside.

2. Combine the tofu and half the diced shrimp in a blender and process until it resembles a rough-textured puree. Transfer the mixture to a medium-size mixing bowl and set aside.

3. In a large wok or medium-size saucepan, heat the oil over medium-high heat. Stir-fry the cilantro paste until quite fragrant, about 30 seconds. Add the shrimp and tofu mix and stir-fry for 30 seconds. Add the coconut milk and stir, scraping up all the cooked bits from the bottom of the pan. Stir in the sugar and fish sauce. Reduce the heat to medium-low and gently boil the mixture until it thickens a little, about 5 minutes, stirring a few more times. Add the remaining diced shrimp and cook for 1 minute, stirring a few more times.

4. Transfer the dip to a serving bowl, sprinkle with chilli powder, and serve warm, with your favorite chips or mini–rice cakes on the side.

Thai Restaurant Perfume

*T*hink back to the last time you visited your favorite Thai restaurant. Do you remember a delicious and unique fragrance hanging in the air, an aromatic signal of pleasures to come?

For years, we supposed that smoky, seductive scent was the distilled essence of all the seasoning mysteries of a Thai chef's repertoire. And then, in one of those great, small discoveries that elegantly unfolds a central truth, we learned about the Thai Spice Trinity—fresh garlic, cilantro, and peppercorns. Convert those three elemental items into a spice paste, which you spoon into a hot wok, and Thai restaurant perfume is created. Simple as that. Elegant and true. It's an ancient sensory experience, predating the sixteenth-century introduction of fresh chillis, when the heat-loving Thais used prodigious amounts of black and white pepper, along with the garlic and cilantro, which have long figured prominently in their lively cuisine.

To create Thai restaurant perfume at home, trim the roots and stems from a fresh bunch of cilantro. Put them in a mortar, and add 2 or 3 large cloves of garlic, and $1/2$ teaspoon or so of black peppercorns. Use the pestle to crack and grind the ingredients until they are mashed into a paste.

Now heat up a wok or large, heavy frying pan. When it gets hot, add 1 or more tablespoons of vegetable oil and swirl the oil around the pan before adding the contents of the mortar. The instant those three ingredients kiss the heat, Thai restaurant perfume will begin to radiate from your stove, throughout the kitchen, and into the dining room. But, of course, you can't stop there, unless you want to face down family and guests who suddenly, inexplicably, find that they're desperate to have a Southeast Asian meal right away. Add a few other ingredients—some cold cooked rice, say, or fresh shrimp, or bite-size pieces of pork or chicken. Stir-fry the mixture, adding a splash or two of fish sauce and a little palm sugar to taste, and present them with a fresh, flavorful feast with flavors just as inviting as the perfume in the air.

California Summer Rolls

We call these soft rice paper roll-ups California summer rolls in honor of everyone's favorite sushi—the California roll—which is also made with fresh crab and avocado.

A summer roll is a spring roll served fresh instead of fried. A fresh noodle salad rolled into rice papers and served with a tangy dipping sauce is a Vietnamese specialty, which other Southeast Asians have also learned to love. In a marriage of East and West, we've dressed the salad in a scrumptious blue cheese vinaigrette, with extra served on the side for the dipping sauce.

NOODLES:

1 small bundle (1.7 or 2 ounces) bean thread vermicelli

BLUE CHEESE VINAIGRETTE:

1 tablespoon cider vinegar or aged red wine vinegar

$1/2$ teaspoon Worcestershire sauce

$1/2$ teaspoon salt

Big pinch of freshly ground black pepper

6 tablespoons extra virgin olive oil

$1/2$ cup crumbled blue cheese

TO ASSEMBLE THE SUMMER ROLLS:

8 Vietnamese rice papers

$1/2$ cup packed fresh Thai, sweet, or purple basil leaves

1 medium-size ripe, but not soft, Hass avocado, peeled, pitted, and finely diced

$1/2$ pound fresh lump crabmeat, picked over for shells and cartilage

Freshly ground black pepper

1. Soak the bean threads in warm water to cover until soft and translucent, about 20 minutes.
2. Meanwhile, make the dressing: Combine the vinegar, Worcestershire, salt, and pepper in a medium-size mixing bowl and whisk until smooth. Slowly whisk in the olive oil, then stir in the blue cheese. Set aside.
3. When the noodles are soft, drain well, lay them out on a cutting board, and chop coarsely. Transfer the noodles to a small mixing bowl and add half of the blue cheese dressing. Toss to mix well and set aside. Pour the remaining vinaigrette into a small dish and set aside.
4. To assemble the summer rolls, organize a work area so all the elements for softening and filling the rice papers are within easy reach. Have a small cutting board or dry dish towel in front of you on which you will wrap the summer rolls. Fill a wide, shallow pan or a pie plate with hot water and set it next to the cutting board or dish towel. Place a tray nearby to hold the finished summer rolls, and have a damp dish towel there to cover them. Arrange the rice papers and all the filling ingredients within easy reach.
5. Dip one rice paper into the pan of hot water and gently submerge until soft and pliant, about 15 seconds. Remove it carefully and place on the board or towel. At the bottom third of the circle, make a row of the dressed noodles (about 1 heaping tablespoon) topped with 3 or 4 basil leaves. Next, scatter about 1 tablespoon diced avocado on top and finish with about 2 tablespoons crabmeat and a few grinds of black pepper. Roll the wrapper edge closest to you up and over the filling, tucking it under the ingredients to form a cylinder shape. Fold in the right and left sides, then finish rolling. Set the completed roll, seam side down, on the tray and cover with the damp dish towel. Continue filling and rolling the rice papers.

    The rolls can be prepared a few hours in advance, covered with a damp towel or plastic wrap, and kept at room temperature until serving time.
6. To serve, arrange the summer rolls on a platter, either whole or sliced in half crosswise with a very sharp knife to cut cleanly and keep the rice paper from tearing. Serve at room temperature, with the remaining vinaigrette on the side.

Vietnamese-Style Summer Rolls with Shrimp and Mango

Makes 16 summer rolls

*T*he Vietnamese name for their light, soft spring rolls is *goi cuon*, which means "salad roll." Most spring rolls are made with pastry wrappers and are fried to a crisp. Vietnamese cooks use dried rice papers, circular sheets that are just as perfect for frying as pastry wrappers, but can also be served uncooked for a beautiful, delicate, translucent roll.

Like the Thais, who have adopted this Vietnamese favorite, we call them summer rolls to differentiate them from fried spring rolls. In our version, the translucent rolls reveal bright pink shrimp and orangey shreds of ripe mango.

Whether served fresh or fried, all spring rolls are paired with a dipping sauce. We've dabbed our shrimp and mango rolls with a favorite Asian-inspired sandwich spread, Red Chilli Mayo, to accent the sweetness of mango and shrimp, reserving some extra "mayo" to serve as a dipping sauce.

The packages of rice paper have more than you need, which is fine, because the first ones may be like the first pancake off the griddle; it may take you one or two summer rolls to become comfortable with the process of making them.

1 pound large shrimp, peeled and deveined if desired

2 medium-size ripe but not soft mangoes

16 Vietnamese rice papers

Red Chilli Mayo (page 78)

1 bunch fresh mint

1 bunch fresh cilantro

1. In a medium-size saucepan of boiling salted water, cook the shrimp until bright pink, 1 to 2 minutes. Drain in a colander. Rinse under cold running water and pat dry. Cut each shrimp in half lengthwise. Place the cut shrimp on a plate and cover with plastic wrap. Set aside in the refrigerator.

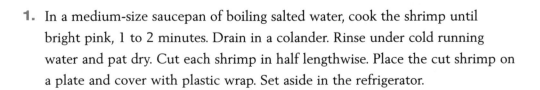

2. Peel the mangoes and cut the flesh into julienne strips. (For slash-cut method, see page 127.)

3. Organize a work area so all the elements for softening and filling the rice papers are within easy reach. Have a small cutting board or dry dish towel in front of you, on which you will wrap the summer rolls. Fill a wide shallow pan or a pie plate with hot water and set it next to the cutting board or dish towel. Place a tray nearby to hold the finished summer rolls and have a damp dish towel to cover them. Arrange the rice papers, chilled shrimp, mango, mayo, and herbs within easy reach.

4. Dip one rice paper into the pan of hot water and gently submerge it until soft and pliant, about 15 seconds. Remove it carefully and place on the board or towel. At the bottom third of the circle, place a row of julienned mango (6 to 8 pieces). Dab the mango with about a heaping $1/4$ teaspoon mayo and pinch off 5 or 6 mint leaves and 5 or 6 cilantro leaves and set them on top. Roll the wrapper edge closest to you up and over the filling, tucking it under the ingredients to form a cylinder shape. Fold in the right and left sides, make one complete roll, then place 3 shrimp halves, cut side down, in a line on top of the cylinder. Finish rolling and set the completed roll, seam side down, on the tray. Cover with the damp dish towel. Continue filling and rolling the rice papers.

The rolls can be prepared a few hours in advance, covered with a damp towel or plastic wrap, and kept at room temperature until serving time.

5. To serve, arrange the summer rolls on a platter, either whole or sliced in half with a very sharp knife to cut cleanly and keep the rice paper from tearing. Serve at room temperature, with extra mayo on the side.

Fried Spring Rolls Filipino Style

*P*eople in the Philippines call their spring rolls *lumpia*. In this version, the filling is made from ground beef and vegetables, which are stir-fried with *sukang paombong*, an opaque white Filipino vinegar with a mellow tang.

Making the filling takes slightly less than half an hour, but the job of wrapping and frying the rolls will extend this recipe beyond our usual limit of 30 minutes. To make it a quick dish, simply spoon the hot filling into pita bread for delicious sandwiches.

Another good option is to make up the rolls, then freeze them for a quick meal at a later date. Just wrap the freshly made rolls in plastic wrap and put them in a covered container in the freezer. They will keep for up to two months, and they don't need to be defrosted before you fry them; they'll just take a few minutes longer to cook.

Serve the *lumpia*—or pita pockets—with Filipino Garlic Dipping Sauce (page 85), or with plain ketchup, as Filipinos do. We like to serve both, but we spice the ketchup with *Sri Racha* Hot Sauce (page 81) for a dash of chilli heat.

1¹/₂ quarts plus 1 tablespoon peanut or vegetable oil

²/₃ cup finely chopped onions

2 large cloves garlic, finely chopped

1 pound ground beef

¹/₄ cup grated carrot (about 1 large carrot)

1 large red potato, peeled and cut into julienne strips (about 1 cup)

¹/₂ cup shredded cabbage

3 tablespoons coconut palm vinegar, or substitute 2 tablespoons distilled white
   vinegar mixed with 1 tablespoon water

1¹/₂ teaspoons salt

¹/₄ cup water

1 large egg, beaten

One 1-pound package frozen spring roll wrappers, defrosted in the refrigerator

Filipino Garlic Dipping Sauce (page 85) and/or plain ketchup, or ketchup spiced with a favorite hot sauce

1. In a large wok or heavy skillet, heat 1 tablespoon of the oil over medium-high heat. Add the onions and garlic and cook, stirring, until translucent, about 1 minute. Increase the heat to high, add the ground beef, and stir-fry until the meat begins to brown, about 2 minutes. Add the carrot and potato and stir-fry for 5 minutes. Add the cabbage, vinegar, salt, and water and stir to mix well. Cover and cook until the carrots and potato are tender, about another 5 minutes. With a slotted spoon, transfer the mixture to a medium mixing bowl and set aside to cool to room temperature.

2. Meanwhile, organize a work area so all the ingredients for making the spring rolls are within easy reach. Have 2 barely damp dish towels on hand—1 for the completed spring rolls, 1 for the remaining wrappers. Put the beaten egg in a saucer and set it on a tray or sheet pan close at hand. Place the stack of spring roll wrappers on a cutting board and slice off the edges on all four sides with a sharp knife. This will make it easy to separate them. Set the wrappers on a clean work surface next to the cutting board. Peel off a wrapper and cover the others with a damp dish towel.

3. Place the wrapper on the cutting board, smooth side down, with one point toward you, forming a diamond shape. Place 2 heaping teaspoons of the filling in the center of the lower half of the diamond, the half closest to you. Use your fingers to shape the filling into a log about 4 inches long. Fold the wrapper point closest to you up, over, and around the filling. Roll halfway up toward the top point, then fold the left and right sides in and continue rolling. When you reach the top point, moisten it well with some of the beaten egg to seal the roll like an envelope. Set the completed roll, seam side down, on the tray or pan and cover with a dish towel. Continue to make rolls until you've used up the filling. Space the finished rolls so they are not touching.

4. Pour the remaining $1^1/2$ quarts of oil into a large wok or deep, heavy skillet, to a depth of $1^1/2$ inches. Heat over medium-high heat to 360 to 375 degrees F. Meanwhile, line a baker's rack or large colander with paper towels. Tear a

corner off a leftover wrapper and drop it into the hot oil. If it sizzles immediately, the oil is ready.

5. Carefully slip a spring roll into the hot oil, then 2 more. Cook, turning a few times, until golden brown all around, 3 to 5 minutes total. Remove the spring rolls from the hot oil with a slotted spoon or long-handled mesh scoop. Hold them over the oil a moment to drain, then transfer to the rack or colander. Cook the remaining spring rolls, 3 at a time, until all are done.

6. Arrange the spring rolls on a serving platter and serve hot with the garlic dip and/or ketchup on the side.

Crispy Peppercorn Shrimp

Serves 6 to 8 as an appetizer

It's amazing that a dish can be this tasty and flavorful and also be so fast and easy to make. The batter requires just four ingredients. The shrimp need no peeling or deveining and they fry up in minutes.

This is a popular appetizer throughout Thailand and Vietnam, where people eat the whole shrimp—shells, tail, legs, and all—for the extra flavor and crunchiness. In fact, the shells are necessary for this dish. The batter is too light to stick to peeled shrimp.

To ensure that the crisp, delicate coating stays intact, drain the shrimp on a baker's rack rather than paper towels. The batter comes together very quickly and should be made right before frying. Tapioca starch is used in Asia, but cornstarch is a perfect substitute.

One 24-ounce bottle peanut oil

3 tablespoons cornstarch

3 tablespoons Asian fish sauce

2 tablespoons white peppercorns, crushed in a mortar or ground in a spice mill

4 small Thai chillies, finely sliced into thin rounds

1 pound medium-size shrimp, legs, tails, and shells left on

Classic Vietnamese Dipping Sauce (page 82)

1. Heat the oil in a 14-inch wok or a large, heavy pot over medium-high heat to 375 degrees F. (To test the oil temperature, dip a wooden spoon in the hot oil. It should bubble and sizzle around the bowl of the spoon.)

2. While the oil is heating, mix together the cornstarch, fish sauce, peppercorns, and chillies in a large mixing bowl.

3. Toss the shrimp in the coating mixture with your hands to evenly distribute the chillies and crushed pepper. Each shrimp should have a thin layer of the coating.

4. Add the coated shrimp to the hot oil, a few at a time. Cook until nicely browned, about 3 minutes. As they fry, use a wooden spoon to keep them from sticking together. With a wire skimmer or slotted spoon, transfer the fried shrimp to a baker's rack.

5. Retest the oil temperature occasionally, letting it heat up if necessary between batches, and continue cooking until all the shrimp are fried.

6. Serve warm with the dipping sauce.

Bangkok-to-Bali Shrimp Cocktail

Serves 4

Southeast Asia is famous for its composed salads. This one is inspired by the classic seafood cocktails of Mexico, but adds Southeast Asian citrus and spice. Avocado and cilantro are both well known and loved in places such as Bali, just as they are in Mexico.

Deveining shrimp is a time-consuming little chore that we're happy to discard. Both in Asia and Latin America most cooks see no reason to devein shrimp, and neither do we.

We serve Bangkok-to-Bali Shrimp Cocktails in parfait glasses, with iced-tea spoons for mounding the avocado-and-onion-studded cocktail sauce onto corn chips or saltines. The white onion is rinsed under cold water to make it a little milder. You want enough onion to add flavor and crunch, without overwhelming the entire preparation.

1 pound medium-size shrimp

$1/2$ cup ketchup

$2^1/2$ tablespoons fresh lemon juice

1 teaspoon Worcestershire sauce

$1/2$ teaspoon Chinese chilli-garlic sauce

$1/2$ teaspoon Tabasco sauce, plus more for serving

$1/2$ teaspoon salt

1 tablespoon minced serrano chillies

$1/2$ cup chopped white onion

1 small bunch fresh cilantro, chopped, including the stems, plus a few sprigs
   for serving

1 large ripe avocado, peeled, pitted, and cut into $1/2$-inch cubes

Tortilla chips or saltine crackers for serving

1. Bring a 1-quart pot of salted water to a boil. Add the shrimp and cook until firm and bright pink, 3 to 4 minutes. Drain and set aside.

2. To make the sauce, combine the ketchup, lemon juice, Worcestershire, chilli-garlic sauce, Tabasco, salt, and chillies in a small mixing bowl. Cover and chill the sauce in the refrigerator until ready to serve.

3. Put the chopped onion in a fine-mesh strainer and rinse under cold running water. Drain on paper towels. Pat dry, transfer to a small bowl, and set aside.

4. To peel the shrimp, remove the shells, but leave the tails intact.

5. In a large mixing bowl, toss the shrimp with the onion and chopped cilantro. Stir in the sauce and mix gently. Spoon the shrimp cocktail into 4 parfait or large martini glasses (small serving bowls will do, if need be). Place an iced-tea spoon in each glass and top each serving with cubes of avocado and a sprig of cilantro. Serve with Tabasco sauce and tortilla chips or saltine crackers on the side.

Bangkok-to-Bali Beer-Battered Shrimp

Serves 6

o make this recipe faster, you can buy your shrimp already peeled and de-veined. You can also roll the shrimp in grated coconut before frying.

1½ pounds jumbo shrimp

1 recipe Bangkok-to-Bali Beer Batter (page 288)

3 cups unsweetened dried shredded coconut (optional)

One 24-ounce bottle peanut or vegetable oil

Tangy Citrus *Sambal* (optional, see page 220)

1. Shell the shrimp, leaving the tails on. If you wish, with a small sharp knife, cut a slit along the back and devein. Toss the shrimp with the beer batter in a large mixing bowl and set aside. If using the coconut, put it in a shallow dish. Dip

the shrimp in the batter, then press them into the coconut. Put them on a baker's rack.

2. Heat the oil in a deep fryer, large wok, or deep, heavy pot to 365 degrees F. (To test the oil temperature, dip a wooden spoon in the hot oil. It should bubble and sizzle around the bowl of the spoon.) Using tongs, take several shrimp out of the batter and fry them, turning twice so they become golden brown and crispy on all sides, 3 to 4 minutes. Use tongs to transfer the shrimp to a baker's rack or paper towels to drain. Repeat with the remaining shrimp, checking the oil temperature and letting it reheat in between batches, if necessary.

3. Serve with the *sambal*, if desired.

Cambodian Steamed Mussels with Pineapple and Thai Basil

Serves 4

Reflecting on the many years his nation was part of French Indochina, King Sihanouk of Cambodia once said, "I am an anticolonialist, but if you must be colonized, it is better to be colonized by gourmets."

He may have been thinking about tantalizing dishes such as this one. We've taken *moules à la crème*, a traditional French dish of fresh mussels steamed with wine, butter, and cream, and given it a taste of Southeast Asia by using coconut milk instead of cream, and adding chunks of fresh pineapple to create the sour-sweet flavor you find in tropical Asian seafood soups.

The French also sparked local enthusiasm for their breads, so we serve the mussels with a fresh, crusty baguette to dunk into the wonderful sauce.

4 to 5 pounds mussels

1 teaspoon olive or vegetable oil

1 teaspoon finely chopped garlic

$1\frac{1}{2}$ to $2\frac{1}{2}$ teaspoons minced small Thai or serrano chillies, to your taste

$2\frac{1}{2}$ cups Chicken Stock (page 289) or canned low-sodium chicken broth

One 14-ounce can unsweetened coconut milk

$\frac{1}{4}$ cup dry white wine, such as Sauvignon Blanc

$\frac{1}{2}$ teaspoon turmeric

$1\frac{1}{2}$ tablespoons Asian fish sauce

$1\frac{1}{2}$ teaspoons palm sugar or light brown sugar

1 cup fresh or canned $\frac{1}{2}$-inch pineapple chunks

$\frac{1}{4}$ cup torn fresh Thai, sweet, or purple basil leaves

1 baguette, sliced

1. Wash the mussels thoroughly in 2 or 3 changes of water in your sink or in a large bowl. Tug off the beards attached to the shells. You can use a knife for any that resist pulling off by hand. Sort through the mussels and discard any with broken shells. Live mussels open and close, so discard any that don't fully close when you tap on the shells. Let the mussels stand in clean cold water while you prepare the broth.

2. Heat the oil in a large pot over medium-high heat. Stir-fry the garlic and chillies until the garlic begins to turn golden, about 1 minute. Stir in the chicken broth, coconut milk, and wine, then add the turmeric, fish sauce, and sugar. Bring to a boil, stirring occasionally. Add the mussels, cover, and cook until the shells open, 4 to 8 minutes, shaking the pot after 1 or 2 minutes to give them all room to open. Any mussels that won't open should be discarded.

3. Ladle the mussels and broth into wide serving bowls. Top each serving with pineapple chunks and basil. Serve hot, with bread on the side for dipping into the broth.

Filipino-Style Ceviche with Salmon and Green Mango

Serves 4 to 6

Filipinos have an ancient culinary tradition called *kinilaw*, in which raw ingredients are "cooked" by marinating them in one of their numerous local vinegars or with some other souring agent, such as citrus juice.

The same thing is done in Mexican cookery, where fresh fish and shellfish are marinated in lime juice for the dish Mexicans call ceviche, a treat many North Americans are familiar with. *Kinilaw* encompasses dozens of possible ingredients, including red meats, but is typically made from fish or shellfish—whatever is local and freshly caught.

Regardless of the regional variations and spicing secrets, *kinilaw* is always made with the belief that freshness is paramount, and whoever cooks least, cooks best. It expresses an ultimate respect for the great ingredients nature provides. We like the tangy, low-acid, flavorful vinegar made in the Philippines from coconut sap, but you can substitute a mixture of white vinegar and water.

$1/2$ cup coconut palm vinegar, or 5 tablespoons distilled white vinegar mixed with
   3 tablespoons water

$1/3$ cup chopped red onion

$1^1/2$ tablespoons finely chopped serrano chillies

1 pound salmon fillet, skin and any small bones removed, cut across the grain into
   strips about $1/4$ inch wide

$1/2$ cup canned unsweetened coconut milk

1 teaspoon peeled and grated fresh ginger

1 medium-size green mango, peeled, flesh cut away from the stone, then cut into
   matchsticks (for slash-cut technique, see page 127)

Saltine crackers or a favorite snack chip for serving (optional)

1. Place the vinegar, onion, and chillies in a medium-size nonreactive (glass, ceramic, or stainless steel) bowl. Stir well and add the strips of salmon. Cover the bowl with plastic wrap and place in the refrigerator to "cook" the salmon until done, 40 minutes to 1 hour, stirring it several times. After 30 minutes, check to see whether it is done. It should be nearly opaque throughout and firm, yet tender. If it needs more time, check at 10-minute intervals to catch it at its peak: barely transformed, still fresh and bright.

2. Drain and squeeze the salmon gently to remove any excess liquid. Combine the "cooked" salmon with the coconut milk, ginger, and mango in a medium-size serving bowl and toss gently but thoroughly.

3. Serve cold or at room temperature, with saltines or chips, if desired.

Stir-Fried Pork, Shrimp, and Coconut in Lettuce Leaves with Crushed Peanuts

Serves 6

*T*raditionally, this delicious stir-fry would be folded into a lacy web made from fried egg (see Egg Nets, page 287). But we love it just as well when it's served in lettuce leaves—a simple change that means much less work for the cook.

However you choose to present this wonderfully savory stir-fry, Hot 'n' Cool Cucumber Relish (page 256) is a perfect accompaniment.

1/4 pound medium-size shrimp, peeled, deveined if desired, and finely chopped

1/2 pound ground pork

One 7-ounce package sweetened shredded coconut

1 tablespoon vegetable oil

4 large cloves garlic, crushed and chopped

6 scallions (white and tender green parts), sliced

20 fresh or frozen kaffir lime leaves, very thinly sliced, or grated zest of 1 lime

2 tablespoons light soy sauce

1 tablespoon seasoned rice vinegar

2 1/2 tablespoons unsalted dry-roasted peanuts, crushed in a mortar or chopped

12 cup-shaped butter lettuce leaves (from about 2 heads)

2 cups crisp, fresh bean sprouts

1 small bunch fresh cilantro

Hot 'n' Cool Cucumber Relish (optional, page 256)

1. Put the shrimp, pork, and coconut in a large mixing bowl and mix well. Set aside.

2. Heat a wok over medium-high heat. When it is hot, add the oil and rotate the wok a bit to coat it evenly. When the oil is hot, add the garlic and stir-fry a few seconds, until fragrant. Add the shrimp and pork mixture and stir-fry just until the meat begins to color, about 2 minutes. Mix in the scallions and lime leaves,

then add the soy sauce and vinegar and stir-fry for 2 minutes. Remove the wok from the heat and stir in the crushed peanuts.

3. Arrange the lettuce "cups" on a large serving platter. Spoon the filling into each one, about $1/3$ cup filling per lettuce cup. Scatter some bean sprouts over each serving and garnish with small sprigs of cilantro.

4. Serve with the relish, if desired.

Minced Pork and Pineapple Tidbits with Red Chilli and Cilantro

Serves 6 to 8

This traditional Thai appetizer is great party food, featuring sophisticated flavors and textures. It contrasts the sweetness of pork, pineapple, and palm sugar with the salty tang of fish sauce and peanuts—plus a dash of chilli heat. Serve it casually, as a finger food, at room temperature. With the red chilli ovals, yellow pineapple, and green cilantro leaves, it looks like an assortment of pretty puzzle pieces.

1 teaspoon black peppercorns, ground in a mortar or peppermill (see step 1)

2 tablespoons finely chopped garlic

2 tablespoons chopped fresh cilantro, including the stems

$1^1/_2$ tablespoons vegetable oil

$1/_2$ pound coarsely ground pork

2 tablespoons Asian fish sauce

3 tablespoons palm sugar or light brown sugar

$1/_4$ cup unsalted dry-roasted peanuts, ground in a mortar or finely chopped

1 small to medium-size pineapple

6 to 8 small Thai chillies, preferably red, to your taste, angle-cut into thin ovals

Leaves from 1 small bunch fresh cilantro for garnish

1. Put the peppercorns in a mortar, add the garlic and cilantro, and pound the mixture into a fairly smooth paste. Alternatively, process freshly ground peppercorns, garlic and cilantro into a paste in a mini–food processor.

2. Heat a wok or medium-size sauté pan over medium heat. When it is hot, add the oil and rotate the wok or pan a bit to coat it evenly. When the oil is hot, add the spice paste and stir-fry about 1 minute to release its fragrance, then crumble in the ground pork with your hands. Increase the heat to medium-high and stir-fry the mixture until the pork begins to brown, about 2 minutes. Add the fish sauce and sugar and stir-fry until the meat is broken up, well blended, and lightly browned, 3 to 4 minutes.

3. Remove the pan from the heat and transfer the pork mixture to a medium-size mixing bowl. Stir in the peanuts and let the mixture cool to room temperature.

4. Using a large, sharp knife, trim the pineapple's base just enough to allow the fruit to stand up on a cutting board. Cut off the top. Slice away the tough skin and green rind with a series of downward strokes. Remove any remaining traces of skin and rind, then use the tip of your knife to remove any "eyes" still attached to the fruit. Cut the pineapple in half lengthwise through the core. Cut away the core from each half, then cut crosswise into 1/4-inch-thick slices. Cut the slices into bite-size pieces, about 1 inch square. Transfer the pineapple squares to a large serving platter. Mound a little of the stir-fried pork onto each square, about a rounded 1/2 teaspoon per piece. Accent each tidbit with some fresh chilli ovals and cilantro leaves and serve.

Malay Pork Saté with Spicy Peanut Sauce

Saté has become well known in America in recent years, but in Southeast Asia it is more than simply popular. It is one of the most universal dishes and quite possibly the favorite late-night snack throughout the entire region, found in open-air markets and at carts parked along sidewalks almost everywhere you may go. It probably originated on the island of Java, but is now considered the national specialty of all Indonesia. It migrated into Malaysia, and from there into Thailand, where people like their food very spicy. However, the Javanese version is still the hottest saté of all.

Satés resemble kebabs, usually of some type of meat, shellfish, or spiced fish paste grilled on a skewer. But unlike kebabs, satés never include vegetables. Pork saté goes especially well with the richness of coconut milk blended into a marinade spiced with shallots, chillies, and ginger.

One 5.5-ounce can (scant ³/₄ cup) unsweetened coconut milk

3 tablespoons finely chopped shallots or red onion

1 tablespoon peeled and minced fresh ginger

1 teaspoon salt

¹/₄ teaspoon freshly ground black pepper

¹/₂ teaspoon sliced small Thai or serrano chillies

2 pounds pork tenderloin, trimmed of any fat and silverskin and cut into 1-inch cubes

1 tablespoon vegetable oil

Spicy Peanut Sauce (page 88), heated

16 ten-inch bamboo skewers, soaked in cold water for at least 30 minutes and drained

1. In a blender, combine the coconut milk, shallots, ginger, salt, black pepper, and chillies and blend until smooth, stopping once or twice to scrape down the sides of the jar. Pour the mixture into a large mixing bowl. Add the pork and

stir until the cubes are evenly coated. Cover with plastic wrap and marinate the pork for at least 1 hour and up to 2 hours in the refrigerator, stirring occasionally.

2. When the pork is ready, remove it from the marinade and thread tightly onto the bamboo skewers, 4 to 5 pieces per skewer. Set aside.

3. Preheat an outdoor grill, or preheat a grill pan for 3 to 5 minutes over medium-high heat. Brush the skewered pork with the oil and grill, turning the skewers occasionally, until the pork is crisp-edged and browned on the outside and just cooked inside, 8 to 10 minutes total.

4. Arrange the saté sticks on a serving platter and serve immediately, with warm peanut sauce on the side.

Indonesian Chicken Saté with Spicy Peanut Sauce

Makes about 16 skewers of saté

For chicken saté, we prefer a marinade based on the ubiquitous Indonesian soy sauce called *kecap manis*, sharpened with fresh lime juice and garlic. It's our favorite type of sweet dark soy sauce, made with molasses, a type of ginger powder called *laos*, and ground coriander. Look for it the next time you visit an Asian grocery. When you need only a small amount, however, maple syrup makes a very good substitute.

2 teaspoons chopped garlic

1 teaspoon salt, preferably coarse

10 white peppercorns, or ¼ teaspoon ground white pepper

1 teaspoon coriander seeds or ground coriander

1 teaspoon fresh lime juice

1 tablespoon *kecap manis*, sweet dark soy sauce, or pure maple syrup

2¹/₂ pounds boneless, skinless chicken breasts, trimmed of any fat and cut into
  1-inch cubes
2 tablespoons peanut or vegetable oil
Spicy Peanut Sauce (page 88), heated

16 ten-inch bamboo skewers, soaked in cold water for at least 30 minutes
  and drained

1. Make a spice paste: Combine the garlic, salt, peppercorns, and coriander seed
   in a mortar and pound the mixture into a fairly smooth paste. Or, combine the
   garlic, salt, and ground spices on a cutting board and mash with a fork, stirring
   and scraping the mixture to form a fairly smooth paste.

2. Transfer the spice paste to a large mixing bowl and stir in the lime juice and
   kecap manis, mixing well. Add the chicken and mix to coat evenly. Cover with
   plastic wrap and let the chicken marinate for 30 minutes at room temperature
   or in the refrigerator for 2 hours.

3. When the chicken is ready, remove it from the marinade and thread tightly
   onto bamboo skewers, 4 to 5 pieces per skewer. Set aside.

4. Preheat an outdoor grill, or preheat a grill pan for 3 to 5 minutes over
   medium-high heat. Brush the chicken with the oil and grill, turning frequently,
   until the chicken is lightly charred outside and just cooked inside, about 5
   minutes total.

5. Arrange the saté sticks on a serving platter and serve immediately, with the
   warm peanut sauce on the side.

Sauces and Condiments

RED CHILLI MAYO

BIG EASY REMOULADE

SWEET HOT THAI CHILLI SAUCE

SRI RACHA HOT SAUCE

CLASSIC VIETNAMESE DIPPING SAUCE

THAI CHILLI DIPPING SAUCE

BALINESE DIPPING SAUCE

HEAT WAVE DIPPING SAUCE

FILIPINO GARLIC DIPPING SAUCE

CHILLI-VINEGAR SAUCE

VEGETARIAN CHILLI-VINEGAR SAUCE

CAMBODIAN PEPPER DIP

SPICY PEANUT SAUCE

BANGKOK-TO-BALI BBQ SAUCE

SPICED COCONUT SAMBAL

TOMATO SAMBAL

TROPICAL-STYLE CRANBERRY RELISH

SPICE ISLAND SALSA

THAI COCONUT, LEMON, AND GINGER CHUTNEY

SWEET VEGETABLE PICKLES

TOASTED RICE POWDER

TOASTED SESAME SALT

TOASTED COCONUT

CRISP-FRIED SHALLOTS

THAI FRIED GARLIC CHIPS

CRISPY GARLIC IN OIL

CRISPY BASIL LEAVES

Here is where much of the magic happens

in tropical Asian cuisine, with simple but versatile concoctions of spice and savor that can make everyday dishes memorable and memorable dishes unforgettable. And their magic can translate beautifully to your all-American cooking as well.

In fact, some of these sauces and condiments are reimaginings of familiar dishes, given a refreshing lift with Southeast Asian accents. Tropical-Style Cranberry Relish (page 94), for example, rises out of the ordinary with rich helpings of ginger and pineapple. It has become a must-have at holiday times for us, our families, and for many of our friends. Red Chilli Mayo (page 78), laced with the Thai hot sauce called *sri racha*, provides an incredibly easy way to make any sandwich more exciting. Bangkok-to-Bali BBQ Sauce (page 95) is a richly satisfying blend of Asian and Western ingredients that requires no lengthy cooking—in fact, no cooking at all, just an appetite for complex flavor born of simple ingredients.

Many more recipes in this chapter, however, are going to be brand new to you. They derive directly from the various Southeast Asian countries whose cuisines inspire this book, and all of them are much-loved essentials in their native lands. We think they'll bring you tremendous enjoyment, not only when they're served traditionally, but also when paired with Western favorites such as hamburgers, meat loaf, fried chicken, vegetable dishes, soups, and salads, plus many more uses you'll discover for yourself.

For example, throughout tropical Asia you'll find dipping sauces on practically every table, for dunking finger foods or for spooning over whatever is on your plate. We've given you quick recipes for lime-tart Cambodian Pepper Dip (page 87), sweet soy and chilli–spiked Balinese Dipping Sauce (page 83), Classic Vietnamese Dipping Sauce (page 82), and homemade *Sri Racha* Hot Sauce (page 81), the world-class hot sauce from Thailand. All of them come together in minutes, keep quite well, and instantly "lively up" any meal you serve.

Many other recipes in this chapter are for enticingly savory items to be sprinkled over soups, salads, rice, side dishes, or main courses. Crisp-Fried Shallots (page 100), for example, are quite addictive and a suitable sprinkle for a wide variety of dishes, from curries to salads. So are Thai Fried Garlic Chips (page 101) and Crispy Garlic in Oil (page 102). Toasted Coconut (page 99) is also extremely versatile, to be showered over salads as well as sweets and desserts. Sweet Vegetable Pickles (page 97), a colorful

mosaic of baby corn, pearl onions, and sliced carrots, are easily made refrigerator pickles with a perfect balance of sweet and sour tang and crunch. Chutney-like *sambals* and, of course, Spicy Peanut Sauce (page 88) all demonstrate the pleasures inherent in adding striking new flavor-packed goodies, both traditional and modern.

Pleasure, in fact, is the entire reason behind every recipe in this chapter. These sauces and condiments enhance, entice, and enliven. We're betting that they will become regulars at your table.

Red Chilli Mayo

his is a great, simple condiment. We created it to go with the Philly-Style Vietnamese Hoagies with Poached Chicken (page 203), but it's a versatile spread for all kinds of sandwiches, made with or without meat.

3 tablespoons mayonnaise

1 tablespoon *Sri Racha* Hot Sauce (page 81), or prepared *sri racha*, or any favorite
   hot sauce

1 or 2 pinches of salt, to your taste

1/2 teaspoon fresh lemon juice

Whisk all the ingredients together in a small mixing bowl. This will keep about 2 weeks, tightly covered, in the refrigerator.

Big Easy Remoulade

*H*ere's a recipe for big flavor, real easy. We call this Big Easy in honor of New Orleans, where a remoulade sauce made from mayonnaise, Worcestershire, and Creole mustard (a coarsely ground variety) is traditionally spread on baguettes for "po' boy" sandwiches. We added white pepper, a favorite spice in Southeast Asia, to create this version for our Philly-Style Vietnamese Hoagies with BBQ Pork (page 186). We believe you'll find dozens of other uses for it. For example, you could try Big Easy Remoulade with cooked shrimp for a kickin' shrimp salad.

$^1/_4$ cup mayonnaise

1 tablespoon Creole mustard

$^1/_2$ teaspoon Worcestershire sauce

Pinch of salt

2 big pinches of white pepper

2 dashes of Tabasco sauce

1. Whisk the mayonnaise and mustard together in a small mixing bowl. Add the remaining ingredients and mix well.

2. Transfer the remoulade to a covered container and refrigerate until chilled, about 1 hour. This will keep about 2 weeks, tightly covered, in the refrigerator.

Sweet Hot Thai Chilli Sauce

*T*his is a delicious sauce for barbecued chicken and many other grilled and fried dishes. Try it on fish kebabs, spring rolls, or pan-fried soft-shell crabs. If the small Thai chillies known as *phrik khee nu* are not readily available, add a tablespoon or so of Chinese chilli-garlic sauce, which is available in most supermarkets in the ethnic foods section. It will also take the place of the fresh garlic.

1 teaspoon salt, preferably coarse

1 tablespoon roughly chopped garlic (omit if using Chinese chilli-garlic sauce)

1 teaspoon sliced small Thai chillies or 1 tablespoon plus 1 teaspoon Chinese
  chilli-garlic sauce

3/4 cup distilled white vinegar

1 1/4 cups white sugar

1. Use a mortar and pestle or a mini–food processor to coarsely crush the salt, garlic, and chillies together, or combine the ingredients on a cutting board and chop until minced and well blended.

2. In a medium-size saucepan, combine the chilli paste with the vinegar and sugar and cook over medium heat, stirring often. Bring to a simmer, then reduce the heat to the lowest setting that will keep the mixture simmering gently. Cook, stirring often, until the mixture thickens, about 10 minutes.

3. Transfer the sauce to a heat-proof bowl and let cool to room temperature before serving. This will keep, tightly covered, in the refrigerator for about 2 weeks.

Sri Racha Hot Sauce

*T*his sauce was first made in the coastal town of Sri Racha, in southern Thailand, and its combination of sweetness and spice is a classic example of how Thai people balance flavors. The popularity of *sri racha* is global. We've seen it on taco stand counters in California.

Sri racha has a consistency like that of ketchup, but the flavor is more complex, thanks to the sun-dried chillies which are the foundation of its recipe. Although commercial brands are excellent, it's easy to make your own and wonderful to put in bottles to give as gifts.

6 large dried red chillies, such as New Mexico or California

4 small dried red chillies, such as chile de arbol or Japanese chillies

One 28-ounce can peeled whole plum tomatoes, preferably San Marzano

6 large cloves garlic, crushed and chopped

$1/3$ cup distilled white vinegar

3 tablespoons plus 2 teaspoons sugar

1 tablespoon plus 1 teaspoon salt

1. Snip the chillies into 1- to 2-inch pieces with kitchen shears or break them up with your hands. Some cooks wear gloves when working with hot peppers; we simply wash our hands very well afterward with soap. Place all the chillies in a medium-size mixing bowl, cover with hot water, and let soak until soft and flexible, about 20 minutes.

2. Meanwhile, drain the canned tomatoes. Squeeze out the excess juice from each tomato. Put 2 or 3 tomatoes in a blender and add all the garlic. Process until the mixture is pureed and the garlic is smoothly incorporated into the mix.

3. Drain the chillies, add them to the blender, and process until the mixture is nearly smooth. Add the remaining tomatoes, the vinegar, sugar, and salt and process until smooth. You can use right away or store, tightly covered, in the refrigerator for up to 1 month.

Classic Vietnamese Dipping Sauce

Makes about 1 cup

*N*uoc cham, as this table condiment is known in its homeland, is present at almost every Vietnamese meal. It's tangy and sweet, hot and sour—terrific over rice and noodles, or for dipping spring and summer rolls.

1/2 cup fresh lime juice (about 6 limes)

1/2 cup Asian fish sauce

1 small Thai or 2 serrano chillies, minced

1 medium-size clove garlic, crushed and finely chopped

1/2 teaspoon *sambal oelek*, *Sri Racha* Hot Sauce (page 81) or prepared *sri racha*, or
  Tabasco sauce

1 1/2 tablespoons sugar

1. Combine all the ingredients in a small serving bowl. Mix well until the sugar has dissolved.
2. Let stand for 10 to 15 minutes to allow the flavors to mix and marry before serving. This will keep for 2 to 3 weeks if stored, tightly covered, in the refrigerator.

Thai Chilli Dipping Sauce

*T*his smooth and spicy chilli sauce, fragrant with citrus and garlic, is a well-balanced potion, wonderful any time you want to add heat and sharpness to just about any dish—whether it's a stir-fry, noodles, a curry, steamed or grilled seafood, or barbecued beef.

¹/₂ cup fresh lime or lemon juice

¹/₄ cup Asian fish sauce

8 small Thai or 4 serrano chillies, thinly sliced

1 clove garlic, minced

Combine all the ingredients in a small bowl. Set aside for about 10 minutes to let the flavors develop, then serve. This sauce will keep for 2 weeks if stored, tightly covered, in the refrigerator.

Balinese Dipping Sauce

Makes 3/4 cup

*T*his confetti-flecked, dark sauce is fiery hot, sweet, and salty. Try it with satés, over Savory Yellow Rice (page 148), or with grilled meats and fish.

¹/₃ cup light soy sauce

¹/₂ cup sweet dark soy sauce, or substitute 2 tablespoons light soy sauce mixed with

   ¹/₄ cup pure maple syrup

2 tablespoons thinly sliced small Thai or serrano chillies

1. Mix all the ingredients together in a small bowl.
2. Let stand for 10 minutes before serving to let the flavors develop. If stored, tightly covered, in the refrigerator, this will keep 2 to 3 days.

Heat Wave Dipping Sauce

*T*his is an example of the Thai category of dipping sauces called *nam phrik*, which means "chilli water." It's a natural accompaniment for grilled or garden-fresh vegetables. The hot and pungent flavor is balanced with a little palm sugar and fresh lemon juice.

$^1/_2$ cup fresh lemon juice

$^1/_4$ cup Asian fish sauce

1 tablespoon plus 1 teaspoon palm sugar or light brown sugar

1 small clove garlic, chopped

4 small Thai or 2 serrano chillies, finely sliced

Combine all the ingredients in a blender and process until the garlic is smoothly incorporated into the mix. Set aside for about 10 minutes to let the flavors marry. Any leftover sauce will keep for 2 weeks if stored, tightly covered, in the refrigerator.

Filipino Garlic Dipping Sauce

*H*ere's another simple but memorable sauce, perfect for broiled and grilled meats and fish. You can substitute another vinegar, diluted with a little water, for the native Filipino vinegar, but it's quite a nice, subtle ingredient and you'll enjoy having it handy for salad dressings, marinades, and other uses.

2/3 cup coconut palm vinegar, or 1/4 cup plus 3 tablespoons rice or distilled white
   vinegar mixed with 1/4 cup water
1 tablespoon minced garlic
1 1/2 teaspoons salt

Combine all the ingredients in a small mixing bowl. Stir to dissolve the salt and let stand 10 minutes to let the flavors develop before serving.

Chilli-Vinegar Sauce

You'll find a version of this dipping sauce in many tropical Asian countries. Throughout Thailand, Vietnam, Malaysia, Indonesia, and the Philippines, for example, people like its piquant heat over stir-fried noodles. Use chilli-vinegar sauce as you would most hot sauces, as a table condiment for any dish to which you'd like to give a sharp, lively accent. Splash on just a bit of the liquid for more tang and less heat, or spoon both the liquid and the sliced chillies over your food for the full effect.

1/2 cup distilled white vinegar
2 teaspoons Asian fish sauce
2 serrano chillies, thinly sliced

1. Combine the ingredients in a small serving bowl.
2. Let stand for 10 to 15 minutes to allow the flavors to mix and marry before serving. This will keep for 2 to 3 weeks, tightly covered, in the refrigerator.

Vegetarian Chilli-Vinegar Sauce

Vegetarians may prefer this dipping sauce, which omits a key Southeast Asian ingredient, fish sauce. It will make flavors sparkle whenever you spoon some on a dish.

1/2 cup distilled white vinegar
1/2 teaspoon light soy sauce
1/2 teaspoon fresh lime juice
3 serrano chillies, thinly sliced

Combine all the ingredients in a small serving bowl. Let stand 10 minutes so the flavors will marry. This will keep for about 1 week, tightly covered, in the refrigerator.

Cambodian Pepper Dip

Cambodians augment our well-known duo of salt and pepper with the tang of fresh lime juice for their signature dipping sauce. *Tik marij* is the name of the condiment created when all three combine. It sharpens the flavors of entrées such as grilled or stir-fried beef, and also enlivens plain steamed rice.

1/4 cup freshly ground black pepper
2 tablespoons salt
2 limes

1. Put 1 tablespoon of the pepper and 1 1/2 teaspoons of the salt in little mounds on each of 4 small side dishes.
2. Roll the limes on a cutting board with the palm of your hand to help release their juice. Cut each lime in half and add 1 half to each side dish.
3. Each person should squeeze their lime half over the pepper and salt and stir until the salt dissolves.
4. Serve as a dipping sauce or spoon over rice to taste.

Spicy Peanut Sauce

*S*picy peanut sauce is the traditional accompaniment to grilled meat satés, and also serves as the dressing for the delightful Indonesian vegetable salad called *gado gado* (page 121). It's based on just four ingredients, but what flavor, especially if you use ingredients of the best quality. With homemade Thai Red Curry Paste (page 292), a natural unsalted chunky peanut butter (from a health food store or a well-stocked supermarket), and real *kecap manis* or sweet soy sauce, you'll have the gold standard for peanut sauce. Don't be too surprised if you find yourself raiding the refrigerator for a spoonful now and then. The first time one of our friends tasted this, she said, "I don't need saté to go with this sauce. I'd be happy to lick it off my arm!"

One 14-ounce can unsweetened coconut milk
$1/4$ cup plus 1 tablespoon Thai Red Curry Paste (page 292) or a commercial brand
1 tablespoon *kecap manis* or sweet dark soy sauce, or substitute $1^1/2$ teaspoons light
soy sauce mixed with $1^1/2$ tablespoons pure maple syrup
$1/3$ cup natural unsalted chunky peanut butter

1. Pour the coconut milk into a medium-size saucepan and slowly bring to a gentle boil over medium heat. Add the remaining ingredients and simmer, stirring occasionally, until the mixture thickens enough to coat the back of a wooden spoon, 12 to 15 minutes.

2. Transfer the sauce to a serving bowl and serve warm. This will keep, tightly covered, in the refrigerator for about 2 weeks.

Bangkok-to-Bali BBQ Sauce

This is a rich, delicious barbecue sauce with a lot of depth and plenty of smoky white pepper heat. It's absolute simplicity to make, requiring no cooking, and it's especially good for beef and pork ribs, chops, and steaks. For a more savory burger, mix a little of this sauce into the ground beef or turkey.

1/4 cup molasses

1/4 cup Asian fish sauce

1/4 cup *Sri Racha* Hot Sauce (page 81) or prepared *sri racha*

1/4 cup plus 2 tablespoons ketchup

2 teaspoons white pepper

1 tablespoon plus 1 teaspoon ground coriander

1 tablespoon plus 1 teaspoon ground cumin

1 tablespoon plus 1 teaspoon palm sugar or light brown sugar

Combine all the ingredients in a small mixing bowl. Mix well, until the sugar is dissolved and blended into the sauce. This will keep for 2 weeks, tightly covered, in the refrigerator.

Bastes and BBQ Sauces

BARBECUE SAUCES ARE OFTEN USED TO FLAVOR MEATS AND SEAFOOD AS THEY GRILL. BRUSH SOME SAUCE ONTO RED MEATS SUCH AS STEAKS AND RIBS DURING THE LAST 5 TO 10 MINUTES OF GRILLING, BUT NOT BEFORE, IN ORDER TO AVOID SCORCHING THE SUGAR IN THE SAUCE. FISH, HOWEVER, COOKS VERY QUICKLY AND CAN BE BASTED AS SOON AS YOU PUT IT ON THE GRILL. COOK UNTIL DONE, WITHOUT TURNING. SERVE THE REMAINING SAUCE AT THE TABLE.

Spiced Coconut Sambal

Makes 1 cup

Spiced and toasted coconut is a condiment found throughout Southeast Asia. This version is in the Malaysian style, a *sambal* perfect for accompanying a wide range of rice and curry dishes. It's light and crispy, with subtle heat and the fragrance of ginger and lime. The flavors are more alive if you make this *sambal* with a mortar and pestle, but a mini–food processor will also do a good job.

Try sprinkling some of this delicious condiment over a platter of Fragrant Malay Rice with Mixed Fresh Herbs (page 150).

8 small dried red chillies

1 cup hot water

1 plump stalk lemon grass

2 large fresh or frozen kaffir lime leaves

3/4 cup unsweetened dried shredded coconut

1 tablespoon peeled and chopped fresh Siamese ginger (*galanga*) or regular ginger

1¹/₂ teaspoons fresh lime juice

¹/₄ teaspoon ground fennel seeds

Big pinch salt

¹/₂ teaspoon sugar

1¹/₂ tablespoons peanut or vegetable oil

¹/₈ teaspoon turmeric

1. Break the chillies into bits and place them in a small mixing bowl. Add the hot water and set aside to soak for about 10 minutes while you prepare the other ingredients.

2. Trim the root end of the lemon grass and discard the tough outer leaves. Cut a 4-inch length from the bulb end and discard the rest. Mince the lemon grass, then set aside. Stack the lime leaves. With a kitchen shears or a small sharp knife, cut them crosswise into thin slivers and set aside. In a dry wok or heavy skillet, toast the coconut over low heat, shaking the pan and stirring frequently until the flakes are fragrant and golden brown, 4 to 6 minutes. Transfer the toasted coconut to a small bowl and set aside. Strain the chillies, reserving the soaking liquid.

3. Place the chillies, lemon grass, lime leaves, and ginger in a mortar and pound with the pestle into a fairly smooth paste, and transfer the spice paste to a small bowl. Or, using a mini–food processor, place the chillies, lemon grass, lime leaves, and ginger in the work bowl and blend, scraping down the sides of the bowl often. Add up to 3 tablespoons of the reserved soaking liquid from the peppers to aid the grinding, as necessary. Process into a fairly smooth paste. Transfer the spice paste to a small bowl.

4. In another small bowl, mix together the lime juice, fennel, salt, and sugar.

5. Set a wok or skillet over medium-high heat. When it is hot, add the oil and rotate the wok or pan a bit to coat it evenly. When the oil is hot, fry the spice paste, stirring, until fragrant and well blended, about 3 minutes. Add the lime juice mixture, then the toasted coconut. Turn off the heat. Stir until the mixture is well blended. Stir in the turmeric.

6. Transfer the *sambal* to a small serving bowl and let cool to room temperature before serving. It will keep at room temperature for up to 4 to 6 hours.

Sambal Savvy

People on the island of Java tell young girls that they will find a good husband if they know just two things—how to brew a good cup of coffee and how to mix up a fine *sambal*.

In both Indonesia and Malaysia, the art of cuisine rests on creating the right *sambal* for the dishes being served. There are many, many *sambals*, each used in quite a few different ways.

Sambals essentially are pastes of fiery hot chillies and other ingredients, often including lime juice, shallots, and/or garlic, traditionally ground in stone mortars to create a moderately rough texture. They usually accompany blander items, such as rice. Many *sambals* are raw, but some are cooked. While they're typically presented as a dipping sauce or hot sauce, they may also be an ingredient in another recipe, often an even more complex *sambal*, or served alone.

Sambal oelek, for example, is a simple paste of crushed red chillies with a splash of vinegar and a pinch of salt. It can be presented as a table condiment, or substituted for fresh chillies in a recipe, or used as the base for many sauces. With the addition of fresh lime juice, it becomes *sambal jeruk*, a condiment that's perfect for steamed fresh fish. If you also add lemon basil, you'll create *sambal kemanji*, often chosen to enliven a dish of steamed vegetables.

Sambal ketjap, whose name was borrowed by Dutch traders for the table condiment we call ketchup, is a sweet-hot condiment for plain rice, fried tofu, and lamb saté. It blends chillies, limes, and *kecap manis*, Indonesia's sweet dark soy sauce.

Sambal trassi is a classic all-purpose *sambal* made with shrimp paste, chillies, lime juice, and garlic. It goes with almost any Indonesian or Malaysian dish.

Pineapple *sambal*, made with red and green chillies, fresh pineapple, and a touch of rice vinegar, is usually paired with seafood. *Sambal bajak*, a chilli paste with tamarind and palm sugar, is the seasoning ingredient for *terong bajak*, a fiery stir-fry of eggplant and shrimp.

Sambals that can be served as a dish include *sambal udang*, which we call Malay Chilli Shrimp (page 211), made with chillies, ginger, garlic, and macadamia nuts, which are cooked with coconut milk, lime juice, and palm sugar. Our simple Tomato *Sambal* (below) can be served as a condiment, and it can also be stir-fried with meat or seafood to make a main dish.

Tomato Sambal

Makes 1 cup

This simple *sambal* packs plenty of flavor and plenty of spice! It's great with grilled fish, and mixes well with a little mayonnaise for a tangy sandwich spread. We often make it with canned San Marzano whole peeled tomatoes. They're rich in flavor, more so than some fresh tomatoes, especially when out of season.

1 tablespoon plus 1 teaspoon vegetable oil

$1/4$ cup sliced shallots

$2^1/2$ tablespoons sliced garlic

$1/2$ cup sliced serrano or jalapeño chillies

1 teaspoon anchovy paste

1 cup chopped fresh plum tomatoes or drained and chopped canned peeled tomatoes, preferably San Marzano

1 teaspoon fresh lime juice

Salt to taste

1. Heat a wok or skillet over medium heat. When it is hot, add the oil and rotate the wok or pan a bit to coat it evenly. When the oil is hot, add the shallots, garlic, and chillies and stir-fry until softened, about 5 minutes. Add the anchovy paste and tomatoes and cook, stirring often, until the tomatoes are soft and the mixture is fragrant and well blended, 8 to 10 minutes.
2. Transfer the mixture to a blender and puree coarsely.
3. Transfer the *sambal* to a small serving bowl. Stir in the lime juice and season with salt. Let cool to room temperature before serving. This will keep 3 or 4 days, tightly covered, in the refrigerator.

Tropical-Style Cranberry Relish

ith a small assist from the tropics, you can surprise your guests with a lush, updated version of this holiday classic: fruity, gingery, delicious.

One 20-ounce can pineapple chunks in their own juice
About 1$^1/_4$ cups fresh orange juice
One 12-ounce bag fresh cranberries, picked over for stems and rinsed
1$^1/_2$ cups sugar
One 2-ounce jar crystallized ginger, minced

1. Drain the pineapple and reserve the juice. Chop the pineapple into bite-size pieces and set aside. Pour the pineapple juice into a large measuring cup (you should have about $^3/_4$ cup). Add enough orange juice to make 2 cups of liquid.
2. Combine the cranberries, sugar, and orange-pineapple juice in a large, heavy nonreactive saucepan. Bring the mixture to a boil over medium-high heat, stirring until the sugar dissolves. Let boil gently until the cranberry skins break

and the berries are tender, 6 to 8 minutes, stirring occasionally. Remove the pan from the heat and let the mixture cool to room temperature. Mix in the pineapple and ginger.

3. Transfer the cranberry relish to a storage container with a tight-fitting lid and refrigerate until ready to serve. You can make this relish up to 3 days in advance.

Spice Island Salsa

his spicy pineapple salsa has a couple of tricks up its sleeve—toasted sesame oil and red wine vinegar, for added savor and fragrance.

2½ cups peeled and cubed fresh pineapple or one 20-ounce can pineapple chunks in their own juice, drained

2½ cups chopped fresh plum tomatoes

1 small yellow bell pepper, seeded and chopped

½ small red onion, finely chopped

3 to 4 small Thai or serrano chillies, to your taste, minced

2 tablespoons toasted sesame oil

3 tablespoons red wine vinegar

Salt and freshly ground black pepper to taste

Gently toss all the ingredients together in a medium-size serving bowl until well mixed and serve. This will keep, tightly covered, in the refrigerator for 4 to 6 hours.

Thai Coconut, Lemon, and Ginger Chutney

*T*here is an exotic and lush Thai salad called *miang kam* that is a colorful mosaic of diced lemon, ginger, toasted coconut, sliced hot chillies, and peanuts. It's meant to be rolled up in Thai leaf lilies and dabbed with a sweetly pungent shrimp sauce. *Miang kam* takes a while to create. Once, when we longed for the flavorful experience of *miang kam* but didn't have the time to make it, we simply blended its key ingredients into this delicious chutney—perfect as an accompaniment for pan-fried or grilled fish, barbecued shrimp, or Bangkok-to-Bali Beer-Battered Shrimp (page 63).

1 small lemon

1 small knob fresh ginger, about $^1/_2$ inch

1$^1/_2$ teaspoons finely chopped shallots

1 tablespoon palm sugar or light brown sugar

$^1/_3$ cup unsalted dry-roasted peanuts, crushed in a mortar or finely chopped

2 tablespoons Chilli-Lemon Vinaigrette (page 294)

1$^1/_2$ tablespoons Toasted Coconut (page 99)

1 or 2 pinches pure chilli powder or paprika

1. Scrub the lemon well, then trim the ends, but leave the peel. Slice the lemon into $^1/_2$-inch-thick rounds. Pick out and discard any seeds, then stack the rounds and cut them into small dice.

2. Peel the ginger and cut it into thin slices. Stack them and cut into small dice.

3. In a small serving bowl, mix together the lemon, ginger, shallots, and sugar. Toss with the peanuts and stir in the vinaigrette. Sprinkle the chutney with the coconut and a little chilli powder and serve immediately.

Sweet Vegetable Pickles

*T*his type of crisp, sweet vegetable pickle is popular throughout the Asian tropics. In Vietnam, these pickles are served with French-style sandwiches made with baguettes. Indonesians always have them at their feasts, and often present them encircling a cone of spiced yellow rice. They're also eaten alone as a snack, or with leftover meat dishes. Many different kinds of vegetables can be used, including shredded cabbage and cauliflower florets.

We've chosen baby corn, carrot slices, and pearl onions because they make a beautiful combination and because the flavors complement one another so well. Once you've tried this recipe, you may want to bring a jar of Sweet Vegetable Pickles as a delicious gift the next time you're invited to a barbecue.

Make these pickles a day ahead of serving, and allow them to marinate in the refrigerator overnight. They will keep in the refrigerator up to one month.

1 cup cider vinegar or distilled white vinegar

1 cup water

$^1/_2$ cup sugar

$^1/_2$ teaspoon salt

One 14-ounce can baby corn, drained

1 medium-size carrot, angle-cut into thin slices

1 cup pearl onions

1. Combine the vinegar, water, sugar, and salt in a medium-size nonreactive saucepan and cook over medium heat, stirring occasionally, until the sugar dissolves, 3 to 4 minutes. Remove the pan from the heat and let cool completely.

2. Meanwhile, bring another medium-size saucepan of water to boil over medium-high heat and cook all the vegetables, separately, just until tender: about 30 seconds for the baby corn, 1 minute for the carrot slices, and 1 to 2 minutes for the pearl onions. As each vegetable is done, remove it from the

boiling water with a slotted spoon and place in a 1-quart mason jar. Peel the onions after draining, then add them to the jar.

3. Pour the cooled vinegar mixture into the mason jar and screw on the lid. Refrigerate overnight. Keep the pickles refrigerated after opening.

Toasted Rice Powder

Makes about 1/4 cup

A nutty, roasted flavor is the signature of this easy-to-make and very useful ingredient. Toasted rice powder originated in Laos, but it is also quite popular in Thailand and Vietnam. Its crunchiness and flavor are a highlight in many salads and summer rolls. Sticky rice is traditionally used, but any raw white rice will do just fine.

Because a fresh batch can be made so quickly, we usually make toasted rice powder the same day we plan to use it. But you can make it in advance, if you wish. It will keep for several weeks at room temperature in a tightly sealed jar.

$\frac{1}{4}$ cup raw white rice

1. Toast the rice in a small, dry skillet over medium-high heat for about 3 minutes, shaking the pan often to toast the grains evenly. They should develop a deep, golden color.
2. Set aside to cool slightly.
3. Transfer the rice to a mortar or spice mill and grind to a somewhat coarse powder. Store at room temperature in a tightly sealed jar until ready to use.

Toasted Sesame Salt

*T*his fragrant salt is a favorite condiment of the Burmese, who sprinkle it over their rice. You'll find that it can be a delicious addition to many kinds of dishes. We especially love to put it on steamed vegetables and on roasted chicken.

3 tablespoons sesame seeds
$1/2$ teaspoon salt

1. Heat a small skillet over medium-low heat. Add the sesame seeds and salt and stir constantly until the seeds are light golden brown, 3 to 4 minutes.
2. Transfer the mixture to a mortar or spice mill and grind to a coarse powder. It will keep about 1 week, tightly covered, at room temperature.

Toasted Coconut

*T*he simple act of frying unsweetened coconut yields crispy golden flakes full of nut-like flavor. Those flakes become a wonderful addition to many dishes—from tropical Asian salads to all-American desserts such as ice cream sundaes, fruit salads, cakes, and pies.

Unsweetened dried shredded coconut can be found in most natural food stores and specialty shops. Sometimes, instead of shredded coconut, you'll find packages labeled coconut chips or flakes. These will work also. Just chop them to bits of nearly uniform size before frying, so they'll brown evenly.

1 cup unsweetened dried shredded coconut

1. In a dry wok or heavy skillet, toast the coconut over low heat, shaking the pan and stirring frequently until the flakes are fragrant and light golden brown, 4 to 6 minutes.

2. Transfer the toasted coconut to a small bowl and let cool completely before serving. If stored in an airtight container at room temperature, toasted coconut will keep indefinitely.

Crisp-Fried Shallots

Makes a scant 1/2 cup

Crisp and crunchy, and rich with flavor, these fried shallot rings are the traditional accent for numerous soups, salads, curries, and noodle dishes throughout tropical Asia. In Burma you'll see them on fried fish and vegetables. They're sprinkled over chicken noodle soup in Vietnam, and over curries and salads from Bali to Bangkok.

Try sprinkling a handful of these crispy shallots (and perhaps some Thai basil, too) over a bowl of tomato soup as well as on everyday favorites such as baked potatoes, home fries, and scrambled eggs.

1/4 cup vegetable oil

1/2 cup thinly sliced shallots

1. Pour the oil into a small saucepan set over medium-high heat. When hot, add the shallots. (Test the oil with a shallot ring: it should sizzle in the hot oil.) Fry the shallots, stirring often, until crisp and brown, about 5 minutes.

2. Remove with a wire skimmer or slotted spoon and drain on paper towels. Let cool to room temperature. The shallots will keep for 1 week if stored in an airtight container at room temperature.

Thai Fried Garlic Chips

nyone who loves garlic will find these golden little chips addictive. The Burmese use them generously in salads, as do the Thai. Beyond salads, they're also great on a wide variety of curries and on steamed vegetables.

1 cup peanut or vegetable oil
1/4 cup thinly sliced garlic (about 12 cloves)

1. Heat the oil in a small skillet over medium heat. When hot, drop in a slice of garlic. If it sizzles, the oil is hot enough. Add the rest of the garlic and stir-fry just until it becomes aromatic and turns a pale golden color, about $1^1/_2$ minutes.

2. Remove the skillet from the heat, lift the garlic chips out of the oil with a wire skimmer or slotted spoon, and transfer to paper towels to drain. Serve warm, or at room temperature. The chips will keep for a few days if stored in an airtight container.

Crispy Garlic in Oil

T his is simply a great little condiment from Thailand, where it is called *kratiem jiew*. Use it as the Thais do—over noodles and soups, or on any dish you think might get a flavor lift from a spoonful or two of this crispy garlic–laced oil. It's even better than butter on baked potatoes or Italian bread, and omelets, sliced tomatoes, and steamed vegetables are all enhanced mightily by this simple pairing.

The garlic bits should be roughly uniform in size so they will cook evenly.

¹/₄ cup plus 2 tablespoons vegetable oil
3 tablespoons finely chopped garlic

1. Heat the oil in a small sauté pan over medium heat. Drop a bit of garlic into the oil. It should sizzle right away. When sizzling hot, add all the garlic and stir-fry until it is pale gold in color and quite fragrant.
2. Remove the pan from the heat. Let the mixture cool, then transfer to a glass jar with a tight-fitting lid. This will keep for about 1 week in the refrigerator. However, if you're going to use it the same day you make it, you can store it at room temperature.

Crispy Basil Leaves

*H*ere is an exceptionally pretty garnish from Thailand. Fresh basil leaves, when fried, become translucent, slightly brittle jewels. They almost appear to be stained glass in the form of leaves. The Thais use *bai horapha*, which we call Thai basil, but any fresh basil leaf can be used. You will see variations in the color, depending on the type you choose. For example, sweet Italian basil turns a rich, grassy green.

The Thais like to sprinkle crispy basil over stir-fries. Try it with Thai-Style Crab Fried Rice (page 154), or on American favorites such as baked potatoes, tomato soup, or sliced tomatoes drizzled with olive oil.

Thai basil is a delicate variety, and gets bedraggled if you wash and dry it. We use it without rinsing. If you use another variety and want to wash it, be extra sure to pat it completely dry. Any residue of moisture will cause the oil to splatter even more than usual.

Peanut or vegetable oil for frying
1 cup lightly packed fresh Thai, sweet, or purple basil leaves

1. In a large, heavy saucepan, heat $1/2$ inch of oil over medium-high heat to 350 degrees F. (To test the oil temperature, dip a wooden spoon in the hot oil. It should bubble and sizzle around the bowl of the spoon.)
2. Standing back from the pan, carefully add a small handful of basil to the hot oil. (The oil will bubble and sputter almost immediately.) Fry until the basil is translucent and crisp, 10 to 15 seconds, then transfer with a slotted spoon to paper towels. Continue frying in small batches until all the basil is cooked. You can prepare Crispy Basil ahead of serving time. Keep the leaves at room temperature, and use them the same day you make them.

Soups and
Salads

BURMESE-STYLE RED LENTIL SOUP

THAI CHICKEN AND COCONUT SOUP,
FESTIVAL STYLE

LAOTIAN SPICED GAZPACHO

SCALLOP AND BABY CORN CHOWDER

VIETNAMESE-STYLE HOT-AND-SOUR SHRIMP
SOUP WITH PINEAPPLE

BURMESE-STYLE POTATO SALAD

BANGKOK-TO-BALI CAESAR SALAD WITH
GRILLED HEARTS OF ROMAINE

GRILLED EGGPLANT SALAD WITH
CILANTRO-CHILLI VINAIGRETTE

INDONESIAN VEGETABLE SALAD WITH
CURRIED PEANUT DRESSING (GADO GADO)

INSALATA SIAM

BALINESE STAR FRUIT, PAPAYA, AND PINK
GRAPEFRUIT SALAD WITH AVOCADO DRESSING

GREEN PAPAYA SALAD WITH
FRESH CHILLI AND LIME

MANGO AND STAR FRUIT SALAD WITH PEANUTS

AVOCADO, ORANGE, AND GRAPEFRUIT SALAD WITH
SWEET SYRUP AND CILANTRO

SEARED SCALLOPS AND FRESH ORANGE SALAD WITH
MINT LEAVES AND CRISP-FRIED SHALLOTS

DANCING SHRIMP SALAD

SHRIMP AND PAPAYA SALAD WITH
PAPAYA SEED DRESSING

SPICY CHICKEN SALAD WITH TOASTED COCONUT

GREEN MANGO AND BABY GINGER SALAD
WITH GRILLED CHICKEN

VIETNAMESE COLESLAW WITH
SHREDDED CHICKEN AND PEANUTS

FIERY GRILLED BEEF SALAD

In the vast menu of tropical Asian cuisine,

there are tempting soups and salads beyond counting. Southeast
Asian soups and salads typically have rich, multilayered flavors.
In salads, that often means featuring both fruits and vegetables in
the same dish, along with meat and perhaps seafood, plus a light,
oil-free dressing.

Among the many examples in this chapter, you'll find Seared
Scallops and Fresh Orange Salad with Mint Leaves and Crisp-Fried
Shallots (page 130), where the interplay of herbs, fruit, and grilled
scallops is luscious and bright. Dancing Shrimp Salad (page 131), as
its name suggests, is alive with the heat of chillies and the punch of
citrus. Insalata Siam (page 123) is a marriage of Southeast Asian
ingredients and a classic Italian salad, *insalata caprese.* Instead of

layering tomato slices with *mozzarella di bufala* and Italian basil, we've featured slices of firm tofu and Thai basil, and added a garlicky vinaigrette and the intriguingly nut-like crunch of Toasted Rice Powder (page 98). Another Western classic in a new incarnation in this chapter is Bangkok-to-Bali Caesar Salad with Grilled Hearts of Romaine (page 118). Here, olive oil, anchovies, and Worcestershire sauce meet up with lime juice and chilli powder.

The tropical Asian technique of combining fruits and vegetables in a salad pays off deliciously in Avocado, Orange, and Grapefruit Salad with Sweet Syrup and Cilantro (page 129), while Fiery Grilled Beef Salad (page 139) and Shrimp and Papaya Salad with Papaya Seed Dressing (page 132) both show how Southeast Asian cooks combine a much wider range of salad ingredients than we do.

Its softly interwoven flavors make Thai chicken coconut soup a favorite of almost everyone who tries it. We've added even one more bright note, incorporating julienned mango with our Thai Chicken and Coconut Soup, Festival Style (page 109). The Vietnamese also have a tremendous repertoire of lushly flavored soups. One that is irresistible, and easy to make, is Vietnamese-Style Hot-and-Sour Shrimp Soup with Pineapple (page 115). Simpler yet, and perhaps the homiest recipe in this chapter, is Burmese-Style Red Lentil Soup (page 108), with an inviting pale yellow broth from the chicken stock and turmeric, flecked with carrot-colored red lentils in each spoonful.

Like the salads, some of our soup recipes are new inventions
in the Southeast Asian tradition of cross-cultural adaptation. Scallop
and Baby Corn Chowder (page 114) lends a Thai accent to the
Eastern Seaboard staple with a coconut milk–enriched broth and
Thai basil topping. The idea for Laotian-Spiced Gazpacho (page 112)
came naturally, since the people of Laos use lots of tomatoes,
chillies, herbs, and vegetables, and long ago, Spanish colonialists
brought gazpacho to Filipino tables. Toasted cumin and coriander
seeds scent and flavor the pureed garlic croutons and give this
herb-laden cold vegetable soup its East-West character.

Burmese-Style Red Lentil Soup

Burma lies just across the Bay of Bengal from India, and the red lentils in this simple, healthy, and easy-to-make soup reflect India's culinary influence. Mellow and mild, and suffused with gingery warmth, this soup is a homey favorite.

Unlike beans, lentils do not need soaking. They don't hold their shape as well as cooked beans, but that makes them perfect for soups and rice dishes. These red ones, often called *masoor* lentils, come from the Punjabi region of India. When uncooked, they're a beautiful deep orange. They become pale when cooked, but the addition of turmeric reinvigorates them and gives the soup a golden hue. You can find red lentils in health food stores and Indian groceries or in well-stocked supermarkets.

We like to accent each bowl with Toasted Sesame Salt (page 99) and/or Crisp-Fried Shallots (page 100) to taste, both of which are traditional Burmese condiments. You will have enough time to make them while the lentils cook.

1/2 cup dried red lentils

1 tablespoon peanut or vegetable oil

2 teaspoons finely chopped garlic

2 teaspoons peeled and minced fresh ginger

1/4 teaspoon turmeric

4 cups water

1/2 teaspoon salt, or more to taste

Toasted Sesame Salt (optional, page 99) to taste

Crisp-Fried Shallots (optional, page 100) to taste

1. Rinse the lentils in a colander under cold running water. Remove any tiny stones, and drain well.
2. Heat the oil in a large saucepan over medium heat. Add the garlic, ginger, and turmeric and stir-fry for 1 minute. Add the lentils and stir-fry until they begin to change color, 2 to 3 minutes. Add the water. Turn up the heat to medium-high and bring the water to boil. Reduce the heat immediately to medium-low and maintain a steady simmer. Cook, stirring occasionally, until the lentils are soft, 20 to 25 minutes. Do not overcook. Add salt to taste and stir.
3. Serve with the sesame salt and fried shallots, if desired, on the side.

Thai Chicken and Coconut Soup, Festival Style

Serves 6 to 8

This coconut and spice–infused soup, known as *tom kha kai*, is one of Thailand's classic dishes. It's comfort food of a high order. Americans have been won over by its creamy and fragrant blend of ginger, lemon grass, lime leaves, and sliced mushrooms, simmered until meltingly tender, with pieces of chicken added at the last moment for just-cooked flavor and texture.

Endless variations of this wonderful soup are possible. An elegant Thai-French establishment in our area serves a version featuring wild mushrooms and heavy cream. But our favorite "alternate" *tom kha kai* was discovered at the Dusit Resort on Pattaya Beach in Thailand during a summertime mango festival, when every dish on the menu featured that lush tropical fruit. At the Dusit, chefs subtly enhanced their chicken coconut soup with mango juice, but we prefer julienned fresh ripe mango, added just before serving for more bursts of flavor.

2 plump stalks lemon grass or strips of zest from 1 small lemon

4 cups Chicken Stock (page 289) or canned low-sodium chicken broth

12 slices fresh Thai ginger (*galanga*) or regular ginger, roughly half-dollar-sized coins,
   1/4 inch thick

16 fresh or frozen large kaffir lime leaves or strips of zest from 1 small lime

Two 19-ounce cans unsweetened coconut milk

2 tablespoons Thai roasted chilli paste (*nam phrik pao*), or a few good shakes
   of paprika

3 tablespoons Asian fish sauce

1/4 cup fresh lemon juice

3 1/2 tablespoons palm sugar or light brown sugar

1/2 pound mushrooms, thinly sliced

1 1/2 pounds boneless, skinless chicken breasts, trimmed of any fat and cut into bite-
   size pieces

1 large ripe mango, peeled, flesh cut away from the stone, and cut into matchsticks

1. If using lemon grass, trim the ends, discard the tough outer leaves, and angle-
   cut the bulb and stem into 4-inch pieces.

2. Put the chicken stock, ginger, lemon grass, and lime leaves in a soup pot, bring
   to a boil over medium-high heat, and let boil for 2 minutes. Stir in the coconut
   milk and return to a boil. Add the chilli paste, fish sauce, lemon juice, and
   palm sugar and stir until blended. Add the mushrooms and simmer until quite
   tender, about 10 minutes. (You can make the soup ahead up to this point; cool
   and refrigerate overnight or let stand for several hours to allow the flavors to
   marry and intensify.)

3. Add the chicken to the hot soup and simmer just until cooked through, 2 to 3
   minutes. Stir in the mango and serve at once.

Note: The ginger, lemon grass, and lime leaves are flavoring elements that you remove
as you eat the soup, so we like to set a bowl on the table to catch these items, much
as you'd offer a bowl for discarded shells when serving mussels.

At Home and Abroad

We love Thai Chicken and Coconut Soup, Festival Style (page 109) and make it even when our Asian cupboard is bare and we need a quick fix too urgently to take the time to go "abroad" (make a special trip to the Asian grocery). Coconut milk, fish sauce, and, of course, lemons and limes are readily at hand from the home pantry or the local supermarket. Thai roasted chilli paste (*nam phrik pao*), heady with roasted onions, shallots, chillies, and the sweet-and-sour tang of tamarind, can be omitted—resulting in a more subtle and mild broth. Or you can spice the soup with a little Hungarian paprika for a sweet-hot accent in the spirit of *nam phrik pao*. Other chilli pastes and hot sauces would overpower the broth, even when used sparingly, so we don't recommend them as substitutes here.

Laotian Spiced Gazpacho

This has traditional Spanish elements, such as tomatoes, chillies, olive oil, and garlic toast, to thicken the soup. Its Laotian personality comes from the coriander and cumin and copious amounts of fresh herbs, including Thai basil, mint, and cilantro. Fresh tomatoes are a staple in Laos, and French colonists introduced their breads to the local cuisine.

This soup is served cold, as a gazpacho should be, yet it is richly aromatic, thanks to the toasted spices and fresh herbs. Your guests will find this very inviting on a warm summer day, especially with a cold beer and perhaps some sliced avocados and corn or shrimp chips on the side.

Laotian-Spiced Gazpacho is at its best in the first hour or two after it's made, but will keep well in the refrigerator, tightly covered, for up to 24 hours.

3 slices (about 3 x 6 x $3/4$ inch) good-quality white bread, such as an Italian or French country loaf or baguette

$1/2$ teaspoon ground coriander

1 teaspoon ground cumin

$1 1/2$ teaspoons salt

$1/2$ teaspoon white pepper

3 large cloves garlic, minced

$1/4$ cup extra virgin olive oil

3 tablespoons aged red wine vinegar

6 large, ripe red tomatoes or a mixture of red and yellow, seeded and chopped

2 cups vegetable juice, such as V-8, chilled

1 medium-size yellow bell pepper, seeded and cut into $1/2$-inch dice

1 small red onion, cut into $1/4$-inch dice

1 medium-size cucumber, peeled, seeded, and cut into $1/2$-inch dice

2 to 4 tablespoons minced serrano chillies, to your taste

¼ cup chopped fresh Thai, sweet, or purple basil leaves

¼ cup chopped fresh mint leaves

¼ cup chopped fresh cilantro, including the stems

1. Preheat the oven to 350 degrees F. Place the bread slices on a baking sheet. Sprinkle them evenly with the coriander, cumin, salt, white pepper, and garlic. Drizzle evenly with 1½ tablespoons of the olive oil. Toast in the oven until light golden brown, about 15 minutes. Remove the pan from the oven.

2. Place the remaining 2½ tablespoons of olive oil in a blender and add the vinegar and garlic toast, breaking it up with your hands before dropping it in the blender. Process until the mixture is ground fairly smooth, stopping once or twice to scrape down the sides of the jar, if needed.

3. Transfer the pureed garlic toast to a large mixing bowl. Stir in the chopped tomatoes, vegetable juice, bell pepper, red onion, cucumber, and chillies and mix well. Stir in 2 tablespoons each of the basil, mint, and cilantro. Reserve the rest for garnishes.

4. Refrigerate the gazpacho until chilled, about 15 minutes.

5. Ladle the gazpacho into soup bowls and top with the remaining 2 tablespoons each of basil, mint, and cilantro.

Scallop and Baby Corn Chowder

This is a nourishing medley of Western and Southeast Asian soup styles. We've crossbred the corn and seafood chowders of the Eastern Seaboard with the coconut milk- and-tamarind-infused broths found beneath fresh basil leaves in Thai seafood and chicken soups. The result is a great all-seasons chowder. In summer, use fresh corn cut from the cob instead of baby corn. Either way, it's delicious.

3 medium-size ears fresh corn or one 14-ounce can baby corn, drained

1 tablespoon unsalted butter

1 medium-size onion, cut into $1/3$-inch dice

$1/2$ large red bell pepper, seeded and cut into $1/2$-inch dice

$1/8$ teaspoon turmeric

1 pound Yukon Gold or new potatoes, peeled and cut into $1/2$-inch dice

3 cups Chicken Stock (page 289) or canned low-sodium chicken broth

1 cup canned unsweetened coconut milk

1 tablespoon Thai roasted chilli paste (*nam phrik pao*), or substitute 1 teaspoon
   Chinese chilli-garlic sauce mixed with $1/2$ teaspoon light brown sugar

$1^{1}/_2$ tablespoons Asian fish sauce

1 teaspoon palm sugar or light brown sugar

1 tablespoon fresh lemon juice

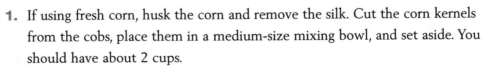

1 pound sea scallops

$1/3$ cup torn fresh Thai, sweet, or purple basil leaves

1. If using fresh corn, husk the corn and remove the silk. Cut the corn kernels from the cobs, place them in a medium-size mixing bowl, and set aside. You should have about 2 cups.

2. Heat a heavy 3- to 4-quart pot over medium-low heat and add the butter. When the butter melts, add the onion, bell pepper, and turmeric and cook,

stirring occasionally with a wooden spoon, until the onion and pepper are soft but not browned, 5 to 8 minutes. Add the corn, potatoes, and chicken stock. Increase the heat to medium-high, cover, and bring to a boil, 5 to 8 minutes. Boil, covered, until the potatoes are softened, 8 to 10 minutes. Use the back of the spoon to mash some potatoes against the side of the pot, just enough to thicken the mixture to a chowder-like consistency.

3. Stir in the coconut milk and return the mixture to boil. Immediately reduce the heat to low and add the Thai chilli paste, fish sauce, sugar, and lemon juice. Stir until the sugar is dissolved and the mixture is well blended. Add the scallops, increase the heat to medium-high, return to a boil, and cook for 1 minute.

4. Ladle the chowder into serving bowls. Sprinkle with Thai basil leaves and serve hot.

Vietnamese-Style Hot-and-Sour Shrimp Soup with Pineapple

Serves 4 to 6

*J*ust about every part of Southeast Asia has its own piquantly hot-and-sour soup. Thailand's *tom yum kung* uses a roasted chilli paste and kaffir lime leaves. *Sinigang na*, the Filipino version, is made tart with underripe fruits, such as guavas. In Burma, they enjoy *hipon*, a vegetable soup given its sour tang by young tamarind leaves instead of the pulpy sauce made from the fruit. Hot-and-sour soup is called *chin hin* in Cambodia, where it is seasoned with fresh lime juice and soy sauce.

Our favorite from this great array is *can chua tom*, from southern Vietnam, which is featured here. Its excellence is based on absolutely fresh ingredients and the fruity tang of tamarind, which flavors the homemade chicken stock. Lemon grass also adds its citrus perfume, while pineapple chunks lend sweetness. Squeezes of fresh lime accent the broth further at the table.

Everything about this soup is bright and lively. If the bean sprouts in your market aren't fresh and crisp, leave them out. Take care not to overcook the shrimp. And if the shrimp don't look terrific on the day you buy your ingredients, you can substitute chunks of catfish, red snapper, or any other firm-fleshed white fish.

We grace our *can chua tom* simply, with mint leaves. The Vietnamese use many herbs, including the aromatic, sour-flavored *ngo om*, which grows in rice paddies, and sliced stems of *rau rap mong*, an aquatic plant with a crisp yet spongy texture. These can sometimes be found in Vietnamese markets, so do add them if they are available.

$^1/_2$ pound medium-size shrimp, peeled, deveined if desired, and halved lengthwise

1 teaspoon finely chopped garlic

$^1/_4$ teaspoon freshly ground black pepper

3 tablespoons Asian fish sauce

1 plump stalk fresh lemon grass or strips of zest from $^1/_2$ lemon

1$^1/_2$ tablespoons vegetable oil

2 medium-size shallots, thinly sliced

2 plum tomatoes or 1 large ripe tomato, seeded and cut into wedges

1 cup $^3/_4$-inch pineapple chunks, preferably fresh

3$^1/_2$ tablespoons sugar

1 cup Chicken Stock (page 289) or canned low-sodium chicken broth

$^1/_4$ cup Tamarind Sauce (page 290) or liquid tamarind concentrate

2 tablespoons minced small Thai or serrano chillies, preferably red, or a dash or two
    of a favorite hot sauce

$^1/_2$ cup crisp fresh bean sprouts (optional)

1 scallion (white and tender green parts), angle-cut into thin slices

$^1/_4$ cup fresh mint leaves

1 lime, cut into wedges

1. In a medium-size mixing bowl, combine the shrimp, garlic, black pepper, and 1 tablespoon of the fish sauce. Let stand at room temperature while you prepare the soup.

2. If using fresh lemon grass, trim the root ends and discard the tough outer leaves. Cut a 6-inch length from the bulb end and discard the rest. Crush the lemon grass with a pestle (or any heavy object, such as a rolling pin, hammer, or mallet) and angle-cut into 2-inch pieces.

3. Heat the oil in a 3- to 4-quart saucepan over medium-high heat. Add the lemon grass and shallots and cook, stirring, without browning, just until fragrant, 2 to 3 minutes. Add the tomatoes, pineapple, and sugar and cook for 1 minute. Add the chicken stock and bring to a boil over high heat. Stir in the remaining 2 tablespoons of fish sauce and the tamarind sauce. Reduce the heat to medium-low and simmer for 5 minutes.

4. Stir in the shrimp and $1/4$ teaspoon of the chillies. If using bean sprouts, stir them in now. Add the sliced scallion and cook just until the shrimp are just cooked through, 30 seconds to 1 minute.

5. Ladle the soup into serving bowls and garnish with the mint leaves. Serve hot, with lime wedges and the remaining minced chillies on the side.

Burmese-Style Potato Salad

Serves 4 to 6

For summer, or for any time of year, it's wonderful to have a fresh, new interpretation of potato salad. The Burmese make theirs with chickpeas, sliced onion, and a supremely light dressing flavored with tamarind and soy sauce. We've added just enough olive oil to make it smooth. Use sweet Vidalia onions and baby Yukon Gold potatoes, which cook quickly, don't need peeling, and have a wonderful creamy flavor.

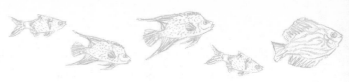

4 cups water

1¹/₂ pounds baby Yukon Gold or red potatoes

1 tablespoon salt

¹/₄ cup light soy sauce

1 cup cooked or canned chickpeas, drained

¹/₃ cup thinly sliced sweet onion, such as Vidalia

1 tablespoon Tamarind Sauce (page 290) or liquid tamarind concentrate

1¹/₂ tablespoons extra virgin olive oil

1 teaspoon ground cumin

Salt and freshly ground black pepper to taste

¹/₂ cup chopped fresh cilantro, including the stems

1. Bring the water to boil in a large saucepan and add the potatoes, salt, and soy sauce. Return the water to a boil, then reduce the heat to medium and simmer just until the potatoes are fork-tender, 12 to 15 minutes. They should still be firm and hold their shape.

2. Drain the potatoes, spread them on a baking sheet in a single layer, and let cool a few minutes. Cut the potatoes in half and put them in a large mixing bowl. Add the chickpeas, onion, tamarind sauce, olive oil, and cumin and mix well. Season with salt and pepper and top with the cilantro. Serve at room temperature.

Bangkok-to-Bali Caesar Salad with Grilled Hearts of Romaine

Serves 4

This salad has all the attributes of a great, classic Caesar, yet with a distinctly Southeast Asian flair. It's garlicky and earthy with anchovies, which are often the main ingredient in Asian fish sauce. The tamarind accent in the Worcestershire sauce also adds an Asian note. We've enlivened the dressing with fresh lime juice, and discovered that adding just a little bit of mayonnaise allows you to omit the traditional eggs.

Grilling the romaine softens the leaves and gives the salad a smoky flavor. Toasted rice powder, so often used in tropical Asian salads, adds a flavorful crunch.

2 large cloves garlic, crushed and chopped

$1/2$ teaspoon coarse salt

4 oil-packed anchovy fillets, rinsed and patted dry

2 tablespoons fresh lime juice

1 teaspoon mayonnaise

1 teaspoon Worcestershire sauce

2 big pinches of salt

2 big pinches of freshly ground black pepper

$1/3$ cup extra virgin olive oil

2 hearts of romaine lettuce, each halved lengthwise, core left in

Toasted Rice Powder (page 98) to taste

Pure chilli powder to taste

1. Crush the garlic, salt, and anchovies to a paste in a mortar, or mash them together on a cutting board with a wooden fork or spoon. Scrape the paste into a small mixing bowl. Whisk in the lime juice, mayonnaise, Worcestershire, salt, and pepper. Add the olive oil in a slow, steady stream, whisking constantly.
2. Brush the romaine halves with some of the dressing.
3. Preheat an outdoor grill, or preheat a grill pan for 3 to 5 minutes over medium-high heat. Place the romaine halves, cut side down, on the grill rack or pan. Grill until slightly wilted and golden, $1^1/2$ to 2 minutes. Turn them over and let sit for another 1 to 2 seconds before removing from the grill.
4. Arrange each of the romaine halves, grilled side up, on the center of a serving plate. Spoon more dressing over each serving. Sprinkle with toasted rice powder and chilli powder and serve at once.

Grilled Eggplant Salad with Cilantro-Chilli Vinaigrette

e love to serve this salad all year long. When the warm weather is gone and our barbecue is packed away, a grill pan takes its place.

A nontraditional but thoroughly delicious way to serve this Thai-inspired salad is to chill the vegetables after grilling them. It will enhance their smoky-sweet flavors and sharpen their contrast with the chilli-spiced dressing.

CILANTRO-CHILLI VINAIGRETTE:

1/4 cup fresh lime juice (about 3 limes)

1 tablespoon Asian fish sauce

1 tablespoon palm sugar or light brown sugar

2 tablespoons chopped fresh cilantro, including the stems

2 cloves garlic, crushed and chopped

1 tablespoon chopped serrano chillies

SALAD:

12 plump cherry tomatoes, quartered

2 medium-size eggplants, left unpeeled and cut crosswise into 1/2-inch-thick slices

1 large red onion, cut crosswise into 1/2-inch-thick slices

1 to 2 tablespoons vegetable oil, as needed

1/4 teaspoon salt

1/4 cup loosely packed torn fresh mint leaves

1/4 cup loosely packed torn fresh Thai, sweet, or purple basil leaves

1. Combine the vinaigrette ingredients in a blender and process until smooth and the sugar is dissolved.

2. Transfer the vinaigrette to a medium-size mixing bowl and mix in the tomatoes. Let stand while you complete the salad.

3. Preheat an outdoor grill, or preheat a grill pan for 3 to 5 minutes over medium-high heat. Brush the rack or pan with oil. Then brush or mist the eggplant and onion slices on both sides with a little vegetable oil and season with the salt. Grill until done, about 5 minutes on each side. The eggplant slices should be cooked through but still retain their shape. The onion slices should be cooked until tender but still retain their shape.

4. Arrange the vegetables on a serving platter, alternating the eggplant and onion slices so that they overlap and the eggplant slices fan out. Cover with plastic wrap and chill in the refrigerator, if desired. To serve, use a slotted spoon to lift the tomatoes out of the dressing and scatter them over the salad. Pour on the dressing, shower the herbs on top, and serve immediately.

Indonesian Vegetable Salad with Curried Peanut Dressing (Gado Gado)

Serves 4 as a main course or
6 to 8 as a side dish

Some Thai restaurants serve this popular Indonesian salad with a topping of lightly crushed potato chips. It may sound crazy, but it's an inspired idea; the chips add a delightful bit of crunch and a trace of saltiness. We learned to love it this way, and think you will, too.

All sorts of vegetables are used in *gado gado*, so choose any ones that you like, or simply use whatever you have on hand. Some variations add fried or boiled potatoes and hard-boiled eggs, plus fried bean curd. We prefer to add chopped fresh pineapple whenever we have it.

The whole, healthful melange is tossed with spicy peanut sauce—the richly delicious accompaniment to grilled meat satés. Moisture from the freshly cut vegetables thins the sauce into a dressing.

The salad is often served with shrimp chips, and it's a good idea to have some extra peanut sauce on the side.

1/4 pound yard-long or green beans, ends trimmed and angle-cut into 2-inch lengths
1 medium-size carrot, cut into 2-inch strips
1/2 head Napa or green cabbage, cored and cut crosswise into long shreds
1/4 pound bean sprouts
1 medium-size red bell pepper, seeded and cut into thin 2-inch-long strips
1 medium-size yellow bell pepper, seeded and cut into thin 2-inch-long strips
1 cup fresh or canned 1/2-inch pineapple chunks
One 2.5-ounce bag potato chips
1 cup Spicy Peanut Sauce (page 88), plus more for the table
Homemade Shrimp Chips (page 285) or one 2.5-ounce bag shrimp chips (optional)

1. Bring a medium-size saucepan of salted water to a boil over medium-high heat. Add the green beans and carrots, return to a boil, and cook just until crisp-tender, about 3 minutes. Remove from the heat. With a slotted spoon, transfer the vegetables to a colander to drain. Refresh them under cold running water, drain thoroughly, and place them on a platter.

2. Return the water to boil and cook the cabbage about 30 seconds. Drain and refresh under cold running water, then blot with paper towels to draw off any excess moisture. Place the cabbage next to the beans and carrots.

3. Arrange the beans, carrots, cabbage, bean sprouts, bell peppers, and pineapple on 4 individual plates. Crush the potato chips slightly and shower some over each serving. Add a dollop (about 1/4 cup) of the peanut sauce over each serving and let each guest toss his or her own salad.

4. Serve at room temperature with more peanut sauce and shrimp chips, if desired, on the side.

Insalata Siam

Visitors to Italy are often captivated by the essence-of-summer composed salad known as *insalata caprese*, or Capri-style salad. It is a colorful layering of ripe red tomato slices and white medallions of *mozzarella di bufala*, with a profusion of green basil leaves, drizzled with the finest olive oil.

We've borrowed the salad's classic form, but given the ingredients list a Southeast Asian transformation. Extra-firm tofu, for example, is a more healthful replacement for the mozzarella cheese, while toasted rice powder adds a nut-like crunch and the Thai variety of basil, easily found in most Asian markets, contributes a note of anise not found in Italian basil.

1 large clove garlic, crushed and finely chopped

1 tablespoon aged red wine vinegar

2 tablespoons fresh lemon juice

$1/2$ teaspoon salt

$1/2$ teaspoon freshly ground black pepper

One 15-ounce package extra-firm tofu, drained

2 medium-size garden-ripe tomatoes

A few handfuls of assorted fresh basil leaves, such as Thai, purple, or sweet basil

$1/4$ cup extra virgin olive oil

$1/4$ cup Toasted Rice Powder (page 98)

1. Combine the garlic, vinegar, lemon juice, salt, and pepper in a small bowl. Stir and let the mixture stand while you prepare the salad.
2. Place the tofu on a cutting board. Cut it diagonally into two triangles. Turn the triangles long edge down and cut each into 4 thin triangular slices. Core the tomatoes and cut them crosswise into 8 slices per tomato.

3. Carefully arrange the tofu triangles on a serving platter, overlapping them slightly. Place a tomato slice between each tofu triangle and circle the remaining tomato slices around the platter. Place one of the larger basil leaves in front of each tomato slice. Tear up the remaining basil leaves and shower them over and around the salad.

4. Whisk the olive oil into the garlic mixture, then drizzle the vinaigrette over the salad. Sprinkle about 1 tablespoon of the toasted rice powder over the salad and serve with the remaining rice powder on the side.

Balinese Star Fruit, Papaya, and Pink Grapefruit Salad with Avocado Dressing

Serves 6

*H*ere we've used some favorite Balinese fruits with a variety of flavors and textures—tart, crisp star fruit; soft, ripe papaya; juicy segments of pink grapefruit (in place of its Asian relative, the pomelo)—for a composed salad that also includes sweet and bitter greens and a tangy avocado dressing.

In Bali, avocados are often used in mixed fruit salads with sugar syrup and shaved ice, but our salad features its creamy flesh as the basis for a lush dressing, spiked with Worcestershire sauce and tamarind, which liquefies after it is spooned on the salad and tossed.

SALAD:

6 cups torn butter lettuce leaves

3 cups torn watercress, including tender stems

3 star fruit, ends and ridges trimmed and sliced crosswise into thin stars

2 small pink seedless grapefruit, peeled and sectioned

1 ripe papaya, peeled, seeded, and cubed

AVOCADO DRESSING:

1 ripe Hass avocado, peeled and pitted

$^1/_2$ teaspoon Chinese chilli-garlic sauce

$^1/_2$ teaspoon Worcestershire sauce

$^1/_2$ teaspoon palm sugar or light brown sugar

$2^1/_2$ teaspoons distilled white vinegar

$2^1/_2$ teaspoons Tamarind Sauce (page 290) or liquid tamarind concentrate, or

    1 teaspoon fresh lime juice, $^1/_2$ teaspoon Worcestershire sauce, and

    $^1/_2$ teaspoon light brown sugar mixed together

3 tablespoons fresh lime juice

1. To make the salad, combine the lettuce and watercress in a large serving bowl. Arrange the fruits in concentric circles on top of the bed of salad greens. Set aside.

2. To make the dressing, in a medium-size mixing bowl, mash the avocado with a fork until smooth and creamy. Add the remaining ingredients and mix well until creamy.

3. Spoon the dressing over the salad, toss at the table, and serve.

Green Papaya Salad with Fresh Chilli and Lime

Serves 4

We have loved green papaya salad since we first heard the thunk! thunk! thunk! of the vendor's stone pestle at a Thai festival, as she pounded a large mortar bowl full of shredded green papaya, fresh hot chillies, peanuts, and lime juice, while an eager line formed in front of her booth. In addition to the appeal of its well-balanced sweet and piquant flavors and its crisp, refreshing bite, this salad lends itself to many ways of serving. It's great with warm Sticky Rice (page 147) to absorb the extra dressing, with cabbage leaves to scoop it up, or with the sweet and mellow contrast of plain Coconut Rice (page 149).

The Thais make the dressing right in the mortar, lightly bruising the strands of green papaya flesh at the same time to make it drink up the dressing. But if you use a blender to make the dressing, you will be able to create all the components ahead of time, then combine them with the dressing just before serving—which makes this salad ideal to bring to a picnic or potluck.

At a Thai festival, you'll find some savory items mixed into the salad, such as dried shrimp or small pickled soft-shell crabs. Don't be afraid to try them. They're terrific.

1 medium-size green papaya (about 1 1/2 pounds)

1 tablespoon fresh lime juice

2 tablespoons palm sugar or light brown sugar

2 to 4 small Thai chillies, to your taste, roughly chopped

2 small cloves garlic, roughly chopped

8 plump cherry tomatoes, halved

1/3 cup unsalted dry-roasted peanuts, crushed in a mortar or finely chopped

1/4 head green cabbage, separated into leaves, or Sticky Rice (optional, page 147)

1. Peel the papaya and halve lengthwise. Scrape out the seeds. Shred the papaya in a food processor fitted with a shredding disk, or with the large holes of a box grater, or using the Southeast Asian technique of slash-cutting (see page 127). You should have about 2 1/2 cups of papaya shreds. Set aside.

2. Combine the lime juice, sugar, chillies, and garlic in a blender and blend until well mixed and smooth.

3. Place the papaya shreds in a large serving bowl. Mix in the tomatoes and peanuts. Add the dressing and toss lightly. Serve at room temperature with green cabbage leaves or sticky rice on the side.

How to Julienne Mangoes and Papayas the Southeast Asian Way

*I*f you saw the beautiful French-Vietnamese film *The Scent of Green Papaya*, you have already seen the easy way to julienne papayas and mangoes. You may recall watching the heroine hold a long knife over a peeled green papaya and lightly flick its blade several times across the fruit, making shallow cuts to release numerous thin shreds into a bowl.

Although she performed this slash-cutting technique with practiced skill, it's quite easy to learn: To cut up a papaya, peel the fruit, then halve it lengthwise and remove the seeds. Hold half of the papaya in one hand, cut side up, while you hold a medium-size knife loosely in the other hand. Position a bowl to catch the julienned shreds. Then, flicking your wrist lightly, make several roughly parallel cuts about 1/4 inch deep on the long axis of the fruit. Next, glide the blade underneath the cuts, releasing thin strips to the bowl beneath. Repeat until all the flesh is julienned; then cut the second half in the same manner.

To slash-cut mangoes, whether green or ripe, first peel the fruit and hold it in the palm of one hand. Because mangoes have a hard, flat pit in the center, you can use the above technique, or make the first series of parallel cuts all the way down to the pit. Then slice off the fruit in shreds of whatever thickness you desire.

Mango and Star Fruit Salad with Peanuts

Serves 4

*T*he star fruit, also known as the carambola, probably originated in the islands of Malaysia. Deliciously tart, it highlights the sweetness of the mango in this luscious fruit salad, which makes a terrific between-meals snack.

2 medium-size mangoes, peeled, flesh cut away from the stone, and cut into 1-inch chunks

2 star fruit, ends and ridges trimmed, and sliced into ³/₄-inch-thick stars, or 2 green apples, peeled, cored, and cut into 2 x ³/₄-inch chunks

¹/₃ cup unsalted dry-roasted peanuts

¹/₄ cup plus 2 tablespoons Bangkok-to-Bali Sweet Syrup (page 294)

Place the mangoes and star fruit in a medium-size serving bowl. Sprinkle the peanuts over the top, then drizzle with the syrup. Toss gently to coat the fruit evenly, then serve.

Mangoes, Inside and Out

Here's the quickest way to carve a ripe mango, whether for eating right out of hand, or for bite-size chunks to toss in a fruit salad.

Hold your mango on end, stem side up, and cut down one side of the fruit, sliding the blade next to the flat pit. You'll cut away what we call a mango cheek. Repeat on the other side, then cut all the fruit from the two ends.

Using the tip of the knife and applying light pressure so you don't cut through the skin, cut two or three evenly spaced, parallel cuts through the flesh of the cheek. Make two or three more cuts, tic-tac-toe-like, at right angles to the first cuts. Then hold the outer corners of the cheek with each hand, between thumb and forefinger, and press the skin side until it turns inside out. You'll see cubes of mango flesh, free on three sides but still connected to the skin. The mango cheek will resemble a hedgehog.

Indulge yourself immediately by nibbling off the juicy cubes of fruit. Or set the hedgehog on a dessert plate, alongside a scoop of ice cream, or some warm sticky rice bathed in coconut cream. For fruit salads, slice the cubes off the skin into individual chunks.

Repeat the procedure for the other mango cheeks, and don't forget to enjoy the fruit clinging to the sides of the pit.

Avocado, Orange, and Grapefruit Salad with Sweet Syrup and Cilantro

Serves 4 to 6

The people of Bali combine slices of ripe avocado with tropical fruits and sweet syrup, which they assemble over a bed of crushed ice, for a refreshing snack in the tropical heat. You can also use this avocado and fruit salad as a refreshment from another type of tropical heat—the fire of a spicy curry or stir-fry. Or it could be part of a buffet, with Spicy Stir-Fried Cashews (page 47).

2 medium-size ripe avocados, peeled, pitted, and sliced
2 pink seedless grapefruits, peeled and sectioned
2 navel oranges, peeled and sectioned
$1/4$ cup Bangkok-to-Bali Sweet Syrup (page 294)
$1/4$ cup chopped fresh cilantro, including the stems, plus a few sprigs for garnish

1. Arrange the avocado slices and grapefruit and orange sections on a shallow serving dish.
2. Stir the syrup to blend in the vanilla seeds and spoon it over the salad. Top with the chopped cilantro, add a few sprigs for garnish, and serve immediately.

Seared Scallops and Fresh Orange Salad with Mint Leaves and Crisp-Fried Shallots

Serves 4

We've borrowed from the spectrum of tropical Asian salad makings to create this sumptuous seafood salad. The citrus dressing is typically Thai, as is the addition of fried shallots. Mixing fruits and vegetables with seafood or meat in a salad is popular throughout tropical Asia. We've added a Continental technique: heating our dressing just enough to lightly wilt the greens and warm the scallops, oranges, and avocado.

DRESSING:

$1/2$ cup fresh lemon juice (about 4 lemons)

$1^1/_2$ tablespoons Asian fish sauce

2 tablespoons palm sugar or light brown sugar

3 cloves garlic, crushed and chopped

1 tablespoon chopped serrano chillies

SALAD:

3 cups torn watercress, including tender stems

3 cups torn curly endive leaves

2 navel oranges, peeled and sectioned

1 large ripe Hass avocado, peeled, pitted, and sliced lengthwise

12 jumbo sea scallops

$1/4$ teaspoon salt

1 teaspoon vegetable oil

$1/3$ cup loosely packed torn fresh mint leaves

Crisp-Fried Shallots (page 100)

1. To make the dressing, combine all the ingredients in a blender and blend until smooth and the sugar is dissolved. Transfer to a small bowl and set aside.

2. To begin the salad, line a serving platter with the watercress and curly endive. Arrange the orange sections and avocado slices on top. Set aside while you prepare the scallops.

3. Season the scallops with salt. Heat the oil in a medium-size nonstick skillet over medium-high heat. Add the scallops and pan-fry until nicely browned, about 2 minutes per side. Arrange them over the fruit.

4. Heat the dressing in a small saucepan over medium heat. Simmer gently until hot, about 1 minute. Pour the hot dressing over the salad to lightly wilt the greens and warm the toppings. (Do not toss the salad.) Sprinkle the mint and shallots on top and serve at once.

Dancing Shrimp Salad

Serves 4

Thai people call this spicy salad dancing shrimp because it should be made with shrimp so recently taken from the water that they're still "dancing" with life. Or perhaps they're dancing from the chilli fire of the dressing. This is hot!

DRESSING:

1 tablespoon Asian fish sauce

2 1/2 tablespoons fresh lime or lemon juice

1 tablespoon palm sugar or light brown sugar

1 tablespoon Thai roasted chilli paste (*nam phrik pao*), or 1 teaspoon Chinese chilli-garlic sauce mixed with 1/2 teaspoon light brown sugar

1 plump stalk lemon grass or 1/4 teaspoon grated lemon zest

1 1/2 tablespoons minced small Thai or serrano chillies

SALAD:

1 pound large shrimp, peeled and deveined if desired

1/2 head romaine or other lettuce, separated into leaves

2 plum tomatoes (optional), sliced into thin wedges

1 to 2 small pickling cucumbers (optional), peeled, seeded, and sliced

1/2 red or yellow bell pepper (optional), seeded and cut into matchsticks

1/2 cup loosely packed fresh mint leaves

1. To make the dressing, combine the fish sauce, lemon juice, sugar, and chilli paste in a blender or small mixing bowl and blend or stir well to dissolve the sugar and chilli paste. Trim the root end of the lemon grass and discard the tough outer leaves. Slice into very thin rounds, using most of the tender lower stalk (about 4 inches). Add the sliced lemon grass to the dressing and stir in the chillies. Set aside.

2. To begin the salad, bring a medium-size saucepan of salted water to a boil. Add the shrimp and cook just until they begin to turn pink, 45 to 60 seconds. Drain well and set aside.

3. Arrange the lettuce leaves and tomatoes, cucumbers, and pepper, if desired, on a serving platter. Arrange the shrimp on top and spoon on the dressing. Sprinkle the mint leaves over the salad and serve.

Shrimp and Papaya Salad with Papaya Seed Dressing

Serves 4 to 6

In Thailand, papaya seeds are sometimes crushed and added to a dressing to give the salad a warm, musky flavor. Whirl the dressing in a blender until the papaya seeds are pulverized just enough to look like bits of crushed black pepper. Their dark speckles lend a beautiful visual contrast to the plump, pink shrimp and the bright yellow papaya.

1 medium-size ripe papaya
12 jumbo shrimp, peeled, and deveined if desired
1 small head butter lettuce, leaves separated and torn into bite-size pieces
1 tablespoon finely diced red onion

PAPAYA SEED DRESSING:
1/4 cup extra virgin olive oil
1 tablespoon plus 1 teaspoon fresh lime juice
1 tablespoon plus 1 teaspoon palm sugar or light brown sugar
1/2 teaspoon chopped small Thai chillies

1. To begin the salad, bring a small saucepan of salted water to boil. Meanwhile, prepare the papaya. Cut the papaya in half. Spoon out the papaya seeds and reserve 1 1/2 teaspoons. Scrape out and discard the rest of the seeds and fibers. Peel the papaya and cut the flesh into 1-inch cubes. Set aside.
2. Add the shrimp to the boiling water and cook just until firm and pink, about 2 minutes. Drain and set aside.
3. Arrange the torn lettuce leaves on a shallow serving dish. Arrange the shrimp in a circle around the platter and pile the papaya cubes in the center. Sprinkle the red onion over the salad and set aside.
4. To make the dressing, put the ingredients in a blender, add the reserved papaya seeds, and process until the seeds resemble crushed black pepper, stopping occasionally to scrape down the sides of the blender. Pour the dressing over the salad and serve immediately.

Spicy Chicken Salad with Toasted Coconut

This modern recipe evokes the traditions of the cuisine served in Thailand's Royal Palace, highlighting the beautifully balanced complexities of taste and texture that are the hallmarks of the best Thai cooking. The bite-size pieces of chicken breast simmer in coconut milk, which reduces to create a rich base for the sweet-and-sour tang of the citrus and spice dressing.

ROYAL THAI DRESSING:

1 tablespoon fresh lemon juice

2 tablespoons fresh lime juice

1 teaspoon Worcestershire sauce

2 tablespoons Asian fish sauce

2 cloves garlic, minced

1 tablespoon minced small Thai or serrano chillies

2 tablespoons minced cilantro stems

2 tablespoons plus 2 teaspoons palm sugar or light brown sugar

SALAD:

1 medium-size head romaine lettuce

1/2 cup canned unsweetened coconut milk

1 pound boneless, skinless chicken breasts, trimmed of any fat and cut into
   bite-size strips

Toasted Coconut (page 99)

Sprigs fresh cilantro for garnishing

1. Combine all the dressing ingredients in a small mixing bowl and stir until the chilli paste and sugar are dissolved and well blended. Set aside.

2. To begin the salad, stem and core the romaine. Set aside the large outer leaves and chop the heart. Place the chopped leaves in the bottom of a large, some-

what shallow serving bowl. Arrange the large leaves, stem ends pointing to the center, in a fan shape going halfway around the bowl. Set aside.

3. Warm the coconut milk in a medium-size saucepan over high heat, but don't let it boil. Add the chicken and bring to a boil, stirring occasionally. Cook until the coconut milk is reduced by about three quarters, 4 to 6 minutes, leaving just enough to coat the bottom of the pan. Remove from the heat and let stand a few minutes to cool slightly. Add the dressing mixture and stir until blended.

4. Transfer the coated chicken to the bowl of romaine. Shower with toasted coconut, top with a few torn sprigs of cilantro, and serve immediately.

Green Mango and Baby Ginger Salad with Grilled Chicken

Serves 4, or 2 as a light meal

Early summer is prime time for tender, translucent-skinned, Hawaii-grown baby ginger, though this dish can also be prepared with mature, brown-skinned ginger. For the best flavor, choose plump, wrinkle-free pieces that haven't begun to dry out.

Mangoes that are firm, with shiny green skins, will be crisp and deliciously sweet-and-sour—perfect with the matchsticks of fragrant, peppery ginger.

INDOCHINE DRESSING:

1/4 cup fresh lemon juice

2 tablespoons Asian fish sauce

1 tablespoon palm sugar or light brown sugar

2 to 3 small Thai or serrano chillies, to your taste, thinly sliced

SALAD:

1 pound boneless, skinless chicken breast halves, trimmed of any fat

1 pound green mangoes (about 2 large) or the least ripe mangoes available

2/3 cup thinly sliced shallots

1/3 cup peeled fresh young ginger or firm, smooth-skinned mature ginger, sliced into
julienne strips

2 cups spring mix salad greens (mesclun)

2/3 cup loosely packed torn fresh mint leaves

1. Combine the dressing ingredients in a blender or small mixing bowl. Blend
    well to dissolve the sugar.
2. To begin the salad, place the chicken on a plate and pour on 1 tablespoon of
    the dressing. Turn the breasts over to lightly coat each side.
3. Peel each mango and cut the flesh from the pit. Cut into thin strips and place
    in a large mixing bowl (see page 128). Add the shallots and ginger and mix
    gently. Set aside.
4. Preheat an outdoor grill, or preheat a grill pan for 3 to 5 minutes over
    medium-high heat. Place the chicken on a well-oiled grill rack or pan and grill
    until cooked through, about 5 minutes on each side. Cut the chicken diago-
    nally across the grain into thin slices. Add to the mango mixture in the bowl.
    Add the remaining dressing and toss gently.
5. Arrange the salad greens on a large serving platter. Transfer the mango mixture
    to the platter, shower the torn mint leaves on top, and serve.

Vietnamese Coleslaw with Shredded Chicken and Peanuts

*H*ere is an incredible crowd pleaser. We brought this to a friend's house recently, as our contribution to a potluck. She said she would host a cooking class for us in her spacious home, but only if we promised to reveal this recipe!

What makes this dish so welcome are its moist shreds of poached chicken breast, served cold and tumbled with a mayonnaise-free slaw of fresh shredded cabbage, carrots, and cilantro, topped with peanuts and mint leaves, all tossed with a chilli-flecked rice vinegar, lime juice, and sesame oil dressing.

If you have access to a Vietnamese market, ask for some *rau rom*, a special Vietnamese fresh coriander with slender, pointed green leaves, and a taste reminiscent of lemons and cilantro, with a peppery aftertaste.

Made entirely from scratch, this salad will take more than 30 minutes, but here are two tips for making it easier: Among the precut and prewashed salad greens at your supermarket, look for packaged coleslaw mix. That saves you the effort of shredding the cabbage and carrots. Secondly, make this recipe when you have leftover cooked chicken on hand.

CHICKEN:

10 cups water

1 pound boneless, skinless chicken breasts, trimmed of any fat

DRESSING:

3 tablespoons fresh lime juice

2 tablespoons plus 1 teaspoon Asian fish sauce

1 tablespoon unseasoned rice vinegar

1 tablespoon sesame oil (not toasted)

1 tablespoon palm sugar or light brown sugar

2 small cloves garlic, minced

2 teaspoons minced small Thai or serrano chillies

COLESLAW:

¹/₂ cup thinly sliced onion (cut in half first, then sliced into half moons)

2 tablespoons sesame seeds

4¹/₂ cups cored and shredded green cabbage

¹/₂ cup shredded carrots

¹/₃ cup fresh mint leaves

¹/₃ cup fresh cilantro leaves

¹/₃ cup Vietnamese coriander (*rau rom*) or mint leaves

Freshly ground black pepper to taste

1 tablespoon unsalted dry-roasted peanuts, crushed in a mortar or finely chopped

Homemade Shrimp Chips (page 285) or one 2.5-ounce bag shrimp chips (optional)

1. To poach the chicken, in a 4- to 5-quart saucepan, bring the water to boil over high heat. Add the chicken and bring to a simmer. Cook for 5 minutes, then reduce the heat to maintain a gentle simmer (the liquid should bubble just enough to break the surface) and cook for 10 minutes. Remove the pan from the heat and let the chicken stand, uncovered, in the liquid until cool enough to handle, or up to 1 hour. (At this point, the chicken will be very nearly cooked through and will finish the last bit of cooking in the hot liquid. It will also keep moist until ready to serve.) Transfer the cooled chicken to a cutting board and pull it apart with your fingers, or slice it into shreds.

2. To make the dressing, combine the ingredients in a small mixing bowl. Stir well, until the sugar is dissolved and the dressing is well blended.

3. To begin the coleslaw, mix the sliced onion into the dressing to marinate and soften a bit.

4. Meanwhile, put the sesame seeds in a small skillet and toast over medium-low heat, stirring often, until light golden brown, about 3 minutes. Transfer to a small bowl and set aside.

5. Combine the shredded chicken, cabbage, carrots, mint, cilantro, and Vietnamese coriander in a large serving bowl. Remove the sliced onion from the dressing and add it to the bowl. Season with black pepper and add the peanuts and toasted sesame seeds. Toss the coleslaw with the dressing until well coated and serve immediately with shrimp chips on the side, if desired.

Fiery Grilled Beef Salad

*H*ere's a salad that features juicy medium-rare beef, served warm. A Southeast Asian would be happiest if served this salad with Sticky Rice (page 147) on the side. But to bring the meal together even more quickly and to satisfy my F.B.I. (Full-Blooded Italian) nature, I often substitute a crunchy-crusted bread to mop up the delicious dressing and steak drippings that collect in the serving dish. Shrimp Chips (page 285) would also make an effective pairing.

It's always important to have the freshest, best-quality ingredients in whatever you cook, but it's vitally important in simple dishes such as this one. To ensure tempting results, you need a peak quality sirloin steak, a garden-fresh tomato, crisp herbs, and juice from plump lemons.

1 pound sirloin steak

$3/4$ teaspoon salt

$1/2$ teaspoon white pepper

1 tablespoon Asian fish sauce

1 small red onion, cut in half and very thinly sliced into half moons

1 medium-large, ripe tomato, cut in half, seeded, and sliced into thin wedges

$1/2$ cup fresh mint leaves

Sticky Rice (optional, page 147)

Italian bread or French baguette (optional)

CHILLI-SPIKED DRESSING:

1 tablespoon fresh lemon juice

1 tablespoon Asian fish sauce

$1^1/2$ tablespoons palm sugar or light brown sugar

1 tablespoon chopped serrano chillies (about 4 chillies) or $1/2$ to 1 tablespoon
    chopped small Thai chillies, to your taste

1 tablespoon chopped fresh cilantro stems

1. Place the steak on a large plate. Mix the salt, pepper, and fish sauce together in a small bowl and pour it over the steak.

2. Prepare an outdoor grill, or preheat a grill pan or a heavy cast-iron skillet for 3 to 5 minutes over medium-high heat. Place the seasoned steak on the grill or in the hot pan and cook until medium-rare, 2 to 3 minutes on each side, or to your preferred degree of doneness. Transfer the steak to a cutting board and let stand for 5 minutes.

3. Meanwhile, prepare the dressing. In a blender or medium-size mixing bowl, combine all the dressing ingredients and blend well to dissolve the sugar. Set aside.

4. Holding your knife at a 45-degree angle, cut the steak crosswise into thin slices. Transfer the meat with its juices to a large mixing bowl. Mix in the onion, tomato, and mint leaves. Add the dressing and mix gently.

5. Serve warm or at room temperature, with sticky rice or bread, if desired.

Rice and Noodles

STEAMED JASMINE RICE

STICKY RICE

SAVORY YELLOW RICE

COCONUT RICE WITH CRISP-FRIED SHALLOTS
AND FRESH MANGOES

FRAGRANT MALAY RICE WITH
MIXED FRESH HERBS

INDONESIAN FRIED RICE

THAI-STYLE CRAB FRIED RICE

CELLOPHANE NOODLES WITH
SCALLIONS AND PICKLED GARLIC

NIGHT MARKET NOODLES

LUNCHTIME NOODLES WITH
GARLIC AND GREENS

THREE SISTERS VEGETARIAN NOODLE STIR-FRY

FAT NOODLES WITH FRESH CHILLIES
AND MINT LEAVES

THAI CHICKEN AND CELLOPHANE NOODLE
SALAD

THAI-STYLE STIR-FRIED RICE NOODLES

VIETNAMESE-STYLE LEMON GRASS CHICKEN
WITH RICE VERMICELLI

FILIPINO-STYLE STIR-FRIED NOODLES WITH
CHORIZO, CHICKEN, AND SHRIMP

Tall mountains separate China from the

Southeast Asian nations and create great rivers in the lands lying south. The Chao Praya, the Irrawaddy, and the Mekong are big, life-giving rivers with numerous tributaries, collectors of the monsoon rains, which bring abundant water to flood the rice paddies of the lowlands. Many scientists believe that rice was the first food humans ever cultivated, judging from evidence unearthed in the mountains of Thailand. Worship of a rice goddess, or rice mother, is practiced throughout Southeast Asia and may well be the oldest form of religion still in practice.

Many Westerners lack confidence about cooking rice well, so they buy "instant." Unfortunately, the process that makes instant rice easy to cook also strips away many key nutrients and makes the rice's texture less satisfying. There is no need to miss out on the nourishment and the quality of "real" rice. The recipes in this chapter will give you perfect rice every time, whether it's the long-grained rice of the lowlands, such as Thailand's superb jasmine rice, or the toothsome sticky rice of the mountains.

Beyond the simple elegance of a bowl of perfectly cooked steamed rice, this chapter offers savory concoctions that will show-case the ingredients and cultural influences that make tropical Asian cooking so memorable. For example, yellow is the color of royalty in

much of Southeast Asia, and Savory Yellow Rice (page 148), rich with sweet onions and mellow spices, is tinted yellow with turmeric to signify celebration.

As you'll discover, it is both customary and practical to prepare a lot more rice than you need for the meal at hand. That's because a supply of cold cooked rice gives you a head start on tomorrow's lunch or dinner. Stir-fried rice recipes—such as Thai-Style Crab Fried Rice (page 154) or Indonesian Fried Rice (page 153)—depend on having plenty of cold leftover rice, which has the right texture to withstand a return trip to the hot stove.

The wealth of noodle dishes beloved in Southeast Asia reflects the Chinese influence on the region. Over time, traditional Chinese noodle recipes have undergone profound changes in their new homes. Local herbs, spices, and preferred cooking techniques of people from Bangkok to Bali have transformed Chinese dishes into many of the Southeast Asian favorites we know and love today. These include *phat Thai*, the national dish of Thailand, made with rice stick noodles, and the summer rolls of Vietnam, made with a cellophane noodle salad and the translucent circles of rice paper unique to Vietnamese cuisine, for rolling up into delicate, savory bundles of contrasting flavor, color, and texture. Other tempting dishes are made with fresh, wide, soft rice noodles—Fat Noodles with Fresh Chillies and Mint Leaves (page 163), for example. And we like egg noodles for the Filipino stir-fry of spicy chorizo sausage, chicken, shrimp, and vegetables called *pancit guisado* (page 172).

Some of these dishes require extra time, beyond the 30-minute limit promised in this book's title. Dried noodles, for example, must be soaked, or sometimes boiled, before incorporating them into stir-fries and salads. But the actual working time for the cook will

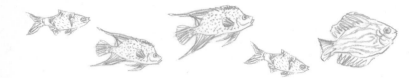

usually be 30 minutes or less. Others, such as Vietnamese-Style Lemon Grass Chicken with Rice Vermicelli (page 169), which the Vietnamese call *bun*, have numerous components that you can make in advance, then quickly put together at serving time. With a little planning, or with some helping hands in the kitchen, these dishes will be a treat to make as well as to serve.

Whether you choose the faster recipes, such as Lunchtime Noodles with Garlic and Greens (page 161) or Coconut Rice with Crisp-Fried Shallots and Fresh Mangoes (page 149), or a more complex dish such as *bun*, this chapter will awaken your taste and talent—not just for that always-welcome bowl of perfectly steamed jasmine rice, but also for spring rolls, summer rolls, wok-browned rice noodles, savory fried rice, and more.

Steamed Jasmine Rice

*T*hai jasmine rice is preferred throughout Southeast Asia, but truly adored in Thailand. It's fluffy, white, and long-grained, with a delicate scent of jasmine blossoms and a pleasingly nutty taste. In many countries, such as Bali, the native strains of rice are disappearing. Thai jasmine rice is appreciated there for its close kinship to their traditional grains.

Asian home cooks usually make a good deal more rice than is needed for the meal at hand. Cooked rice is saved, cold, as a mainstay of stir-fried meals to come. Hot, freshly cooked rice would become mushy if stir-fried. Cold leftover rice has the "strength" to be tossed in a hot wok.

Jasmine rice can now be found in supermarkets, though it costs less in Asian markets. In a pinch, any long-grain white rice, except converted rice, can be substituted.

2$\frac{1}{2}$ cups (1 pound) jasmine or other long-grain white rice
3$\frac{1}{2}$ cups water

1. Wash the rice in a colander under cool running water until it runs clear, and drain.
2. Put the drained rice and water in a heavy-bottomed pot with a tight-fitting lid. Bring to a full boil, uncovered, over medium-high heat. Stir, cover the rice, and reduce the heat to its lowest setting. Simmer for 20 minutes without lifting the lid. Turn off the heat. Keep the pot covered and let stand, undisturbed, for at least 5 minutes, or up to 30 minutes, before serving.
3. To serve, gently fluff the rice with a fork or rice paddle.

Goddess of Rice

*N*on Nok Tha and Ban Chien, in Thailand, are believed to be the sites of the world's first known rice fields, cultivated around 6,000 years ago. In any country you may visit throughout Southeast Asia, a high percentage of the population—often 50 percent or more—works at either growing, packing, or selling rice. When it comes to cooking and eating, the popular level of involvement reaches 100 percent. Rice is the central pillar of life in this part of the world. Centuries-old rituals keep its place secure.

An eighteenth-century Thai writer, trying to explain Westerners to his people, singled out what he seemed to think was the most startling fact: "They do not grow rice." That would certainly be astounding to a people who frequently say, "Rice is our mother" and who invite you to the table by saying "*kin khao*," which means "come eat rice."

Balinese rice farmers organize cooperatives, called *subaks*, to provide shared watering systems for their individual fields. Each *subak* also keeps a small temple for rituals devoted to *Dewi Sri*, the Balinese rice goddess, whose counterpart in Thailand is *Mae Phosop*. She is prayed to with these words: "You are as beautiful as a star. Please come into our rice bin. Please come out of the hot sun, come and rest in our shade." As soon as their seedbeds are ready, farmers wrap food and flowers in banana leaves for the rice goddess, so she will enter the fields and become pregnant with new life.

Throughout Southeast Asia, rice is personified in female form. When the rice is growing, the goddess is said to be living within the plants. The rest of the time, she abides in the temples. The Balinese also make offerings to *Dewi Nini*, the masculine aspect of the rice divinity, and scatter rice grains soaked in palm wine to distract evil spirits who might otherwise bring harm to the crop.

Nature made Southeast Asia the perfect place for rice. First there is the warm sun. Then there are the annual monsoon rains, caught by mountains so they can flow down to create enormous floodplains. Southeast Asians have made rice their perfect food, an easily digested counterpoint to the exciting flavors that nature also provides via abundant spices, wildlife, and fish and shellfish. The chefs of tropical Asia are great artists, and rice is the ever-renewing canvas upon which they've painted masterpieces daily for thousands of years. It's little wonder that they see an eternal and holy being in the fragrant, pearlescent grains.

Sticky Rice

Serves 4

T his plump, short-grain rice is high in gluten, which allows it to be rolled into little round clusters that you can dip in the curries and savory sauces on your plate, much as you might use a piece of bread. Also known as sweet rice or glutinous rice, sticky rice is a staple throughout Asia, but is very popular in mountainous northern Thailand and in neighboring Laos.

Sticky rice needs to be soaked overnight. The longer you soak it, the quicker it will cook, so it can easily become a 30-minute recipe. We like to cook sticky rice in a Thai steamer with a double-handled rack, but you can also use a colander set over a pot or a bamboo steam basket set on a wok rack. Serve sticky rice from a lovely basket lined with banana leaves (or a fresh tea towel), as the Laotians often do, or on a serving platter. Everyone takes a good-sized handful to start, adding more as the meal progresses.

2 cups sticky rice

1. Soak the rice overnight in a large mixing bowl with enough water to cover by 2 to 3 inches.
2. The next morning, drain the rice and transfer it to a steaming rack or basket that can be suspended over boiling water. Set aside. Fill a 4-quart saucepan or wok half full with water. Cover and bring the water to boil over high heat.
3. Nearby, keep a smaller saucepan filled with water at a simmer so you can quickly bring it to boil as needed, to replenish the steamer pot.

4. Place the rice-filled steaming rack over the boiling water. It should be suspended an inch or more above the water. Cover and steam the rice for 15 minutes. Check the water level of the steamer pot occasionally and replenish it with boiling water as needed to maintain the original water level. Wearing an oven mitt, uncover the rice and turn it over with a spatula for even cooking. Cover and steam the rice 10 minutes more. It should be tender and sticky enough to be pressed into small lumps.

5. Serve hot, warm, or room temperature, either from a basket or a serving platter.

Savory Yellow Rice

Serves 4 to 6

O n most Southeast Asian tables, center stage is held by the simple wonder of a heaping bowl of pristine white rice. Indonesians, however, like to embellish their rice with additional flavor and color. Throughout Asia, the color yellow is associated with godliness, royalty, and feasting. Savory Yellow Rice takes its "heavenly" hue from turmeric, while onions, cinnamon, coriander, and cumin deliver the earthy flavors.

2 tablespoons peanut or vegetable oil

1 large onion, halved and thinly sliced into half-moons

1 cup jasmine or other long-grain white rice

1/2 teaspoon turmeric

1 teaspoon ground coriander

1 teaspoon cinnamon

1 teaspoon ground cumin

1 1/2 teaspoons salt

3 1/2 cups Chicken Stock (page 289) or canned low-sodium chicken broth

1. Place a large, heavy-bottomed saucepan over medium heat. Heat the oil, then add the sliced onion and stir-fry until softened, 3 to 4 minutes. Add the rice, turmeric, coriander, cinnamon, cumin, and salt and stir-fry until all the grains of rice are glistening with oil and the ingredients are well mixed, about 2 minutes.

2. Stir in the chicken stock and bring to a boil. Reduce the heat to its lowest setting, cover, and simmer until the liquid is absorbed and the rice is tender, about 20 minutes.

3. Turn off the heat, keep covered, and let the rice stand for at least 5 minutes, or up to 30 minutes, before serving. Transfer the rice to a serving bowl and serve either hot or warm.

Coconut Rice with Crisp-Fried Shallots and Fresh Mangoes

Serves 4 to 6

Eating this creamy, fragrant rice—sprinkled with crispy fried shallot rings and encircled by juicy mango slices—is like taking a quick trip to Bangkok or Bali. Serve it with grilled fish or chicken, roast pork, or crab cakes and a simply dressed salad for a sumptuous yet easy meal.

1 cup jasmine or other long-grain white rice

1 cup canned unsweetened coconut milk

1/2 cup water

1 teaspoon sugar

1/4 teaspoon salt

3 firm, ripe mangoes, peeled, flesh cut away from the stone, and thickly sliced

Crisp-Fried Shallots (page 100)

1. Rinse the rice well under cold running water until it runs clear, and drain. Put the rice in a large saucepan. Stir in the coconut milk, water, sugar, and salt and bring to a boil over medium-high heat. Cover, reduce the heat to its lowest setting, and simmer for 18 minutes. Lift the lid and check for doneness. Cook 1 or 2 minutes or longer if needed. Turn off the heat, keep covered, and let stand for 5 minutes, or up to 30 minutes, before serving.

2. Fluff the rice gently with a fork or wooden spoon, blending in any coconut cream that may have risen to the top. To serve, mound portions of the rice in the center of small individual serving dishes. Arrange mango slices around the rice and sprinkle with the shallots.

Fragrant Malay Rice with Mixed Fresh Herbs

Serves 6

*T*his simple yet elegant centerpiece dish features aromatically-infused jasmine rice steamed with coconut milk to create a lemon, ginger, and cream feast for the senses. The trio of chopped fresh cilantro, basil, and mint is an herbal counterpoint for the fragrant rice. To serve this traditional Malaysian dish in festive tropical style, mound the rice in a simple cone shape, encircle it with the green herbs, then sprinkle the whole creation with a bright orange dusting of turmeric. Edible flowers from the garden such as nasturtiums, pansies, or calendulas can complete the presentation.

Tell your guests to scoop up some rice along with the fresh herbs and mix them together on their plates. In a Malay household, this dish would be accompanied by a selection of *sambals* and chutneys, such as Spiced Coconut *Sambal* (page 90).

2¹/₂ cups jasmine or any long-grain white rice

1 cup water

³/₄ cup canned unsweetened coconut milk

1/2 teaspoon salt

2 plump stalks lemon grass or 1/2 teaspoon grated lemon zest

6 quarter-size slices fresh Siamese ginger (*galanga*) or regular ginger

4 fresh or frozen kaffir lime leaves, or 1/2 teaspoon grated lime zest

1/3 cup chopped fresh cilantro, including the stems

1/3 cup thinly sliced fresh Thai, sweet, or purple basil leaves

1/3 cup chopped fresh Vietnamese coriander (*rau rom*), mint, or cilantro leaves

Turmeric for dusting

1 to 2 handfuls fresh nasturtium blossoms or other edible flowers (optional)
   for garnish

1. Rinse the rice well under cold running water until it runs clear and drain. Pour the water into a heavy-bottomed saucepan and stir in the coconut milk, salt, and rice. Set aside.

2. Trim the root ends of the lemon grass and discard the tough outer leaves. Cut the tender stalks into 4-inch lengths. With a pestle or rolling pin, lightly bruise the lemon grass and ginger.

3. Add all the lemon grass, ginger, and lime leaves to the rice and stir to mix well. Bring the mixture to boil over medium-high heat. Cover, reduce the heat to its lowest setting, and simmer for 18 minutes. Lift the lid and check for doneness. Cook 1 or 2 minutes longer, if needed. Turn off the heat, keep covered, and let the rice stand for at least 5 minutes, or up to 30 minutes, before serving.

4. At serving time, remove and discard the lemon grass, ginger, and lime leaves. (If you've used lemon and lime zest, simply remove the ginger.) Mound the rice on a large serving platter. Moisten your hands with water and form it into a tall cone shape. Arrange the cilantro, basil, and coriander around the base of the rice. Sprinkle the rice with the turmeric so that all sides are lightly dusted with color. If using edible flowers, decorate the platter, reserving the showiest blooms for the top of the rice.

Rice and Ritual

Most Indonesians and Malaysians are Muslim, but they still love to mark their celebrations with a tradition dating to earlier times, when they believed in gods who resided in a sacred mountain.

For important occasions of all kinds, Indonesian cooks prepare a *tumpeng*, a cone of rice to symbolize that holy mountain. They build it with *nasi kuning*, a simple dish of rice cooked in coconut milk. It may include raisins or almonds, but it will always have the tint of yellow-gold from turmeric. Sunny yellow hues are used in many Asian cultures to signify happiness.

For the most elaborate occasions, the rice mound is surrounded by a host of side dishes, which may include omelet shreds, hard-boiled eggs, crispy fried potato sticks, spiced toasted coconut, roast chicken, and spicy shrimp. When such dishes as these encircle a rice mound, the presentation is called *nasi kuning lenghop*, which means "yellow rice complete." To be deeply traditional, *nasi kuning lenghop* must have side dishes chosen to represent the four forms of life on earth—something that swims the waters, something that walks the earth, something that flies in the air, and something that grows in the earth.

A *tumpeng* can also be made without turmeric, and surrounded by richly colorful foods and "flowers" made from artfully carved chilli peppers. The stark purity of white rice allows celebrants to balance the symbolic power of all the other colors. For example, although the color yellow symbolizes good fortune, when combined with other colors it becomes negative, signifying greed. Red may symbolize anger; black may connote violence. But a *tumpeng* of white rice subordinates their powers and ensures that beneficence will rule.

Similarly, Malaysians who have emerged from a streak of ill fortune will prepare and serve a dish that they call "red rice–white rice." First, rice is prepared with coconut milk and fragrant *pandanus* leaves. Half the batch is then sweetened with a palm sugar called *gula merah*. Because *merah* means "red," the sweetened rice is considered to have become red. The combination of white with red is a way of signifying a victory of good forces over evil ones.

Indonesian Fried Rice

*H*ere is one of Indonesia's most popular dishes and another way to make great use of leftover rice. The Chinese, of course, are famous for fried rice. But many Indonesians, especially in the countryside, once believed that it was disrespectful to the divine Rice Mother to fry grains of rice. The influence of Dutch colonists, who absolutely loved fried rice, gradually persuaded Indonesians to make an exception for this dish, which they call *nasi goreng* and often serve for breakfast. Now it is widely thought of as Indonesia's national dish.

Although a Chinese influence is present, Indonesians have expanded the usual list of ingredients for fried rice to create a main meal rather than a side dish. We've used Vietnamese-Style Oven-Roasted BBQ Pork (page 183), but you could substitute almost any leftover cooked meat or fresh shrimp or ground pork. Either way you've got a great meal, especially when you pair it with a side dish of Hot 'n' Cool Cucumber Relish (page 256) or toppings such as Crisp-Fried Shallots (page 100) or Omelet Shreds (page 167). And we always serve *nasi goreng* with *Sri Racha* Hot Sauce (page 81).

1 tablespoon sesame oil (not toasted) or vegetable oil

1 large onion, finely chopped

2 large cloves garlic, crushed and chopped

$1^{1}/_{2}$ cups sliced Vietnamese-Style Oven-Roasted BBQ Pork (page 183), or substitute a 1-pound mixture of ground pork and chopped peeled fresh shrimp

5 cups cold cooked jasmine or other long-grain white rice

2 tablespoons *kecap manis* or sweet dark soy sauce, or substitute $1^{1}/_{2}$ teaspoons light soy sauce mixed with $1^{1}/_{2}$ tablespoons pure maple syrup

1 tablespoon light soy sauce

2 slender scallions (white and tender green parts), angle-cut into $^{1}/_{2}$-inch pieces

Hot 'n' Cool Cucumber Relish (optional, page 256)

Crisp-Fried Shallots (optional, page 100)

Omelet shreds (optional, see page 167)

Sri Racha Hot Sauce (page 81) or prepared *sri racha*, or any favorite hot sauce

1. Heat a large wok or deep, heavy skillet over medium-high heat. When it is hot, add the oil and rotate the wok or pan a bit to coat it evenly. When the oil is hot, add the onion and garlic and stir-fry until they begin to color, about 1 minute. If using ground pork and shrimp, stir them in and cook for 1 minute. If using cooked BBQ pork, stir in and cook just until mixed. Add the rice and stir-fry until all the ingredients are well mixed and the rice is getting crispy on the bottom, about 3 minutes. Mix in the *kecap manis* and light soy sauce and the scallions.

2. Serve hot, with the cucumber relish and/or fried shallots and omelet shreds, if desired, and *sri racha* or other hot sauce on the side.

Thai-Style Crab Fried Rice

Serves 2 as a main course,
4 as a side dish

*T*hai stir-fried rice is never heavy or oily. This one, with fresh crabmeat, is especially light and elegant.

Thai cooks like to set out a selection of herbs and spices to complement their fried rice dishes. Here we've paired the delicate flavors of the dish with fresh cilantro, pineapple, and sliced tomatoes, plus the all-important dipping sauce for its bracing, pungent spice.

3 cups cold cooked jasmine or other long-grain white rice

3 tablespoons vegetable oil

3 teaspoons finely chopped crushed garlic

3 tablespoons finely chopped shallots

2 tablespoons minced fresh cilantro stems

1/2 pound lump crabmeat, picked over for shells and cartilage

2 tablespoons Asian fish sauce

$^1/_2$ teaspoon palm sugar or light brown sugar

$^1/_2$ teaspoon freshly ground black pepper, plus extra for sprinkling on tomatoes

$^1/_4$ cup chopped fresh cilantro leaves

2 medium-size ripe tomatoes, halved and thinly sliced

Salt to taste

1 cup fresh or canned chopped pineapple

Thai Chilli Dipping Sauce (page 83)

1. Put the cold rice in a large mixing bowl and use your hands to crumble the mass into grains. Set a large wok or deep, heavy skillet over medium-high heat. When it is hot, add the oil. Rotate the wok a bit so the oil coats the sides. When it is hot, add the garlic, shallots, and cilantro stems and stir-fry until the garlic is pale golden brown, about 1 minute.

2. Add the rice and stir-fry briskly, making sure to mix it well with the aromatics, about 2 minutes. Add the crabmeat, fish sauce, sugar, and $^1/_2$ teaspoon pepper and stir-fry gently for 1 minute, keeping the crabmeat lumps as whole as possible.

3. Transfer the fried rice to a serving platter and top with the cilantro leaves. Sprinkle the tomatoes with salt and pepper. Set out small serving plates of tomatoes and pineapple and a bowl of dipping sauce on the side. Serve immediately.

Soul Food: Spirit Houses, Temple Offerings, and "Making Merit"

In any Thai home, restaurant, or other business, there will be—almost without exception—a small symbolic dwelling known as a spirit house. Every day, as a way of staying on peaceful and benevolent terms with any spirits that their homes or businesses may displace, Thais offer food as well as coins and incense on the "doorsteps" of their spirit houses. Wrapping and tying the offerings in beautiful little packages is a cherished art, a way to add sweet grace to the observances.

Beautifully presented offerings are key to an annual festival known as *Loy Krathong*, but sometimes called the water festival. It dates back at least 700 years and takes place during full moon in November. The purpose of *Loy Krathong* is to ask pardon from water spirits for constantly using their waters. Everyone, from peasants to royalty, participates, vying to be as creative as possible in building tiny paper lanterns. These are set adrift at night on canals and rivers throughout the country, carrying offerings of coins, flowers, and food.

Something tremendously important to a Thai community, such as a pregnancy or a harvest, calls for special ceremonial dishes. One of these, brought forth and dedicated to *Maeya*, the mother of the sun king, is a pig's head that has been boiled and spiced with fish sauce, vinegar, and chillies. By contrast, when an individual is depressed or beset by troubles, they may enlist the help of a village expert to perform rituals designed to draw a helpful spirit into a bowl of rice. The person needing that spirit's help is fed the rice, and thereby the spirit joins with them.

Although many ceremonies and rituals prove that belief in spirits is still a powerful part of Thai culture, Therevada Buddhism is the formal belief system of nearly all Thais. It is a branch of Buddhism that places special emphasis on taking personal responsibility for one's own salvation. For a Therevada Buddhist, the goal of life is becoming a "worthy one," a person who travels the Noble Eight-Fold Path and breaks free of errors in his or her thoughts.

Food is a basic and often-used means for building one's worthiness, a practice known as "making merit." Monks go out into the streets, carrying bowls with them to accept donations of food. They always find people eager to present them with rice and other things to eat. It's the most direct way that common people can make merit.

At certain times of the year, girls will put on their prettiest dresses and carry trays of food to the monks in the temple, highlighting fruits that are in season. They carry the trays at the ends of bamboo carrying poles balanced on their shoulders, striving to be highly graceful. Their efforts are considered to be most beautiful when the poles flex rhythmically under their loads as the girls walk to the temple.

Cellophane Noodles with Scallions and Pickled Garlic

*T*his piquant, vegetarian version of a favorite Thai dish has just enough vegetable broth to help create a light, garlicky sauce. And the bean thread vermicelli (also known as cellophane noodles) have a talent for mopping it all up. Adding scallions at the end gives them a crisp, *al dente* texture that contrasts nicely with the soft noodles. The pickled garlic, called *kratiem dong* by the Thai, is both sweet and sour. It's one of their favorite accompaniments to soups, curries, fried rice, and noodle dishes. *Kratiem dong* is sold in Asian markets and specialty stores.

One 3.5-ounce package dried bean thread vermicelli

5 small bulbs prepared pickled garlic

2 tablespoons vegetable oil

5 large cloves garlic, crushed and chopped

2 tablespoons sugar

1/4 cup vegetable broth or water

1 tablespoon Thai mushroom soy or light soy sauce

6 scallions (white and green parts), greens angle-cut into 1-inch pieces and bulbs
   halved lengthwise

Sprigs fresh cilantro for garnish

1. Put the noodles in a large bowl of warm water and soak until soft and translucent, 12 to 15 minutes. As the noodles become pliable, spread them out with your fingers to ensure even soaking. Put the noodles in a colander, drain well, and turn out onto a cutting board. Using a knife or scissors, cut the mound of noodles into thirds. Set aside.

2. Trim away any stems of the pickled garlic and cut the bulbs crosswise into thin slices. You should have about 3/4 cup.

3. Place all the ingredients within easy reach of the cooking area.

4. Set a wok over medium-high heat. When it is hot, add the oil. Rotate the wok a bit so the oil coats the sides. When the oil is hot, add the fresh and pickled garlic and stir-fry for a few seconds, just until golden and aromatic. Add the noodles, tossing them into the garlicky oil just until mixed. Add the sugar, vegetable broth, and soy sauce, stirring after each addition. Add the scallions and stir-fry until cooked through and crisp-tender, 1 to 2 minutes.

5. Transfer the noodles to a serving platter. Scatter torn sprigs of cilantro over the top and serve.

Night Market Noodles

Serves 2 as a snack or side dish

This is a great example of the kind of dish Southeast Asians love to snack on late at night, stopping at a vendor's cart in the street or a stall in the local night market as they take in the myriad displays of clothing, household goods, CDs, and everything else found in a present-day Asian bazaar. These noodles are reminiscent of *chee chong fun*, a Singapore favorite. It's a simple and unadorned stir-fry that comes together in a very few minutes—just some soft rice noodles that get browned in a wok, scented with cumin, and spiced with tamarind-accented Thai chilli paste, an ingredient that's quite popular in Singapore.

We enjoy using "fat" noodles, the soft, fresh rice noodles so often found in Thai recipes, but you can also use the thin rice stick noodles that are typical of Singapore stir-fries. Whatever noodle you prefer, just make sure to use fresh noodles for this dish, not dried. They're the best for quick stir-fries. You'll find them in Asian markets, where you'll also find the sweet soy sauce and chilli paste.

One 12-ounce package fresh rice noodles, presliced or uncut sheets

2¹/₂ tablespoons sweet dark soy sauce, or substitute 2 teaspoons light soy sauce
   mixed with 2 tablespoons pure maple syrup

1 teaspoon Thai roasted chilli paste (*nam phrik pao*), or substitute ¹/₂ teaspoon
   Chinese chilli-garlic sauce mixed with ¹/₄ teaspoon light brown sugar

¹/₂ teaspoon peeled and grated fresh ginger

¹/₂ teaspoon ground cumin

1 tablespoon sesame oil (not toasted) or vegetable oil

1. If you bought rice noodles in uncut sheets, slice them lengthwise through the fold to make ribbon-like strips about 1 inch wide. Put the noodles in a colander and rinse them with hot water to remove their light oil coating and soften them a bit. Separate the noodles into individual ribbons. Some may break into shorter lengths—that's okay. Just loosen them up so they can get tumbled into the stir-fry and nicely sauced.

2. Combine the sweet soy sauce, chilli paste, ginger, and cumin in a small mixing bowl.

3. Set a wok over medium-high heat. When it is hot, add the oil and rotate the wok a bit to coat it evenly. When the oil is hot, add the rice noodles and toss them gently, again and again, until heated through, about 2 minutes. Add the sweet soy mixture and stir-fry briskly to coat all the noodles with the sauce, about 1 minute.

4. Transfer the noodles to a serving platter and serve hot.

Greetings

How deep is the love that Southeast Asian people hold for their cuisine? Consider the people of Chuuk, a small island group located in the vastness of the Pacific between the Asian mainland and Hawaii. Their ancestors arrived eons ago, probably from present-day Malaysia or Indonesia. When the people of Chuuk meet one another, very often the first thing they will say is "Have you eaten?" This greeting may be an incredible example of a cultural survival, and a testimony to how thoroughly Southeast Asians have always cared about food.

In present-day Singapore, when two people meet they often say *"In chi bao le ma?"*, which means "Have you eaten yet?" And the same greeting is exchanged when Laotians meet. Laos is a more traditional country, the only tropical Asian nation with no seacoast, a place where old ways are likely to survive. Singapore, though, is one of the world's most cosmopolitan cities. It has been a hub of China-to-India trade for some two and a half centuries. It's people have taken in a huge number of foreign influences, including Chinese, Arabian, and Indian. And still that food-lovers' greeting, which is probably well over a thousand years old, remains a central feature of their social customs.

Lunchtime Noodles with Garlic and Greens

his savory yet quick and healthful lunch is a favorite Thai street snack. It's great any time you'd like a simple, light meal or side dish.

4 ounces thin (1/8 inch) rice stick noodles
1 tablespoon peanut or vegetable oil
1 1/2 tablespoons finely chopped garlic
6 cups fresh young spinach leaves
1 tablespoon light soy sauce
1 teaspoon sugar

1. Soak the rice sticks in a large bowl of boiling hot water until they are soft and pliable, about 20 minutes. Drain and set aside.

2. Heat a large wok or deep, heavy skillet over medium-high heat. When it is hot, add the oil and rotate the wok or pan a bit to coat it evenly. When the oil is hot, stir-fry the garlic until fragrant, about 1 minute. Add the spinach and stir-fry 1 to 2 minutes. Stir in the soy sauce and sugar, then add the noodles and toss thoroughly to mix evenly and heat all the way through, about 2 minutes. Serve hot.

Three Sisters Vegetarian Noodle Stir-Fry

*T*his is a vegetarian recipe we've invented using typical Southeast Asian methods and ingredients. You might think that it's called Three Sisters because it features a trio of fresh, lively herbs: cilantro, Thai basil, and mint. But, in fact, this recipe honors another fresh and lively trio, our wonderful nieces, Lisa, Jennifer, and Kristin, who are all vegetarians and whose preferences have inspired us to create this dish.

There's also another important trio here—rich peanuts, sweet pineapple, and garden-ripe tomatoes—to make this stir-fry appealing even to people who have never thought of trying vegetarian cuisine. To make this dish as spicy as it is sweet and tasty, pair it with Vegetarian Chilli-Vinegar Sauce (page 86), which contains no fish sauce.

6 ounces thin ($1/8$ inch) rice stick noodles

$2^{1}/_{2}$ tablespoons peanut or vegetable oil

1 large clove garlic, crushed and chopped

4 slender scallions (white and tender green parts), angle-cut into 1-inch pieces

$1/8$ teaspoon pure chilli powder

1 tablespoon *kecap manis* or sweet dark soy sauce, or substitute 1 teaspoon light soy
   sauce mixed with 1 tablespoon pure maple syrup

1 tablespoon light soy sauce

$1/2$ teaspoon palm sugar or light brown sugar

1 medium-size ripe tomato, halved, cored, and cut into thin wedges

$1/2$ cup fresh or canned $1/2$-inch pineapple chunks

$3^{1}/_{2}$ tablespoons unsalted dry-roasted peanuts, crushed in a mortar or finely chopped

1 cup mixed chopped fresh herbs, such as cilantro, mint, and Thai basil, plus a few
   sprigs for garnish

Vegetarian Chilli-Vinegar Sauce (optional, page 86)

1. Soak the rice sticks in a large bowl of boiling hot water until they are soft and pliable, about 20 minutes. Drain and set aside.

2. Heat a wok or deep, heavy skillet over medium-high heat. When it is hot, add the oil and rotate the wok or pan a bit to coat it evenly. When the oil is hot, add the garlic and stir-fry until golden, 30 to 45 seconds. Add the scallions and chilli powder and stir-fry for 1 minute. Add the noodles, *kecap manis*, light soy sauce, and sugar and stir-fry briskly, tossing the noodles with the sauce until the noodles are tender and coated with sauce, about 3 minutes. Add the tomatoes and stir-fry for 30 seconds. Add the pineapple and stir-fry for 1 minute. Turn off the heat. Mix in the peanuts and chopped herbs.

3. Transfer the stir-fried noodles to a serving platter and garnish with sprigs of fresh herbs. Serve hot, with the vegetarian dipping sauce on the side, if desired.

Fat Noodles with Fresh Chillies and Mint Leaves

Serves 4 as a light one-dish meal

Back in the 1970s, when the first wave of Thai restaurants in Los Angeles began catering to their growing legion of fans, we were there, falling in love with the intriguing flavors and scents, learning a bit more week by week about one of the world's great cuisines. This dish, known in its homeland as *kwaytiow phat khae mao*, was an early favorite.

In those days the delicate but spicy holy basil, *bai gaprao*, wasn't available to L.A.'s Thai chefs. They used fresh mint instead, which actually works quite well in this fiery hot yet savory noodle dish. Now it's easier to find holy basil, or to grow your own supply. But we loved the mint-accented version and still make it that way today.

One 12-ounce package fresh rice noodles, presliced or uncut sheets

$1/4$ cup plus 1 teaspoon Asian fish sauce

1 tablespoon sweet dark soy sauce, or substitute 1 teaspoon light soy sauce mixed
   with 1 tablespoon pure maple syrup

1 teaspoon sugar

Scant $1/2$ teaspoon salt

$1/4$ teaspoon freshly ground black pepper, or to taste

3 tablespoons peanut or vegetable oil

$1^1/2$ teaspoons chopped crushed garlic

$1^1/2$ to $2^1/2$ tablespoons finely chopped small Thai or serrano chillies, to your taste

$1/2$ pound coarsely ground beef, chicken, or pork

1 cup loosely packed fresh mint leaves, plus a few sprigs for garnish

8 plump cherry tomatoes, quartered

1. If you bought rice noodles in uncut sheets, slice them lengthwise through
    the fold to make ribbon-like strips about 1 inch wide. Put the noodles in a
    colander and rinse them with hot water to remove their light oil coating and
    soften them a bit. Separate the noodles into individual ribbons. Some may
    break into shorter lengths—that's okay. Just loosen them up so they can get
    tumbled into the stir-fry and nicely sauced.

2. Combine the fish sauce and sweet soy sauce in a small bowl. Combine the
    sugar, salt, and black pepper in another small bowl.

3. Heat a wok or deep, heavy skillet over medium-high heat. When it is hot, add
    the oil and rotate the wok or pan a bit to coat it evenly. When the oil is hot,
    add the garlic and stir-fry just until golden, about 30 seconds. Add the chillies
    and stir-fry another 30 seconds. Add the ground meat and stir-fry just until it
    begins to brown, 1 to 2 minutes. Add the fish sauce mixture, then add the
    sugar mixture and stir-fry about 1 minute to let the sauce thicken a bit. Add
    the rice noodles and turn them over gently, again and again, to absorb the
    sauce, about 1 minute. Mix in the mint leaves, then the tomatoes, and remove
    the pan from the heat.

4. Transfer the noodles to a serving platter, garnish with mint sprigs, and serve hot.

Thai Chicken and Cellophane Noodle Salad

hen you soak cellophane noodles, then serve them without cooking, they are the Asian equivalent of pasta *al dente*. That treatment makes them soft and pliant, but with a little crunchy "tooth"—perfect for this quick salad, which the Thais know as *laab woon sen*. You'll notice the interesting way the chicken is cooked—by poaching in a small amount of boiling water rather than stir-frying. The chicken cooks rapidly this way, staying moist and bland, the better to absorb the lively flavors of the dressing.

Here again we've used New Mexico chilli powder, instead of the traditional Thai *phrik pon* chilli powder, because it is likely to be fresher and livelier and it imparts a beautiful crimson color.

1 small bundle (1.7 to 2 ounces) dried bean thread vermicelli

1 cup water

1/2 pound ground chicken

1 small onion, halved and thinly sliced into half-moons, or 2 plump scallions (white
  part and 1 inch of the green), angle-cut into 1/4-inch pieces

1/2 cup loosely packed fresh mint leaves

3 tablespoons Toasted Rice Powder (page 98)

1/4 cup fresh lime juice

1 tablespoon plus 1 teaspoon Asian fish sauce

1 1/2 teaspoons palm sugar or light brown sugar

1/2 teaspoon minced small Thai or serrano chillies (optional)

New Mexico or any pure chilli powder to taste

1. Soak the bean threads in a large bowl of boiling hot water until they are soft and pliable, about 20 minutes. Drain and set aside.

2. Meanwhile, bring the 1 cup of water to boil in a medium-size saucepan over high heat. Add the ground chicken, stirring often to break up the meat and cook it through, about 1 minute. Remove the pot from the heat. Use a slotted

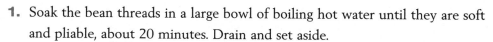

spoon to transfer the meat to a large mixing bowl, leaving any excess liquid behind. Add the onion, mint, and toasted rice powder, mix well, and set aside.

3. Place the noodles on a cutting board. Using a knife or kitchen shears, cut the mound of noodles into thirds. Combine the noodles with the chicken mixture, tossing and stirring until well blended.

4. Combine the lime juice, fish sauce, sugar, and chillies, if desired, in a small mixing bowl. Stir until the sugar is dissolved and blended. Pour the dressing over the noodle salad, tossing and stirring to mix thoroughly. Transfer the salad to a serving platter. Sprinkle with some chilli powder to taste and serve warm or at room temperature.

Thai-Style Stir-Fried Rice Noodles

Serves 2 as a one-dish meal, 4 as a side dish

One of my friends had her six-year-old daughter in the car at lunchtime and, thinking this would please her little girl, offered to take her to MacDonald's. To her surprise, this offer raised a protest: "*Phat Thai*, Mommy, I want *phat Thai!*" We've given this dish an English name, but most lovers of Thai cooking will recognize it as *phat Thai*. It's the national dish of Thailand, first because it is delicious and easy to make, second because it is so easily adapted to personal preferences. This warm, tangy, tamarind-accented tangle of noodles can be an all-shrimp dish, for example, or all-chicken—however you want to customize it. If you're going to shop at an Asian market, you should be able to find the dried shrimp, salted radish, and firm tofu.

Some notes about ingredients: The Thai chilli powder called *phrik pon*, when found in America, is often too old and rather dusty in flavor. We use a pure domestic chilli powder, such as those from New Mexico. And we find that substituting lime juice for tamarind sauce still produces a terrific result.

One 8-ounce package rice stick noodles,

preferably Thai *chantaboon* or a thin, flat variety about $^1/_8$ inch wide

1 tablespoon peanut or vegetable oil

2 large eggs, lightly beaten

3 tablespoons Asian fish sauce

1 tablespoon unseasoned rice vinegar or distilled white vinegar

1 tablespoon Tamarind Sauce (page 290), liquid tamarind concentrate, or fresh lime
    juice

$^1/_4$ cup palm sugar or light brown sugar

1 teaspoon pure chilli powder, plus extra for garnish

3 tablespoons vegetable oil

1 tablespoon chopped crushed garlic

$^1/_4$ pound medium-size shrimp, peeled and deveined if desired

$^1/_4$ pound pork tenderloin or boneless, skinless chicken breast or thigh, trimmed of
    any fat or silverskin and cut into bite-size pieces, about 1 x $^1/_4$ inch

2 tablespoons small dried shrimp (optional)

2 tablespoons shredded salted radish (*hua pak kad khem*, optional)

$^1/_4$ cup diced firm tofu (optional)

4 slender scallions (white and green parts), angle-cut into 1-inch pieces

$^1/_4$ cup plus 2 tablespoons unsalted dry-roasted peanuts, crushed in a mortar or finely
    chopped

$1^1/_2$ cups crisp, fresh bean sprouts

1 lime, cut into wedges

1 tablespoon minced small Thai or serrano chillies or Chilli-Vinegar Sauce (page 86),
    to taste

1. Soak the rice sticks in a large bowl of boiling hot water until they are soft and
pliable, about 20 minutes. Drain and set aside.

2. To make the omelet shreds, if desired, heat the peanut oil in a small nonstick skillet over medium-high heat. Add the eggs and swirl them around in the pan to make an even, thin layer. Cook just until set on one side, about 1 minute, then turn with a metal spatula and cook on the other side until set, about 20 seconds. Transfer the omelet to a cutting board, cut into thin strips, and set aside.

3. Combine the fish sauce, vinegar, tamarind sauce, sugar, and chilli powder in a small mixing bowl and set aside.

4. Heat a large wok or deep, heavy skillet over high heat. When it is hot, add the 3 tablespoons of oil and rotate the wok or pan a bit to coat it evenly. When the oil is hot, add the garlic and stir-fry until soft and fragrant, 5 to 10 seconds. Add the shrimp and pork or chicken and stir-fry until the shrimp and meat begin to color, about 1 minute. Stir in the sauce. Add the dried shrimp, or salted radish, or tofu, if desired, alone or in any combination you like. When the mixture begins to boil, add the noodles and mix well, stir-frying until they absorb the sauce, about 3 minutes. Add the omelet shreds, if desired. Add the scallions, half of the peanuts, and half of the bean sprouts. Mix well, sprinkle with more of the chilli powder to taste, and serve hot with the remaining bean sprouts and peanuts, the lime wedges, and chillies on the side.

Vietnamese-Style Lemon Grass Chicken with Rice Vermicelli

*B*un is the Vietnamese name for rice vermicelli and for dishes such as this one, which features those versatile noodles in a wonderful balancing act of flavors, textures, and temperatures, too. *Bun* showcases the best of Vietnamese cuisine. It's hot, sour, salty, sweet, soft, and chewy all at once—a light, herb-laden, and healthful dish with plenty of noodles and greens, and small portions of grilled pork, beef, or, as in this instance, chicken.

This dish takes a bit longer to prepare, but it's definitely a "must have." And you can prepare nearly everything in advance. The cooked noodles will keep a long time at room temperature. You can compose the greens in individual serving bowls and stash them in the refrigerator, along with the dipping sauce. The chicken marinates in the refrigerator for between 30 minutes and three hours, then takes only a minute to cook. As soon as everyone is ready to eat, you can quickly grill the chicken, then combine all the other ingredients.

LEMON GRASS CHICKEN:

2 plump stalks fresh lemon grass

2 teaspoons sweet dark soy sauce or pure maple syrup

2 tablespoons Asian fish sauce

1/2 teaspoon *Sri Racha* Hot Sauce (page 81) or prepared *sri racha*, or any favorite hot sauce

1 1/2 tablespoons palm sugar or light brown sugar

1/4 cup finely chopped shallots

2 tablespoons finely chopped garlic

1 pound boneless, skinless chicken breasts, trimmed of any fat and cut crosswise into thin strips about 1 1/4 x 4 inches

Peanut or vegetable oil for the grill

8 ounces dried rice vermicelli (*bun*)

GREENS:

1 small head Boston or red leaf lettuce, shredded

1 cup crisp, fresh bean sprouts

1 medium-size carrot, grated

$^1/_3$ cup torn or small fresh cilantro leaves

$^1/_3$ cup torn or small fresh mint leaves

$^1/_3$ cup torn fresh Thai basil, cilantro, or mint leaves

TOPPINGS:

$^1/_2$ cup unsalted dry-roasted peanuts, crushed in a mortar or finely chopped

Classic Vietnamese Dipping Sauce (page 82), to taste (see Note)

16 bamboo skewers (10-inch), soaked in cold water at least 30 minutes and drained

1. To make the chicken, trim off the root end of the lemon grass and discard the tough outer leaves. Cut a 3-inch length from each bulb end and discard the rest. Slice the lemon grass crosswise into thin rounds, then mince. Set aside. Combine the sweet soy sauce, fish sauce, hot sauce, and sugar in a medium-size mixing bowl. Stir well to dissolve the sugar. Mix in the lemon grass, shallots, and garlic. Add the sliced chicken to the marinade and mix with your hands to coat the pieces well. Cover with plastic wrap and marinate in the refrigerator for at least 30 minutes or up to 3 hours.

2. Meanwhile, prepare the noodles: Bring a medium-size saucepan of water to a rolling boil. Add the rice vermicelli and cook, stirring frequently, until the strands are tender and white, but not too soft, 3 to 4 minutes. Drain the noodles in a colander, rinse with cold running water, about 1 minute, and toss with your hands to cool off all the strands. Let the noodles continue draining in the colander. (The noodles can be prepared to this point and kept covered at room temperature for 2 to 3 hours before serving.)

3. To assemble the greens, toss all ingredients together in medium bowl and divide among 4 wide soup bowls. If making the dish in advance, cover each bowl with damp paper towels and refrigerate. About 15 to 20 minutes before serving time, remove the greens from the refrigerator. They should be cool, but not cold, when the meal is ready.

4. At serving time, remove the chicken from the marinade. Weave a bamboo skewer down the center of a slice of chicken so the meat lies flat, with the skewer threaded through several times. Repeat with the remaining chicken pieces, with 1 slice per skewer. Set aside.

5. Mound equal portions of noodles on top of the greens in each bowl, shaking them loose with your fingers as you portion them out. Set aside.

6. Preheat an outdoor grill, or preheat a grill pan for 3 to 5 minutes over medium-high heat. If using a barbecue grill, brush the grill rack well with peanut or vegetable oil. If using a grill pan, heat about 1 tablespoon of oil in the hot pan. (Make sure there is good ventilation.) Space out the skewers of chicken over the grill or pan and cook, turning once or twice, until the chicken is lightly charred and cooked through, about 1 minute on each side.

7. Divide the skewers of grilled chicken among the 4 bowls, laying them across the bowls on top of the noodles. Sprinkle each serving with the peanuts and serve immediately with the dipping sauce on the side. Pass the dipping sauce at the table. Each guest should push the lemon grass chicken off the skewers and drizzle 3 to 4 tablespoons of sauce over the salad, then toss the salad in the bowl with chopsticks or forks and enjoy.

Note: The dipping sauce can be served cold but is best at room temperature.

Filipino-Style Stir-Fried Noodles with Chorizo, Chicken, and Shrimp

Serves 4 to 6 as a one-dish meal

Combining several kinds of meat and seafood in a single dish is customary in the Philippines, just as it is in other Southeast Asian cuisines. What sets this stir-fried noodle dish apart is its use of chorizo, a spicy, smoky, Spanish-style sausage you may be familiar with from Mexican cooking. If it is not available, you can substitute any favorite spicy smoked sausage.

The use of olive oil for the stir-fry is another indicator of the pervasive Spanish influence on Filipino cooking.

Filipinos use extremely thin noodles for this dish. We favor egg noodles, which are available in a one-sixteenth inch width. Filipino rice sticks, called *pancit bihon*, are even thinner.

NOODLES:

8 ounces dried Chinese egg noodles (¹/16 inch wide) or *pancit bihon*

STIR-FRY:

2 to 3 tablespoons olive oil

1 medium-size red onion, finely chopped

1 large clove garlic, crushed and chopped

1 teaspoon peeled and finely chopped fresh ginger

1 to 2 serrano chillies (optional), to your taste, finely chopped

¹/2 pound medium-size shrimp, peeled, deveined if desired, and cut in half

¹/2 pound boneless, skinless chicken breast, trimmed of any fat and cut crosswise
   into thin strips about ¹/2 inch x 2 inches

¹/4 pound uncooked chorizo or other spicy smoked sausage, thinly sliced

1 cup thickly sliced (about 1 inch wide) Napa or green cabbage

1 medium-size carrot, halved lengthwise and angle-cut into thin slices

1 tablespoon light soy sauce, plus more for the table

1 tablespoon Asian fish sauce

$1/4$ cup Chicken Stock (page 289) or canned low-sodium chicken broth

2 slender scallions (white and some of the green part), angle-cut into $3/4$-inch pieces

TOPPINGS:

Freshly ground black pepper to taste

Sprigs fresh cilantro

1 medium-large ripe tomato, halved, cored, and cut into thin wedges

1. To prepare the noodles, soak them in a large bowl of boiling hot water until they are soft and pliable, about 15 minutes. Drain and set aside.

2. To begin the stir-fry, heat a wok or deep, heavy skillet over medium-high heat. When it is hot, add the oil and rotate the wok or pan a bit to coat it evenly. When the oil is hot, add the onion, garlic, ginger, and chillies and stir-fry until soft and fragrant, about 2 minutes. Add the shrimp, chicken, and sausage and stir-fry for 2 minutes. Mix in the cabbage and carrot, then add the soy sauce and fish sauce and mix well. Pour in the chicken broth and cook for 1 minute, stirring frequently. Add the noodles and scallions and stir-fry until the noodles are well mixed and heated through, 1 to 2 minutes.

3. Transfer the stir-fried noodles to a serving platter. Sprinkle with black pepper and garnish with sprigs of cilantro. Encircle the noodles with the tomato wedges and serve hot, with more soy sauce on the side.

Main Dishes

BRAISED PORK TENDERLOIN WITH STAR ANISE,
SWEET SOY, AND BALSAMIC

SAIGON-STYLE PORK CHOPS WITH PAN GRAVY

FIERY BALINESE STIR-FRIED PORK WITH
SWEET SOY AND GINGER

VIETNAMESE-STYLE GRILLED PORK TACOS

VIETNAMESE-STYLE OVEN-ROASTED BBQ PORK

THAI-STYLE SWEET PORK

PHILLY-STYLE VIETNAMESE HOAGIES WITH
BBQ PORK

CHARRED BEEF IN RED CURRY WITH
GREEN PEPPERCORNS

RENDANG-STYLE BEEF CURRY

STIR-FRIED BEEF WITH SWEET SOY
AND ONIONS

BANGKOK-TO-BALI BURGERS WITH
GRILLED ONIONS

BURMESE-STYLE BAKED CHICKEN WITH
YOGURT AND CUMIN

THAI-STYLE BARBECUED CHICKEN

CHICKEN WITH SNOW PEAS

CHICKEN AND FENNEL WITH
THAI GREEN CURRY AND BASIL

BRAISED CHICKEN WITH GREEN PAPAYA

PHILLY-STYLE VIETNAMESE HOAGIES WITH
POACHED CHICKEN

ROAST TURKEY BREAST WITH THAI CILANTRO PESTO

BALINESE ROAST DUCK

MALAY CHILLI SHRIMP

LAOTIAN-STYLE STIR-FRIED SHRIMP WITH
CRISPY LEMON GRASS

CRAB DUMPLINGS WITH THAI GREEN CURRY AND BASIL

SPICY STIR-FRIED SQUID

PAN-SEARED TUNA STEAKS AU POIVRE

ROASTED SALMON WITH INDONESIAN SOY-GINGER
SAUCE, SPINACH, AND BABY CORN

CRISPY SALMON WITH TANGY CITRUS SAMBAL

GRILLED RED SNAPPER WITH THAI TAMARIND SAUCE

RED SNAPPER STEAMED WITH
GINGER AND LEMON GRASS

CRISPY FLOUNDER WITH CHILLI-PEANUT DIPPING SAUCE

BANGKOK-TO-BALI BEER-BATTERED CATFISH

BALI-STYLE MARINATED GRILLED FISH KEBABS

INDONESIAN-STYLE TEMPEH CURRY

GOLDEN TOFU SQUARES WITH SWEET-AND-SOUR
TAMARIND SAUCE AND GARLIC CHIPS

In this chapter you'll find 33 great

new ways to answer the age-old refrain "What's for dinner?"

All eight nations represented in *From Bangkok to Bali* are richly explored within this chapter, including several of their distinct regions. These recipes will transform your dining room and kitchen into passageways to the great and lively traditional entrées of Southeast Asia, from casual family meals to decadent entertaining, from simple stir-fries such as Chicken with Snow Peas (page 199) to the sumptuous, world-class curries of Thailand.

If you want to try your hand at some of the classics, turn to such recipes as Laotian-Style Stir-fried Shrimp with Crispy Lemon Grass (page 213), Burmese Baked Chicken with Yogurt and Cumin (page 194), Thai-Style Barbecued Chicken (page 196), Rendang-Style Beef Curry (page 190), or Balinese Roast Duck (page 207). Or you can choose from the innovative East-West dishes created exclusively for this book, all of them true to the culinary traditions that inspired them. These include Bangkok-to-Bali Burgers with Grilled Onions (page 193), Philly-Style Vietnamese Hoagies (pages 186 and 203), Roast Turkey Breast with Cilantro Pesto (page 205), Crispy Flounder with Chilli-Peanut Dipping Sauce (page 228), Vietnamese-Style Grilled Pork Tacos (page 182), and Pan-Seared Tuna Steaks au Poivre (page 217).

Looking for a new vegetarian dish? You'll want to try Indonesian-Style Tempeh Curry (page 231), or Golden Tofu Squares with Sweet-and-Sour Tamarind Sauce and Garlic Chips (page 233). For an elegant, yet easy and health-conscious entrée, go straight to Red Snapper Steamed with Ginger and Lemon Grass (page 224).

For the pleasures of barbecuing, whether on an outdoor fire or a grill pan, choose from fish kabobs, burgers, and pork and chicken recipes. Bangkok-to-Bali Beer-Battered Catfish (page 229) offers an easy recipe for light yet crispy fried fish. Spicy Stir-fried Squid (page 216) is especially for "chilli heads," with a fiery pan gravy rich in garlic and roasted chilli paste, plus fresh Thai chillies thrown in for added punch.

Not all these dishes feature maximum spiciness, but they all offer lively, fascinating flavors that evoke the best tropical Southeast Asia has to offer. Before long, the refrain you hear nightly might change. Instead of asking what's for dinner, they may be pleading with you for more of the exciting main dishes you'll learn in this chapter.

Braised Pork Tenderloin with Star Anise, Sweet Soy, and Balsamic

*H*ere's a dish that calls upon flavors from several tropical Asian cuisines. From Thailand comes the liberal use of garlic and black pepper, and from Vietnam the complex notes of star anise, which is added to *kecap manis*, the signature sweet soy sauce of Indonesia. There's even a nod to Italy in the complementary tang and depth of balsamic vinegar.

When these condiments and spices are added to the pan juices created from browning the tenderloins, they make a simple, yet vibrant, sweet and savory pan gravy. As you feast, add a squeeze of lime here and there to brighten the lusty flavors.

1¹/₂ pounds pork tenderloin, trimmed of any fat and silverskin

Salt and freshly ground black pepper

1 tablespoon peanut or vegetable oil

3 large cloves garlic, crushed and chopped

3 slices peeled fresh ginger, each about the size of a quarter

3 whole star anise

¹/₂ cup *kecap manis* or sweet dark soy sauce, or substitute 2 tablespoons light soy
   sauce mixed with ¹/₄ cup plus 2 tablespoons maple syrup

¹/₄ cup plus 1 tablespoon light soy sauce

1 tablespoon balsamic vinegar

¹/₄ cup palm sugar or light brown sugar

¹/₂ cup water

1 lime, cut into 4 wedges

1. Season the pork with salt to taste, then season liberally with the black pepper.
2. Heat a large skillet over high heat. When it is hot, add the oil and rotate the pan a bit to coat it evenly. When the oil is hot, add the tenderloin and brown it well, 3 to 5 minutes per side. Cover the pan and reduce the heat to low.

Cook until the internal temperature reads 150 to 155 degrees F on a meat thermometer, about 12 to 15 minutes. Transfer the tenderloin to a plate and cover loosely with aluminum foil. Let stand while you prepare the sauce.

3. Reheat the skillet over high heat and add the garlic, ginger, and star anise to the pan juices. Bring the mixture to boil, stirring and scraping up the bits of garlic and ginger, until the mixture becomes fragrant and the juices are reduced by half, $1^1/_2$ to 2 minutes.

4. Stir in the *kecap manis*, light soy, balsamic, sugar, and water and bring the mixture to boil. Reduce the heat to maintain a low boil and cook, stirring occasionally, until the sauce begins to thicken, 5 to 8 minutes. (If you prefer a syrupy glaze, boil the sauce down further.)

5. Angle-cut the tenderloin into $^1/_4$-inch medallions. Arrange the meat on a serving platter and spoon the sauce on top. Serve hot, with the lime wedges on the side.

Saigon-Style Pork Chops with Pan Gravy

Serves 4

With just a few ingredients, you can transform simple pork chops into a main course that's as intriguingly flavored as it is easy. The chops are sautéed quickly, then kept in a warm oven while you enrich their pan juices—light soy sauce plus a bit of vinegar for sharpness and a little light brown sugar for sweetness, married with fish sauce, which seems to disappear into the mellow flavors of the silky-textured gravy.

Serve this with a platter of Steamed Jasmine Rice (page 145) topped with fresh cilantro and Crisp-Fried Shallots (page 100)—perfect partners to the gravy-rich chops. Make the rice and shallots first, so you can use the shallot-infused oil to sauté the chops. Use a light soy sauce of fine quality. San-J and Eden are two health food store brands that we've used successfully.

To complete the dinner menu, we often serve the rice and pork chops with a chopped tomato, red onion, and cucumber salad dressed in a simple vinaigrette.

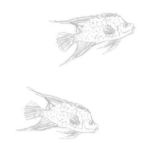

8 thin pork chops (about 2^1/$_2$ pounds total)
Salt and freshly ground black pepper
1 to 2 tablespoons vegetable or peanut oil
^{1}/$_4$ cup light soy sauce
^{1}/$_4$ cup Asian fish sauce
2 tablespoons distilled white vinegar
^{1}/$_4$ cup palm sugar or light brown sugar
Steamed Jasmine Rice (page 145)
Crisp-Fried Shallots (page 100)
Sprigs fresh cilantro for garnish

1. Season the chops on both sides with salt and pepper. Heat 1 tablespoon of the oil in a large nonstick skillet over high heat until sizzling hot. Place 4 chops in the pan and pan-fry until browned and cooked through, about 3 minutes per side. Transfer to a heat-proof serving platter with a 1-inch rim and keep warm in a low oven while you cook the remaining chops. If needed, add a little more oil to the pan and when hot, pan-fry the last 4 chops and transfer them to the platter.
2. Reduce the heat to medium and add the soy sauce, fish sauce, vinegar, and sugar to the skillet. Stir until the sugar dissolves and the sauce is well blended and heated through.
3. Scoop the steamed rice onto a serving platter and sprinkle with the shallots. Tear a few sprigs of fresh cilantro and scatter over the rice and shallots.
4. Pour the hot pan gravy over the pork chops and serve at once with the rice on the side.

Fiery Balinese Stir-Fried Pork with Sweet Soy and Ginger

The Balinese people seem to have more festivals on their calendar than any other nation on Earth. They simply love to celebrate. This dish is a festival favorite. There's no long cooking, just plenty of flavor, thanks to heady amounts of garlic, chillies, and ginger. Any burn the chilli-ginger combination might create is soothed by the sweet soy sauce and onions.

Serve this stir-fry with plenty of Steamed Jasmine Rice (page 145) or Malaysian-Style Flatbread (page 286).

$^1\!/_2$ teaspoon black peppercorns, ground in a mortar or pepper mill (see step 1)

3 large cloves garlic, roughly chopped

3 to 6 small Thai chillies, to your taste, sliced

$^1\!/_3$ cup peeled and roughly chopped fresh ginger

2 tablespoons vegetable oil

$1^1\!/_4$ pounds pork tenderloin, trimmed of any fat and silverskin and cut into $^1\!/_4$-inch-thick medallions

1 large onion, halved and cut lengthwise into thin strips

$^1\!/_4$ cup sweet dark soy sauce, or substitute 1 tablespoon light soy sauce mixed with 3 tablespoons pure maple syrup

$^1\!/_2$ cup Chicken Stock (page 289) or canned low-sodium chicken broth

1 tablespoon palm sugar or light brown sugar

Steamed Jasmine Rice (page 145)

Malaysian-Style Flatbread (optional, page 286)

1. Make a spice paste with the black pepper, garlic, chillies, and ginger. If using a mortar and pestle, use whole peppercorns and pound the ingredients into a fairly smooth paste. Or use a mini–food processor to work freshly ground pepper, garlic, chillies, and ginger into a paste.

2. Heat a wok or deep, heavy skillet over medium heat. When it is hot, add the oil and rotate the wok or pan a bit to coat it evenly. When the oil is hot, stir-fry the spice paste until the mixture is quite fragrant, about 2 minutes. Add the pork and onion and stir-fry over high heat until the meat begins to brown, about 2 minutes. Add the soy sauce and stir-fry for 1 minute. Pour in the chicken stock, add the sugar, and simmer over medium heat for 5 minutes, stirring occasionally.

3. Serve hot over the rice and accompany with flatbread.

Vietnamese-Style Grilled Pork Tacos

Serves 6

We love the Vietnamese way with grilled pork—a syrupy soy- and honey-based marinade laced with garlic and ginger produces a lusty, flavorful char that brilliantly complements the sweet pork. Here it is in an all-American setting: tacos!

Spice Island Salsa (page 95), made with fresh pineapple and tomatoes, is the perfect accompaniment.

SWEET SOY MARINADE:

1/4 cup sweet dark soy sauce, or substitute 1 tablespoon light soy sauce mixed with
   3 tablespoons pure maple syrup
1 tablespoon distilled white vinegar
3 large cloves garlic, minced
1/4 teaspoon ground ginger
1 teaspoon freshly ground black pepper
1 tablespoon vegetable oil
2 1/2 teaspoons honey

1 1/2 pounds pork tenderloin, trimmed of any fat and silverskin

18 small, or 12 large flour tortillas

Spice Island Salsa (optional, page 95)

1. In a large mixing bowl, combine the marinade ingredients and stir until well mixed.

2. Add the tenderloin to the marinade and turn to coat all sides. Cover with plastic wrap and marinate for 1 hour in the refrigerator.

3. Prepare an outdoor grill or preheat a grill pan for 3 to 5 minutes. Remove the pork from the marinade and place on a well-oiled grill rack or pan. Grill, turning once, for a total of about 25 minutes for a pale pink center, or to your preferred degree of doneness. Remove from the grill and let rest for 10 minutes.

4. Meanwhile, heat the tortillas on the grill and keep them warm in a kitchen towel. Cut the pork into thin slices and heap them on a serving platter. Serve with the tortillas and salsa, if desired.

Vietnamese-Style Oven-Roasted BBQ Pork

Serves 6

One look at a map will show why Vietnam's culinary traditions are the most Chinese-influenced in all of Southeast Asia: Tall mountains restrict China's overland routes to Burma, Thailand, and Laos, but northern Vietnam isn't as sealed off geographically, and the flow of peoples and their customs has always been considerable.

Laced with five-spice powder, a favorite Chinese ingredient that includes the licorice-like flavor of star anise, this dish is called *xa xiu* (pronounced something like "zha zhiu") by the Vietnamese. It is quite similar to the Chinese style of barbecued pork called *char siu*.

What's wonderful about this dish, besides its inviting flavors, is how easily the roasted pork can be used in many other dishes, including stir-fried noodles, fried rice, or Philly-Style Vietnamese Hoagies with BBQ Pork (page 186). It's also delightful to serve this pork in the simplest way possible: barely warm, right out of the oven, with Steamed Jasmine Rice (page 145).

1/2 cup light soy sauce

1 tablespoon tomato paste

1 teaspoon Chinese five-spice powder

1 tablespoon finely chopped garlic

1/4 cup firmly packed dark brown sugar

1 pound pork tenderloin, trimmed of any fat and silverskin

1. Combine the soy sauce, tomato paste, five-spice powder, garlic, and sugar in a small mixing bowl. Whisk until the sugar is dissolved and well blended.

2. Lay the pork in a pie plate or shallow dish or place in a zippered-top plastic bag and pour the marinade over it. Cover or seal and refrigerate for at least 4 hours or overnight, turning once or twice.

3. Preheat the oven to 450 degrees F. Line a roasting pan with aluminum foil. If you have a roasting rack, set it in the pan. Arrange the pork on the rack or foil-lined pan. Reserve any marinade left in the pie plate or pan for basting. Roast the pork for 15 minutes, then reduce the oven temperature to 350 degrees F. Turn the pork and baste with the marinade. Roast another 10 minutes, then turn the pork and baste it again. Roast until cooked through, but still a little pink inside, about 10 minutes more.

4. Transfer the roast pork to a cutting board. Let rest 5 to 10 minutes to allow the juices to settle, then cut crosswise into thin slices. Serve warm or at room temperature, for eating with steamed rice or for sandwiches. Or cover and refrigerate, unsliced, until ready to use in other recipes.

Thai-Style Sweet Pork

*I*n Thailand they usually serve this as an accompaniment to other dishes, such as the sweet, crunchy noodle treat called *mee krob*, but there are versions of this dish throughout Southeast Asia. This one is the simplest and we think it's the most delicious of all. We make it for a late afternoon treat, or for a light meal with plenty of Steamed Jasmine Rice (page 145), sauced with generous amounts of the pan gravy and showered with Crisp-Fried Shallots (page 100).

3 tablespoons vegetable oil

3 large cloves garlic, crushed and finely chopped

1 pound pork tenderloin, trimmed of any fat and silverskin and cut crosswise into thin medallions

3 tablespoons plus 1 teaspoon Asian fish sauce

3 tablespoons palm sugar or light brown sugar

1¼ teaspoons white pepper

Steamed Jasmine Rice (page 145)

Crisp-Fried Shallots (optional, page 100)

1. Heat a wok or deep, heavy skillet over medium-high heat. When it is hot, add the oil and rotate the wok or pan a bit to coat it evenly. When the oil is hot, add the garlic and stir-fry a few seconds, then add the pork and stir-fry for 2 minutes. Add the fish sauce, sugar, and pepper and stir-fry just until the pork is cooked through, 2 to 3 minutes.

2. Serve hot or warm, with plenty of jasmine rice and fried shallots, if desired.

Philly-Style Vietnamese Hoagies with BBQ Pork

Serves 4

*I*n this version of *banh mi*, a Vietnamese sandwich, our central ingredient is the Vietnamese-style BBQ pork known as *xa xiu*—the Southeast Asian version of the Chinese favorite *char siu*.

Just as the Chinese often dab *char siu* with hot mustard, you can spread these sandwiches with our Big Easy Remoulade (page 79), which features Creole mustard, a grainy, piquant type used in many New Orleans specialties. *Banh mi* has really caught on in Philadelphia as a more exotic version of the city's famous hoagie (which is also known as a sub or hero).

Tangy Sweet Vegetable Pickles (page 97) or Sweet Hot Thai Chilli Sauce (page 80) will merge with the creamy remoulade to make a supremely flavorful sandwich, one that's outstanding enough to make it worth your while to prepare the barbecued pork and the additional items. For the sake of convenience, you may want to make all the necessary components a day ahead. Or simply bring home some sliced roast pork from your favorite deli. The chilli sauce, like the remoulade, takes just minutes to prepare.

4 Italian hoagie rolls (about 8 inches long) or 2 French baguettes (about 8 ounces each)

SANDWICH FILLING:

1/4 to 1/2 cup Big Easy Remoulade (page 79)

2/3 cup shredded Napa cabbage or prepared coleslaw mix

1 pound thinly sliced Vietnamese-Style Oven Roasted BBQ Pork (page 183) or sliced roast pork from the deli

1 cup Sweet Vegetable Pickles (page 97) or 1/4 cup Sweet Hot Thai Chilli Sauce (page 80)

2 to 3 serrano chillies, to your taste, thinly sliced

Salt and white pepper to taste

1 small bunch fresh cilantro sprigs

1. Preheat the oven to 350 degrees F.
2. Lightly toast the bread in the hot oven for 5 minutes. Split each roll or baguette nearly in half lengthwise, leaving the halves attached on one side. Spread about 1 tablespoon of remoulade in each hoagie roll, or 2 tablespoons in each baguette. Place a layer of shredded cabbage on the bottom of each roll or baguette, then layer the pork on top. Next add a layer of some sweet vegetable pickles, or drizzle with 1 tablespoon or so of the chilli sauce. Sprinkle each sandwich with some sliced chillies and season with salt and pepper. Top with a few sprigs of cilantro and serve.

Charred Beef in Red Curry with Green Peppercorns

Serves 6

*I*n Southeast Asia, people harvest young, green peppercorns right off the pepper vines they find twining up the trunks of trees. Here, we have to be satisfied with soft, brine-packed green peppercorns, which can be found in gourmet specialty stores.

This is an adaptation of a traditional Thai curry called *kaeng phed neua phrik*, using grilled steak instead of allowing the meat to cook in the curry sauce. In Southeast Asia, beef usually comes from water buffaloes, sometimes from older ones that are becoming less useful as work animals. Therefore, it makes more sense for cooks to use the curry sauce as a way of tenderizing the meat. However, with the quality of beef we have available, it seems best not to take the chance of overcooking it, which could easily happen if we followed tradition to the letter. We also love how the charred flavor of seared beef complements the sauce.

For the best results, use homemade curry paste and prepare the curry a few hours, or even a full day, ahead of actual serving time. This will deepen the flavors nicely. If you use commercially prepared curry paste, first add the fish sauce and the sugar, then stir in only two tablespoons and taste the resulting flavors before deciding whether to add more. It's so much better to use homemade red curry paste, and one recipe will give you enough for this beef curry, plus plenty left over to make Spicy Peanut Sauce (page 88) for satés, Indonesian *gado gado* (page 121), and more.

This curry is traditionally served with rice, but it's also terrific with Malaysian-Style Flatbread (page 286) for dunking into the curry and rolling up slices of steak into sandwich-like wraps.

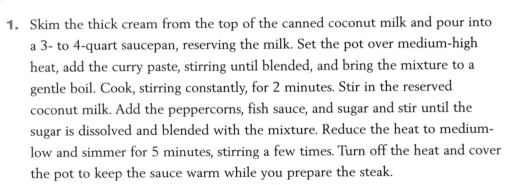

One 14-ounce can unsweetened coconut milk
$^2/_3$ cup Thai Red Curry Paste (page 292)
$^1/_3$ cup brine-cured green peppercorns, drained
2 tablespoons Asian fish sauce
1 tablespoon palm sugar or light brown sugar
1 pound sirloin steak
Salt and freshly ground black pepper to taste
Steamed Jasmine Rice (page 145)
1 cup loosely packed fresh Thai, sweet, or purple basil leaves

1. Skim the thick cream from the top of the canned coconut milk and pour into a 3- to 4-quart saucepan, reserving the milk. Set the pot over medium-high heat, add the curry paste, stirring until blended, and bring the mixture to a gentle boil. Cook, stirring constantly, for 2 minutes. Stir in the reserved coconut milk. Add the peppercorns, fish sauce, and sugar and stir until the sugar is dissolved and blended with the mixture. Reduce the heat to medium-low and simmer for 5 minutes, stirring a few times. Turn off the heat and cover the pot to keep the sauce warm while you prepare the steak.

2. Preheat an outdoor grill, or preheat a grill pan for 3 to 5 minutes over medium-high heat. Season the steak with salt and pepper and place it on the grill or in the hot pan and cook until medium-rare, 2 to 3 minutes per side, or to your desired degree of doneness. Transfer the steak with all its juices to a cutting board. Let stand for 5 minutes to allow the juices to settle. Holding your knife at a 45-degree angle, cut the steak crosswise into thin slices.

3. Uncover the curry sauce and heat it through over low heat without bringing it to a boil. Spoon the hot steamed rice into individual bowls. Divide the sliced steak with its juices among the rice-filled bowls and ladle on the red curry sauce. Top each serving with a handful of basil leaves and serve immediately.

So Civilized

In Vietnamese restaurants, you will be presented with chopsticks. The Vietnamese are the most Chinese-influenced of all tropical Asian people, so they adopted China's eating utensils long ago.

Many people also request chopsticks at Thai restaurants, thinking that they want to eat as Thai people would. Being among the world's most gracious hosts, Thai restaurateurs are glad to provide whatever a customer may request. However, for quite some time it has been the Thai custom to eat with Western-style implements, except when eating Chinese-style noodle dishes.

Of all the nations in Southeast Asia, Thailand (then called Siam) was the only one that was not taken over during the years European colonialists established themselves throughout the region. They managed this feat through a long process of diplomacy, which meant that the royal family often entertained European ambassadors. Through formalized contact with many Westerners, they observed the use at table of knives, forks, and spoons, and they adopted them as their own. But as they so often do, the Thais imparted their own style to the new eating tools.

First, the knives were unnecessary and did not find favor. Who wants an implement at the table that carries a connotation of violence? Whatever is served at a Thai meal is likely to be already carved into bite-size morsels, allowing you to concentrate on enjoying your meal, rather than working to make it edible.

With the hand that would have held a knife now free, it made great sense that in a two-implement system each hand should be permanently in charge of its own implement. And it made even greater sense that the spoon should be larger than the conventional Western teaspoon, more like a tablespoon, so it could capture not only morsels of food but also plenty of the curry sauce or pan gravy.

What a great plan! No more scraping here and there around your plate to corral morsels that elude a solo fork. To try this dining technique, take a tablespoon in your dominant hand, a fork in the other, and push food into the bowl of the spoon with the fork. Your eating experience will be easier and you can concentrate on simply enjoying the luscious flavors, colors, textures, and aromas. What could be more civilized?

Rendang-Style Beef Curry

Serves 4

Rendang beef, the beloved curry from Indonesia, is traditionally a slowly cooked dish made with chunks of beef stewed in fragrant spices and coconut milk until saucy or nearly dry, the coconut milk and spices having cooked down to a dark coating. We've adapted the traditional method to bring out all the flavor of a true beef *rendang* curry in a much shorter time by using strips of sirloin that cook quickly in a simmering bath of coconut milk and spices.

This curry is saucy, and would be perfect served with Malaysian-Style Flatbread (page 286) or ladled over Steamed Jasmine Rice (page 145).

RENDANG SPICE PASTE:

2 plump stalks lemon grass

3 small Thai or serrano chillies, sliced

3 cloves garlic, coarsely chopped

2 tablespoons peeled and finely chopped fresh ginger

1 teaspoon ground coriander

$1/2$ teaspoon ground cumin

$1/4$ teaspoon ground Saigon or regular cinnamon

$1/4$ teaspoon ground cloves

2 tablespoons peanut or vegetable oil

1 pound sirloin steak, trimmed of any fat, halved lengthwise, then cut crosswise into
   $^1/_2$-inch-thick strips

1 medium-size onion

1 cup canned unsweetened coconut milk

1 tablespoon Tamarind Sauce (page 290), liquid tamarind concentrate, or fresh
   lime juice

1 tablespoon plus 1 teaspoon sugar

$^1/_2$ teaspoon salt

1. To make the spice paste, trim the root end of the lemon grass and discard the tough outer leaves. Cut a 4-inch length from the bulb end and discard the rest. Mince the length of lemon grass. Put the lemon grass, chillies, garlic, and ginger in a mortar and pound into a coarse paste, or process in a mini–food processor. Mix in the coriander, cumin, cinnamon, and cloves.

2. Heat a large wok or deep, heavy skillet over medium-high heat. When it is hot, add the oil and rotate the wok or pan a bit to coat it evenly. When the oil is hot, stir-fry the spice paste until it is quite fragrant, about 1 minute. Add the meat and onion and stir-fry just until the meat begins to brown, about 3 minutes. Stir in the coconut milk, then add the tamarind, sugar, and salt. Reduce the heat to medium-low and simmer for 10 minutes, stirring occasionally.

3. Serve hot with rice or flatbread, if desired.

Stir-Fried Beef with Sweet Soy and Onions

*T*his simple, homey dish comes together in minutes, using just a few ingredients, but it creates a luscious pan gravy to mix with your rice. The slivers of onion stay a little crispy as a wonderful counterpoint to the tender strips of sirloin. This savory stir-fry is wonderful with Cambodian Pepper Dip (page 87) and Steamed Jasmine Rice (page 145) or Sticky Rice (page 147).

2 tablespoons vegetable oil

1 pound sirloin steak, trimmed of any fat and cut crosswise into ¼-inch-thick strips

1 large onion, halved and cut lengthwise into thin strips

¼ cup sweet dark soy sauce, or substitute 1 tablespoon light soy sauce mixed with
   3 tablespoons pure maple syrup

1 tablespoon Asian fish sauce

Steamed Jasmine Rice (optional, page 145) or Sticky Rice (optional, page 147)

Cambodian Pepper Dip (page 87)

1. Heat a wok or deep, heavy skillet over medium-high heat. When it is hot, add the oil and rotate the wok or pan a bit to coat it evenly. When the oil is hot, stir-fry the steak and onion until the meat begins to brown, about 2 minutes. Add the soy sauce and fish sauce and stir once. Move the meat and onion to the side and let the sauce boil for about 1 minute to thicken.

2. Serve hot with rice and pepper dip, if desired.

Bangkok-to-Bali Burgers with Grilled Onions

*H*ere's a recipe that shows what Southeast Asian flavors can do for an all-American favorite—burgers spiced up with garlic, yellow curry, and *kecap manis*, served with tangy grilled sweet onions. For the most flavorful burgers, use ground chuck with some fat content, not extra-lean meat.

To make this recipe even more tropical, serve your Bangkok-to-Bali Burgers with Tomato *Sambal* (page 93) or with ketchup spiked with a favorite hot sauce. We recommend the Thai classic, *Sri Racha* Hot Sauce (page 81).

1 tablespoon *kecap manis* or sweet dark soy sauce, or substitute 1 teaspoon light soy
  sauce mixed with 1 tablespoon pure maple syrup
1 tablespoon Asian fish sauce
1 tablespoon curry powder
1 large clove garlic, minced
$1^1/_2$ pounds ground beef, preferably ground chuck
Coarse salt and freshly ground black pepper to taste
1 large sweet onion, such as Vidalia, sliced into 1-inch-thick rounds (see Note on
  page 194)
1 tablespoon unseasoned rice vinegar
4 sesame seed hamburger buns

1. Combine the *kecap manis*, fish sauce, curry powder, and garlic in a small bowl and stir until well mixed.
2. Put the ground beef in a large mixing bowl. Add the *kecap manis* mixture and blend it into the meat with your hands. Gently form 4 patties from the seasoned ground beef. Do not overwork or flatten the patties; keep them loosely formed to make juicy burgers. Season the burgers with salt and pepper. Set aside while you grill the onions.

3. Preheat an outdoor grill, or preheat a grill pan for 3 to 5 minutes over medium-high heat. Grill the onions until they soften a bit and begin to brown, 3 to 4 minutes per side. Transfer to a bowl and drizzle with the rice vinegar. Cover and set aside.

4. Grill the burgers to taste, turning once, 3 to 4 minutes per side for medium-rare, 1 or 2 minutes more per side for medium or well done. Meanwhile, toast the buns on the grill or in a toaster. Place the burgers on the toasted buns, top them with the grilled onions, and serve.

Note: If using an outdoor grill, you'll want to keep the sliced onions from falling through the grates. Use a grill basket if you have one, or secure each slice with a skewer, or use a sheet or two of heavy-duty aluminum foil to make a boxy rectangle you can set on the grill. Poke the bottom full of holes so the onions cook evenly.

Burmese-Style Baked Chicken with Yogurt and Cumin

Serves 4

*I*ndia and Burma have long influenced one another's cuisines. The marinade for this recipe closely resembles a tandoori marinade that you would find in an Indian kitchen—a yogurt base accented with cumin and cardamom, two traditional components of the Indian dry-spice blend called *garam masala*. This is a very healthful dish, since the moist yogurt coating allows you to cook the chicken breasts without their skins. However, do use bone-in breasts; you'll get a more flavorful result.

To intensify the flavors, serve this as they would in Burma, with wedges of fresh lime to squeeze over the chicken. We also recommend another traditional Burmese accompaniment, Toasted Sesame Salt (page 99). If you have any leftover chicken, you have the makings of wonderful sandwiches.

4 chicken breast halves (about 2$^1/_2$ pounds total)

$^1/_2$ cup plain yogurt

1 teaspoon salt

$^1/_2$ teaspoon turmeric

2 tablespoons ground cumin

1 teaspoon ground cardamom

$^1/_4$ teaspoon ground ginger

1 tablespoon vegetable oil

1 teaspoon pure chilli powder or hot paprika

Toasted Sesame Salt (optional, page 99)

1 lime, quartered

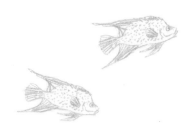

1. Remove the skin from the chicken and put the chicken pieces in a shallow, nonreactive (glass, stainless steel, or ceramic) bowl. Set aside.

2. Combine the yogurt, salt, turmeric, cumin, cardamom, and ginger in a small mixing bowl and whisk until thoroughly mixed. Whisk in the oil. Pour the marinade over the chicken and mix well, using your hands, to coat the pieces evenly. Cover with plastic wrap and marinate in the refrigerator for 2 hours.

3. Preheat the oven to 350 degrees F. Arrange the chicken pieces on a baking sheet or in a roasting pan. Sprinkle with the chilli powder and bake until cooked all the way through, about 30 minutes.

4. Transfer the baked chicken to a serving platter, sprinkle with toasted sesame salt, if desired, and serve hot, with lime wedges on the side.

Thai-Style Barbecued Chicken

This dish, known in its homeland as *kai yang isaan*, originated in the mountainous Isaan region of northern Thailand, where it is eaten with sticky rice, but you'll find a special regional version of this much-loved specialty practically everywhere you go in Thailand. No matter how it may vary, it will always be barbecued with a tangy spice paste and served golden brown and smoky from the grill with *nam jeem yang*, a sweet-and-spicy dipping sauce. This dish is a favorite not only throughout Thailand, but also in every cooking class where we've presented it. And now it's a favorite at backyard barbecues all over our town.

The key to success with this recipe is barbecuing the chickens slowly, over the lowest heat possible. If they do not scorch, they will retain the heady herbal flavors of their marinade.

2 chickens (about 3^1/$_2$ pounds each)

MARINADE:

3 tablespoons Asian fish sauce

1 tablespoon palm sugar or light brown sugar

1 tablespoon peeled and minced fresh ginger

2^1/$_2$ tablespoons coarsely chopped garlic

^{3}/$_4$ cup chopped fresh cilantro stems

1 tablespoon freshly ground black pepper

Sweet Hot Thai Chilli Sauce (page 80)

1. Using kitchen shears or a boning knife, butterfly each chicken by cutting through the ribs on either side of the backbone and removing the backbone. Turn the chickens breast side up and press hard on the breastbones to flatten them slightly. Place each chicken in a shallow pan skin side up. Set aside.

2. Combine the marinade ingredients in a blender and process until smooth, stopping once or twice to scrape down the sides of the jar. Spread equal amounts of the marinade over the two chickens, then turn them skin side down and spoon some of the marinade into the cavities. Marinate for at least 2 and up to 24 hours in the refrigerator, turning occasionally.

3. Preheat an outdoor grill. When it is ready, grill the chickens, skin side up, until brown on the bottom, 6 to 8 minutes. Turn and cook until golden brown, another 6 to 8 minutes. Turn again and finish cooking, skin side up, until the juices run clear when you pierce the leg joint with a fork.

4. Transfer the chickens to a cutting board and let them stand for about 10 minutes before carving to let the juices settle. Cut the chickens into separate pieces with a cleaver or kitchen shears. Transfer to a serving platter and serve immediately with the dipping sauce.

Chicken with Snow Peas

*G*arlic, fish sauce, and white pepper give this Chinese-style dish its Thai character. This is a mild, yet flavorful stir-fry, heady with garlic and mellowed with soft, wok-browned chicken.

1 tablespoon sesame seeds

1 plump stalk lemon grass or 2 teaspoons grated lemon zest

2 tablespoons vegetable oil

8 large cloves garlic, crushed and chopped

1 pound boneless, skinless chicken breast, cut into bite-size strips

3 tablespoons oyster sauce

1½ tablespoons Asian fish sauce

½ teaspoon white pepper

1 tablespoon palm sugar or light brown sugar

½ pound snow peas, tough strings removed

Steamed Jasmine Rice (page 145)

Thai Chilli Dipping Sauce (optional, page 83)

1. In a small dry skillet over medium heat, toast the sesame seeds until fragrant and golden, 2 to 3 minutes, shaking the pan a few times. Transfer to a small bowl and set aside.

2. If using lemon grass, trim the root end and discard the tough outer leaves. Slice into very thin rounds, using most of the tender lower stalk, about 4 inches.

3. Place all the ingredients, except the dipping sauce, within easy reach of the cooking area.

4. Set a wok over medium-high heat. When it is hot, add the oil. Rotate the wok a bit so the oil coats the sides. When the oil is hot, add the garlic and stir-fry a few seconds, just until it is golden and aromatic. Add the chicken and stir-fry until it begins to turn opaque, about 30 seconds. Stir in the oyster sauce, fish sauce, pepper, and sugar. Add the snow peas and lemon grass and stir-fry just until the peas are cooked through, about 5 minutes.

5. Transfer to a serving platter, sprinkle with the toasted sesame seeds, and serve with plenty of rice and the dipping sauce, if desired.

Treasures around Every Corner

With some of the finest fresh seafood, vegetables, and fruit in the world always at hand, Southeast Asians have shopping and eating options that food lovers in America can only dream about. Even their modern supermarkets have heavenly touches. If you were staying in Thailand, you would be able to take home preservative-free TV dinners prepared the same day you bought them. The very best cost about two dollars, and are full of fresh local meat or seafood, herbs, and vegetables. They aren't sealed in foil, or tucked into limp cardboard cartons. They're snugly wrapped in fresh banana leaves and tightly sealed in cellophane.

At the same supermarket's produce counter, you would find all sorts of delicious fruits already peeled, seeded, and ready to be eaten—artistically carved mangoes, watermelons, and papayas, which are scooped out and filled with lychees and other small fruits. There might even be someone standing by to custom carve and prepare whatever fresh fruit you selected from the bins.

Of course, you could bypass the supermarket and shop in the floating markets that convene on canals and rivers everywhere. Longboats are sidled up next to one another, open for business, their crews vending fresh fish, meat, produce, spices and herbs, ready-made snacks hot and cold, as well as refreshments—from spiced teas and coffees to fresh, liquid-filled coconuts. If you lived along a river, you would just wait placidly until those same boats came to you. Wave your hand, and they pull right up to your dock.

More great food is to be had on the streets of almost any city in tropical Asia. They are, for all practical purposes, a tremendous, unwalled restaurant. From daybreak, until well past midnight, entrepreneurial street vendors offer so much variety at wonderfully low prices that you would never really have to rely on cafes, restaurants, or your own kitchen. Some offer simple wares, others specialize in complex dishes that require an expert hand. Such artistry in cooking is deeply appreciated, so the best of the best among street vendors are just as honored locally as the chefs of the most expensive and formal restaurants.

There's yet another great option: Have dinner delivered to your door by one of the best home cooks in the neighborhood. You would learn his (or her) specialties, then commission them to keep you deliciously well fed. Many of these neighborhood caterers serve their regular customers for years and years.

Chicken and Fennel with Thai Green Curry and Basil

Serves 6

*T*his is a traditional Thai chicken curry, richly herbal in flavor, that we've accented with a European vegetable, fennel, which imparts something of a licorice taste. The combination itself might not be traditional, but we think Thai people will approve: It was inspired by their love (and ours) of *horapha*, a.k.a. Thai basil, a licorice-flavored herb. And by combining fennel and Thai basil, we've given this traditionally fiery hot curry a double shot of one of its more intriguing flavor components.

1 small fennel bulb

1 tablespoon sesame oil (not toasted) or vegetable oil

1 large clove garlic, crushed and finely chopped

1 small onion, sliced

Salt and freshly ground black pepper to taste

1/2 cup Thai Green Curry Paste (page 291)

One 14-ounce can unsweetened coconut milk

1/4 cup Chicken Stock (page 289) or canned low-sodium chicken broth

1 tablespoon Asian fish sauce

2 tablespoons palm sugar or light brown sugar

1¼ pounds boneless, skinless chicken breasts, trimmed of any fat and cut crosswise
   into ½-inch-thick slices
Steamed Jasmine Rice (page 145)
¾ cup torn fresh Thai, sweet, or purple basil leaves

1. Cut away the leafy tops of the fennel bulb and trim the bottom. Peel away any bruised or dry-looking outside layers. Cut the bulb in half lengthwise, then cut each half into ½-inch-thick slices. You should have about 1½ cups.

2. Set a large saucepan over medium-high heat and add the oil. When the oil is quite hot, add the fennel, garlic, and onion and cook, stirring, until the mixture softens and becomes fragrant, about 2 minutes. Season with the salt and pepper. Add the curry paste and stir-fry for 30 seconds.

3. Skim the thick cream from the top of the can of coconut milk and pour into the saucepan, reserving the milk. Cook the fennel and cream mixture for 2 minutes, stirring frequently. Stir in the chicken broth, fish sauce, and sugar. Add the chicken, and bring to a boil. Reduce the heat to medium-low, add the reserved coconut milk, and simmer until the chicken is cooked through, about 1 minute.

4. Transfer the curry to a soup tureen or serve directly from the pot over individual serving plates mounded with the steamed rice. Sprinkle each serving with the basil and serve.

Braised Chicken with Green Papaya

*T*his Filipino recipe will easily find a place at your table. A recipe featuring chicken sautéed in olive oil with garlic and onions will seem familiar and comfortable. Now add a little ginger and some green papaya—the under-ripe ones found in our markets are just right—and you've got a new family favorite in the making.

3 pounds chicken breasts or thighs

Salt and freshly ground black pepper to taste

3 tablespoons olive oil

1 medium-size onion, thinly sliced and separated into rings

3 large cloves garlic, crushed and chopped

1 tablespoon peeled and grated fresh ginger

1 cup Chicken Stock (page 289), canned low-sodium chicken broth, or water

1 green papaya (about 1 pound), peeled, halved, seeded, and cut crosswise into thin
  slices

1 tablespoon Asian fish sauce

Steamed Jasmine Rice (optional, page 145)

1. If using chicken breasts, cut them in half diagonally, through the bone, with poultry shears or a heavy chef's knife or cleaver. Season the chicken liberally with salt and pepper. Heat the oil in a large wok or heavy saucepan or Dutch oven over medium-high heat. Stir-fry the onion, garlic, and ginger until the onion is soft, 3 to 5 minutes.

2. Increase the heat to high. Add the chicken pieces and stir-fry until lightly browned on all sides, about 5 minutes. Add the chicken stock and bring to a boil. Reduce the heat, cover, and simmer gently until the chicken is tender and nearly cooked through, about 15 minutes.

3. Add the papaya and simmer briskly, uncovered, until the papaya is tender and the chicken is entirely cooked, 5 to 8 minutes. Stir in the fish sauce and some more pepper, and serve with plenty of rice, if desired.

Philly-Style Vietnamese Hoagies with Poached Chicken

Serves 2

Vietnamese take-out restaurants in Philadelphia serve *banh mi*, the French-influenced, baguette-based sandwiches that are so popular in their Asian homeland. And they've discovered that folks born and raised in Philadelphia have been quick to appreciate these wonderfully multiflavored sandwiches. It's no surprise. These Vietnamese sandwiches are close cousins to the many-ingredient sandwiches introduced to America by Italian immigrants of a previous generation. Hoagies—also called subs, grinders, heroes, or po' boys, depending on what part of the country you come from—are mega-sandwiches designed to pack all the nourishment possible between two slices of bread to sustain workers through a long day of labor. The Vietnamese in Philadelphia have also discovered that the local Italian sub rolls, with their firm crusts and soft, yielding interiors, are even better for these sandwiches than the French baguettes used in Vietnam, which is why we call these sandwiches Philly style.

You can make *banh mi* with several different types of meat. Roasted chicken, barbecued pork, and liver pâté are popular traditional choices. Here we fill the sandwiches with poached chicken breasts and the bright flavors of Red Chilli Mayo.

SANDWICH FILLING:

2 whole boneless, skinless chicken breasts, trimmed of any fat

2 to 4 tablespoons Red Chilli Mayo (page 78), to your taste

²/₃ cup shredded Napa or green cabbage or prepared coleslaw mix

1 cup Sweet Vegetable Pickles (page 97) or 2 tablespoons Sweet Hot Thai Chilli Sauce
   (page 80), or more to taste

2 to 3 serrano chillies, to your taste, thinly sliced

Salt and freshly ground black pepper to taste

1 small bunch fresh cilantro sprigs

4 Italian hoagie rolls (about 8 inches long) or 2 French baguettes (about 8 ounces each)

1. Fill a 4- to 5-quart saucepan with water and bring to a boil. Add the chicken and bring to a simmer. Cook for 5 minutes, then reduce the heat to maintain a gentle simmer (the liquid should bubble just enough to break the surface) and cook 10 minutes. Remove the pan from the heat and let stand, uncovered, until the chicken is cool enough to handle, or up to 1 hour. (The chicken will be very nearly cooked through when removed from the heat and will finish the last bit of cooking in the hot liquid, which will keep it moist until you're ready to serve.)

2. Meanwhile, assemble the remaining sandwich filling ingredients.

3. Preheat the oven to 350 degrees F.

4. Transfer the cooled chicken to a cutting board and pull it apart with your fingers, or slice it into shreds.

5. Lightly toast the bread in the hot oven for 5 minutes. Split each roll or baguette nearly in half lengthwise, leaving the halves attached on one side. Spread about 1 tablespoon of mayonnaise in each hoagie roll or 2 tablespoons in each baguette. Place a layer of shredded cabbage on the bottom of each roll or baguette, then layer the chicken on top. Add a layer of sweet vegetable pickles or drizzle with 1 tablespoon or so of the Thai chilli sauce. Sprinkle each sandwich with some sliced chillies and season with salt and pepper. Top with a few sprigs of cilantro and serve.

Roast Turkey Breast with Thai Cilantro Pesto

his year, serve a moist and fragrant holiday turkey with an aromatic pesto under the crisp-baked skin. A turkey breast is the prefect choice when you're hosting a small gathering of family and friends. The garlic-laced cilantro and black pepper pesto vividly accents the mild, mellow taste of the turkey. The perfect accompaniment is Tropical-Style Cranberry Relish (page 94).

THAI CILANTRO PESTO:

1 cup loosely packed chopped fresh cilantro, including the stems

4 large cloves garlic, crushed and chopped

1/2 teaspoon black peppercorns, or freshly ground black pepper

1 tablespoon sesame oil (not toasted) or any vegetable oil

TURKEY:

1 fresh whole turkey breast (5 to 6 pounds)

Sesame oil (not toasted) or other vegetable oil for the skin

Salt and freshly ground black pepper to taste

1. To make the pesto, combine all the ingredients in a mortar and pound until a moist, rough-textured paste forms. Or process in a mini–food processor, stopping once or twice to scrape down the sides of the work bowl. (If using a mortar, include whole peppercorns. If using a food processor, use freshly ground pepper.) Transfer the pesto to a small mixing bowl and set aside.

2. Preheat the oven to 350 degrees F. To begin preparing the turkey, cut away any excess fat, then rinse the turkey and pat it dry with paper towels. Loosen the skin over the turkey breast by slowly working your fingers under the skin, first one side of the breastbone, then the other. You can use a small knife or kitchen shears to snip any string-like membranes that get in your way. Just be careful

to cut close to the meat, leaving the skin intact. Work the cilantro pesto under the loosened skin on each side of the breast bone, patting and smoothing it over the meat as you go. Rub a little sesame oil over the skin and season with salt and pepper.

3. Roast the turkey in a baking dish or roasting pan until cooked through but still moist, about $1^{1}/_{2}$ hours, or 15 to 20 minutes per pound. The meat should release clear juices when pierced with a knife tip and register 160 degrees F on an instant-read thermometer inserted at its thickest point. Transfer the turkey to a platter and let stand for 20 minutes before carving. Meanwhile, skim the fat from the pan juices for a simple au jus, or make your favorite gravy, if desired.

4. To cut both breasts away from the bone, use a long, sharp knife and cut along the length of the breast bone, slightly to one side of the bone so the knife can penetrate the meat. As the blade reaches bone, pry the meat lightly away with the blade or with your hand. Slice a little deeper, keeping the blade close to the bone. Pry the meat away again. Repeat these steps until the meat comes away from the bone in a single large piece. Place the meat on a cutting board, skin side up. Cut crosswise into slices, beginning at the narrowest and holding the knife blade at a 45-degree angle to the board. Cut and slice the other side of the breast in the same manner. Arrange the turkey slices on a large serving platter and serve.

Fresh Cilantro: Leaves, Stems, and Roots

IN MANY CULTURES, THE LEAFY TOPS OF AN HERB PLANT ARE PLUCKED FOR USE IN THE CUISINE. WE USE ONLY THE LEAVES OF HERBS LIKE BASIL, PARSLEY, AND SAGE, FOR EXAMPLE. BUT THE FLOPPY, LACE-EDGED LEAVES OF THE LOVELY CILANTRO PLANT ARE JUST THE BEGINNING OF THE PLANT'S USEFULNESS. THE ROOTS AND STEMS OF THE CILANTRO PLANT HAVE A MORE CONCENTRATED FLAVOR THAN THE LEAVES. ASK THE PRODUCE MANAGER AT YOUR LOCAL SUPERMARKET TO KEEP THE ROOTS ON. THEY'RE VITAL FOR CURRY PASTES AND CAN ENLIVEN MANY OTHER RECIPES. FOR EXAMPLE, IF YOU'RE MAKING A MEXICAN-STYLE SALSA, USE THE WHOLE PLANT.

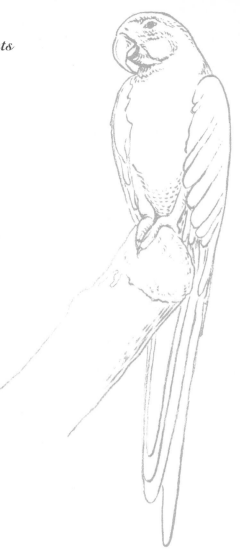

Balinese Roast Duck

Serves 2

In all of Southeast Asia, no one loves duck more than the Balinese. Their specialty is slowly cooking a whole duck over a charcoal fire after coating it in a rich spice paste—called *bumbu*—made of ground nuts, shallots, chillies, and sweet spices, and wrapping the duck snugly in banana leaves. Their name for this flavorful dish is *bebek betutu*.

The cooking process is slow, to produce a succulently spicy result, but in terms of active kitchen work, it is a fast recipe. Heavy-duty aluminum foil is a fine stand-in for banana leaves and allows you the option of oven-roasting the bird. We have also substituted macadamia nuts for the authentic—and hard to get—candlenuts.

An average duck usually yields just enough meat to serve two people, so this is perfect for a special dinner for two. If you wish to serve it at a dinner party, a variation of this recipe follows for roasting two small chickens instead.

1 duck (about 4¹/₂ pounds)

BUMBU SPICE PASTE:

¹/₄ cup plus 1¹/₂ tablespoon peanut or vegetable oil

1 large onion, roughly chopped

3 large cloves garlic, roughly chopped

3 tablespoons peeled and minced fresh ginger

1 tablespoon finely chopped small Thai chillies (about 8)

¹/₄ cup chopped macadamia nuts (about 12)

1 teaspoon ground cardamom

1 teaspoon turmeric

1 teaspoon anchovy paste

1 teaspoon salt

1 teaspoon freshly ground black pepper

1 tablespoon palm sugar or light brown sugar

1 tablespoon light soy sauce

1. Rinse the duck, inside and out, under cold running water. Pat dry. Cut off any excess fat or loose skin. Set aside.

2. To make the paste, heat a large wok or deep, heavy skillet over medium-high heat. When it is hot, add ¹/₄ cup of the oil and rotate the wok or pan a bit to coat it evenly. When the oil is hot, stir-fry the onions until they begin to turn golden brown, 4 to 5 minutes. Add the garlic and ginger and stir-fry for 1 minute. Reduce the heat to low, add the chillies, nuts, cardamom, turmeric,

anchovy paste, salt, pepper, and sugar, and stir-fry just until the ingredients are well blended. Transfer the mixture to a food processor and process it to a fairly smooth paste, stopping once or twice to scrape down the sides of the work bowl, as needed.

3. Preheat the oven to 400 degrees F. Transfer the spice paste to a large mixing bowl. Spread two large sheets of heavy-duty aluminum foil, about 2 feet long, over a roasting pan. Overlap them by about 2 inches to form one large sheet. Set the duck on the foil. Slather the inside of the duck with half of the spice paste. Add the remaining 1^1/$_2$ tablespoons of oil and the soy sauce to the remaining spice paste. Slather the mixture over the outside of the duck. Fold the foil over the duck, crimping the edges together to make a tight seal. Place the pan with the foil-wrapped duck in the oven and roast for 15 minutes. Reduce the oven temperature to 350 degrees F and roast an additional 1 hour and 45 minutes, or until the juices run clear when a thigh joint is pricked with a fork.

4. Remove the pan from the oven. Open the foil package carefully while still in the pan, so the accumulated liquid does not spill; be careful of the steam coming out of the package. Transfer the duck to a cutting board and let stand for 5 minutes to settle the juices. Pour out and discard the liquid from the pan. Spoon the spice paste stuffing into a small bowl and set aside. Carve the duck and arrange the meat on a serving platter. Spoon the spice paste stuffing over the duck and serve immediately.

Balinese Roast Chicken with *Bumbu* Spice Paste: Substitute 2 small chickens (about 3 pounds each) for the duck. Prepare as instructed above, but place each chicken in its own roasting pan. Reduce the oven temperature to 350 degrees F after the chickens have been in the oven for 15 minutes. They will take about an additional 1 hour and 15 minutes to cook. Serves 6.

W herever you travel in Southeast Asia, you'll discover that food is appreciated as a great form of art. But to the Balinese it is much more. It is a link for communication between *sehala*, the visible world, and *nishala*, the spirit world. As Dr. Anak Agung Made Djelantik, a physician-prince who lectures on aesthetics at the College of Indonesian Arts at Denpasar, explains the belief, "The arts are an invitation for the gods to come down and join the people." Indeed, the foods prepared for Balinese ceremonies may be the most ornate and elaborate culinary displays anywhere on earth.

One of the most striking examples is the *bebanten*, a towering, intricate assemblage of various foods, flowers, and woven bamboo decoration. Created to please the deities, it is solemnly carried to temple balanced on the head of a beautiful young woman. Her height may be doubled by the multicolored offering she bears. An individual *bebanten* may hold a whole roast suckling pig, in addition to mangoes, bananas, candy-colored rice cakes, and lengths of bamboo packed with white rice, all decked in garlands of tropical flowers.

As a procession of villagers nears a temple, many *bebanten* will be seen over the heads of the crowd, converging as they enter the courtyard. Each girl kneels in turn, as her *bebanten* is lifted by waiting attendants and placed before a priest, who then chants to the spirits, inviting them to come in and consume the gorgeous offerings. After the spirits have accepted the "essence" of the *bebanten*, the villagers are free to make a feast of the offerings and also enjoy an open-air recital by the best musicians and dancers.

The depth of Balinese devotion to art can be explained by the island's history. Five centuries ago, Bali was a remote portion of the great Hindu-Javanese empire known as Madjapahit. Islam was then becoming the dominant religious culture. A Hindu prince decided to gather as many artists, priests, dancers, musicians, and cooks as possible, and he led them all eastward to Bali, to preserve as much of their culture as they could.

Thanks to Bali's rich volcanic soils, and to seas and mountains that discouraged would-be invaders, these newcomers prospered nearly undisturbed for centuries.

Their embrace of art remained deeply imbedded in their culture, with religion knitting together all their art forms. As the anthropologist Margaret Mead famously observed, everyone in Bali is an artist. The teacher or the fisherman may also be the village's finest sculptor. The architect may be a dancer, the carpenter a musician. And all of them, chefs and home cooks included, create their art with an intention to benefit the whole community by honoring the divine force of creation. To borrow a well-expressed thought from the Sufi poet Jalaluddin Rumi, they let the beauty they love be what they do. This explains why the culture of Bali is so widely admired among creative people everywhere. Daily chores, including the preparation of food, become a chorus of gratitude for the gift of life.

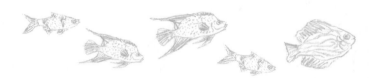

Malay Chilli Shrimp

Serves 4 to 6

This Malaysian classic is an example of a *sambal* that's served as a main dish. The *sambals* of Malaysia and Indonesia are richly flavored and spiced concoctions usually served as relishes or as dips. Malay Chilli Shrimp should be served with Steamed Jasmine Rice (page 145) or scooped up with Malaysian-style flatbread (page 286).

In tropical Asian countries like Malaysia, shrimp is often served straight up—with their heads and shells intact—for more flavor and crunch. It can be awfully hard to find supremely fresh heads-on shrimp here in the States. So, unless we're frying them for a dish like Crispy Peppercorn Shrimp (page 60), we shell ours but don't bother to devein them. You can, though, if you like.

MALAY SPICE PASTE:

1 teaspoon dried shrimp paste or anchovy paste

1 tablespoon chopped unsalted dry-roasted cashews or macadamia nuts

1 large clove garlic, crushed and chopped

1 tablespoon chopped shallots or red onion

1 tablespoon peeled and chopped fresh Siamese ginger (*galanga*) or regular ginger

6 to 10 small Thai or serrano chillies, preferably red, to your taste, sliced

SHRIMP:

1/2 cup canned unsweetened coconut milk

1 tablespoon palm sugar or light brown sugar

1 tablespoon fresh lime juice

1 pound medium-size shrimp, peeled, and deveined if desired

1. To make the spice paste, put the shrimp paste, if using, in the center of a double-thick 6-inch square of aluminum foil. Fold the edges over to make a little packet and set it directly on a gas or electric burner at medium heat. Toast until fragrant, about 20 seconds per side, then unwrap the shrimp paste. Put the shrimp paste and all the remaining spice paste ingredients in a mortar and pound into a fairly smooth paste. Or process in a mini–food processor.

2. Pour the coconut milk into a large wok or large, heavy skillet set over medium heat. Add the spice paste and cook, stirring frequently, until the mixture is well blended and quite fragrant, about 3 minutes. Stir in the sugar, then the lime juice. Add the shrimp and increase the heat to medium-high. Cook, stirring constantly, until the shrimp is firm and pink, 3 to 5 minutes.

3. Transfer to a serving platter and serve immediately, with rice or flatbread, if desired.

Laotian-Style Stir-Fried Shrimp with Crispy Lemon Grass

*T*he Laotian name for this delightful yet simple stir-fry of shrimp, garlic, fish sauce, and soy sauce is *kai takrai krob*. Its most notable component is its thin rounds of fragrant lemon grass, deep-fried until crispy and sprinkled over the entire dish to give it a lemony zing. Instead of fresh chillies, Laotian cooks use small dried red chillies, which flavor the sauce and also give hardcore chilli lovers something pleasantly combustible to nibble on.

CRISPY LEMON GRASS:

3 plump stalks lemon grass

³/₄ cup peanut or vegetable oil for frying

STIR-FRIED SHRIMP:

1 medium-size shallot, thinly sliced

1 tablespoon chopped garlic

1 pound large shrimp, peeled and deveined if desired

¹/₂ teaspoon salt

¹/₄ teaspoon freshly ground black pepper

1 tablespoon light soy sauce

1 tablespoon palm sugar or light brown sugar

3 small dried red chillies, such as chile de arbol

1 tablespoon Asian fish sauce

1. To make the Crispy Lemon Grass, trim the root ends of the lemon grass stalks and discard the tough outer leaves. Cut a 3-inch length from each bulb end and slice them into thin rounds. (You should have about 2 tablespoons. If not, cut more.) Pour the oil into a wok or deep skillet over high heat and heat until the oil is very hot. Add one piece of the lemon grass. It should sizzle briskly.

Add the remaining lemon grass and stir-fry until golden brown, about 2 minutes. Remove the lemon grass from the oil with a wire skimmer or slotted spoon and drain on paper towels.

2. To cook the shrimp, pour off most of the oil, leaving about 1½ tablespoons in the wok. Over high heat, stir-fry the shallots and garlic just until fragrant, about 1 minute. Add the shrimp and stir-fry for 2 minutes. Add the salt, pepper, soy sauce, sugar, chillies, and fish sauce and stir-fry until the shrimp is cooked through, about 30 seconds.

3. Transfer the stir-fried shrimp to a serving platter and top with the stir-fried lemon grass. Serve hot.

Crab Dumplings with Thai Green Curry and Basil

Serves 6

You can keep things simple and just serve this with Steamed Jasmine Rice (page 145) but a lush and elegant main course like this green curry really deserves to have a complete dinner party designed around it. We recommend that you enlist some friends to help you prepare a feast.

You might start it off with Spicy Stir-Fried Cashews (page 47), then serve the green curry over Steamed Jasmine Rice (page 145), with Hot 'n' Cool Cucumber Relish (page 256) on the side. Your dessert could be Sweet Cheeks of Caramelized Mango with Vanilla Bean Ice Cream (page 268).

If you make the curry paste in advance, you'll have less work to do on the day of your dinner party. Curries, like stews, improve when given a little time to let the flavors marry and become more pronounced, so you could even make the entire curry a day ahead, then gently rewarm it for your dinner party.

CRAB DUMPLINGS:

³/₄ cup coarsely chopped fresh cilantro, including the stems

¹/₄ cup coarsely chopped garlic (8 to 12 large cloves)

1¹/₄ pounds fresh lump crabmeat, picked over for shells and cartilage

¹/₄ pound ground pork

¹/₂ teaspoon white pepper

2 teaspoons Asian fish sauce

1 tablespoon palm sugar or golden brown sugar

CURRY:

One 19-ounce can unsweetened coconut milk

¹/₂ cup Thai Green Curry Paste (page 291)

1 tablespoon Asian fish sauce

1 tablespoon palm sugar or light brown sugar

Steamed Jasmine Rice (page 145)

²/₃ cup torn fresh Thai, sweet, or purple basil leaves

1. To begin the dumplings, make a spice paste with the cilantro and garlic by pounding them together in a mortar, or combine them on a cutting board and chop finely. Transfer to a large mixing bowl and combine with the remaining dumpling ingredients, mixing by hand until well blended. Form the mixture into 1¹/₂-inch balls and set aside.

2. To make the curry, skim the thick cream from the top of the can of coconut milk and pour into a medium-size saucepan, reserving the milk. Heat the coconut cream over medium heat until the oil starts to separate from the cream, 1 to 2 minutes. Add the green curry paste and cook for 1 to 2 minutes, stirring often. Add the coconut milk and cook for 1 minute, stirring often. Add the fish sauce and sugar and stir until the sugar is dissolved and well blended with the curry. Carefully add the dumplings. Raise the heat to high and bring the sauce to a boil. Gently boil 2 minutes, stirring once or twice very carefully.

3. Transfer the curry to a soup tureen, or serve directly from the pot over individual serving plates mounded with the rice. Sprinkle each serving with the basil and serve immediately.

Spicy Stir-Fried Squid

*I*n the seaside resorts and ports of Thailand, you will find impeccably fresh seafood, often stir-fried with *nam phrik pao*, a roasted chilli paste, and the small-leaved but intense, almost clove-like holy basil. It's a dish known locally as *pla muek phrik*.

We've added fresh hot chillies to that basic recipe to create layers of both roasted and raw chilli heat and extra depth of flavor. As a counterpoint to all that heat, there's lots of garlic and mint. Best of all, the seafood-flavored juices from the squid make a lush pan gravy for the rice you'll want to serve on the side.

To keep your cooking time short, buy cleaned fresh or frozen squid, which you can defrost in the refrigerator the day before you plan to cook this dish. All you need to do then is cut the squid bodies into rings and leave the tentacles whole, as you would for Italian fried calamari.

1^1/$_2$ pounds fresh whole squid, cleaned, or frozen squid, thawed

2 tablespoons peanut or vegetable oil

^{1}/$_4$ cup sliced garlic (about 6 large cloves)

1 tablespoon thinly sliced serrano chillies, preferably red

2 to 4 small Thai chillies, preferably red, to your taste

2 tablespoons Thai roasted chilli paste (*nam phrik pao*), or substitute 2 teaspoons
    Chinese chilli-garlic sauce mixed with 1 teaspoon light brown sugar

1 slender scallion (white and tender green parts), angle-cut into thin slices

1 tablespoon Asian fish sauce

¼ teaspoon palm sugar or light brown sugar

Steamed Jasmine Rice (page 145)

¼ cup small or torn fresh mint leaves

1. Cut the squid bodies into 1-inch-thick rings. Leave the tentacles whole. Set aside.

2. Heat a large wok or deep, heavy skillet over high heat. When it is hot, add the oil and rotate the wok or pan a bit to coat it evenly. When the oil is hot, add the garlic and stir-fry until it begins to color, about 30 seconds. Add the sliced squid and whole tentacles and stir-fry for 30 seconds. Add the chillies and stir-fry for 30 seconds. Add the chilli paste and cook, stirring frequently to mix the ingredients well, about 1½ minutes. Reduce the heat to medium-low. Add the scallion and stir in the fish sauce and sugar. Stir-fry to dissolve the sugar and blend the ingredients, about 30 seconds.

3. Serve hot over the rice with the mint leaves sprinkled on top.

Pan-Seared Tuna Steaks au Poivre

Serves 4

Peppercorns were the original hot spice of Southeast Asian cooking, the uncontested ruler for eons, until Portuguese traders introduced today's champion, the chilli pepper.

A more recent European influence was the lengthy French occupation of Cambodia, Laos, and Vietnam, which they called, collectively, French Indochina. This dish draws inspiration from the French favorite called steak *au poivre*; at the same time, it recalls that the roots of spicy Southeast Asian food are the roots that lace pepper vines into the native soil.

The French simply use peppercorns on beefsteak; we're also using cumin, ginger, and coriander for even more spice and aroma, and tuna steaks for a more healthful dish. Your objective, as cook, is to keep the tuna steaks moist so they will contrast nicely with the dry heat of the spices.

This is a wonderful dish to serve with Braised Baby Bok Choy (page 245) and/or Golden Mashed Potatoes (page 242).

1 tablespoon black peppercorns

1 tablespoon coriander seeds

$^1/_2$ teaspoon coarse salt

$^1/_2$ teaspoon ground ginger

$^1/_8$ teaspoon ground cumin

4 medium-size tuna steaks (6 to 8 ounces each), 1 inch thick

1 tablespoon peanut or vegetable oil

1. Crack the peppercorns with a mortar and pestle or with a rolling pin until cracked but not powdered. Transfer the cracked pepper to a small bowl. Crack the coriander seeds in the same manner and add them to the pepper. Set aside.

2. Combine the salt, ginger, and cumin in another small bowl. Season both sides of the tuna steaks with the cumin mixture, then coat the steaks all over with the pepper mixture.

3. Heat the oil in a cast-iron or other type of heavy skillet over medium-high heat until very hot. Add the tuna steaks and sear them for 1 minute on each side for rare, $1^1/_2$ to 2 minutes on each side for medium, or to your desired degree of doneness. Serve hot or warm.

Roasted Salmon with Indonesian Soy-Ginger Sauce, Spinach, and Baby Corn

*I*ndonesian-style fish recipes often call for bathing a whole fish in a piquant, spicy sauce, then wrapping it in a banana leaf and roasting it over glowing hot coals. We love Indonesian cooking, but prefer a less exacting and time-consuming cooking method. To that end, we've created this recipe using thick, center-cut fillets of fresh salmon, quickly roasted in a 500-degree oven. The roasted salmon is displayed on a mound of sautéed spinach encircled by ears of baby corn, and basted with a richly spiced soy-ginger sauce.

3 tablespoons sesame oil (not toasted) or vegetable oil

4 center-cut salmon fillets, about 1 inch thick (8 ounces each), skin on

Salt and freshly ground black pepper to taste

1 pound fresh spinach, washed well and stemmed

1/4 cup sweet dark soy sauce, or substitute 1 tablespoon light soy sauce mixed with
    3 tablespoons pure maple syrup

1 teaspoon *sambal oelek* or 1 1/2 teaspoons Tabasco sauce

1 tablespoon fresh lemon juice

1/4 teaspoon ground ginger

1 1/2 teaspoons palm sugar or light brown sugar

One 15-ounce can baby corn, drained

1. Preheat the oven to 500 degrees F. Grease a 9 x 13-inch baking dish (such as a lasagna pan) with 1 tablespoon of the oil. Set the fillets in the pan, skin side down, and season with salt and pepper. Set aside.

2. Heat the remaining 2 tablespoons of oil in a large pot over high heat until the oil shimmers. Carefully add the spinach and stir for 1 or 2 minutes, until wilted. Season with salt and pepper. Remove from the heat and keep covered until serving time.

3. Place the pan of salmon in the hot oven and roast just until cooked through, about 15 minutes, or to your taste. Meanwhile, prepare the sauce.

4. Combine the soy sauce, *sambal oelek*, lemon juice, ginger, and sugar in a small saucepan over medium-low heat and stir until the sugar dissolves and ingredients are well blended. Keep warm until the salmon is cooked.

5. To serve, mound the spinach in the centers of 6 dinner plates and surround with ears of baby corn. Set a salmon fillet on each spinach mound and spoon the soy-ginger sauce on top. Serve at once.

Crispy Salmon with Tangy Citrus Sambal

Serves 4

The salmon takes only minutes to cook in a hot skillet. We score the skin so it doesn't curl from the heat. Instead, it becomes a cracker-crisp counterpoint to the moist salmon flesh.

Based on orange marmalade, the *sambal* also takes just a few minutes, but it adds a flavor contrast that will make your guests think this simply prepared dish is really quite complex.

This is wonderful paired with Golden Mashed Potatoes (page 242).

TANGY CITRUS *SAMBAL*:

1/2 cup orange marmalade

1/4 cup plus 2 tablespoons grapefruit juice

1 teaspoon *sambal oelek* or Tabasco sauce

SALMON:

4 center-cut salmon fillets, about 1 inch thick
   (8 ounces each), skin on

Salt and freshly ground black pepper to taste

1 tablespoon vegetable oil

1. To make the *sambal*, heat the marmalade in a small nonstick skillet over low heat, stirring often, until it begins to soften and melt, about 1 minute. Add the grapefruit juice and mix until smooth. Turn off the heat. Add the *sambal* and mix well. Transfer to a small serving bowl. (You will have about ⅔ cup.)

2. To cook the salmon, with a sharp knife, score the skin side of each salmon fillet in 3 places. Cut right through the skin. Season both sides of the fish with salt and pepper. Heat a large nonstick skillet over medium-high heat. Add the oil. When the oil is hot, place the salmon in the pan, skin side up, and cook for 2 minutes. Using a metal spatula, turn the salmon skin side down and cook until the skin is crisp and brown, 4 to 6 minutes. Serve hot with the *sambal* on the side.

At Home and Abroad

YOUR HOME PANTRY IS LIKELY TO INCLUDE THE KEY FLAVOR COMPONENTS OF TWO WIDELY USED ASIAN INGREDIENTS: SWEET DARK SOY SAUCE—A MOLASSES-TINGED SOY—AND *SAMBAL OELEK*, THE INDONESIAN CHILLI PASTE MADE FROM FRESH RED CHILLIES, VINEGAR, AND SALT. BUT IF THEY AREN'T ON HAND, A SIMPLE HOT SAUCE SUCH AS TABASCO MAKES A GOOD STAND-IN FOR THE *SAMBAL*, AND 1 PART LIGHT SOY SAUCE WITH 3 PARTS PURE MAPLE SYRUP WILL DOUBLE FOR THE SWEET DARK SOY.

Grilled Red Snapper with Thai Tamarind Sauce

*T*his lusty, sensual display of flavors and textures is an adaptation of *sadow nam pla wan*, a classic Thai dish of numerous components—grilled fish, steamed rice, rich tamarind gravy, fried garlic, chillies, shallots, and lots of fresh herbs, plus steamed rice. We've streamlined it a bit to accent a few key elements, and rather than set out the traditional sides, such as tamarind sauce and garlic chips, we include them all on the plate. With its beautiful presentation and memorable flavor and texture, we think this showcases the best of Thai cooking in a single, delicious dish.

If you buy snapper fillets with the skin on, you don't have to turn them on the grill. Just place them on the grill rack, skin side down, cover, and cook until done.

THAI TAMARIND SAUCE:

$1/2$ cup Tamarind Sauce (page 290) or liquid tamarind concentrate

$1/3$ cup Asian fish sauce

$1/3$ cup palm sugar or light brown sugar

3 tablespoons water

HERBS:

1 bunch fresh cilantro

1 bunch arugula or another leafy herb, such as Thai or sweet basil

FISH:

1 pound red snapper fillets, skin on

Vegetable oil for brushing the fish

Steamed Jasmine Rice (page 145)

Thai Fried Garlic Chips (page 101)

1. To make the sauce, combine all the ingredients in a medium-size saucepan set over medium-high heat. Bring to a boil, stirring until the sugar is dissolved and blended. Reduce the heat to medium-low and simmer, stirring occasionally, until slightly thickened, 3 to 4 minutes. Remove the pan from the heat and set aside.

2. To prepare the herbs, tear the cilantro leaves from the stems. (You can save the stems for another dish. Pop them in a food storage bag and store in the freezer.) Tear the arugula leaves from their stems, then tear the leaves into bite-size pieces and put them in a medium-size mixing bowl. Add the cilantro leaves, toss together, and set aside.

3. Preheat an outdoor grill, or preheat a grill pan for 3 to 5 minutes over medium-high heat. To cook the fish, brush the fillets with vegetable oil and place them, skin side down, on the grill or in the pan. Cover and cook for 6 to 8 minutes. Check immediately. The fish should be opaque throughout and firm enough that it begins to flake when you press it with the blade of a knife. Take the fish off the grill just before it's cooked through the way you like it, as it will continue to cook a bit after it is removed from the heat.

4. To serve, make a bed of rice on each individual dinner plate and top with 1 or 2 grilled fish fillets. Sprinkle some mixed herbs over the fish, spoon on some tamarind sauce, and top each serving with garlic chips. Serve immediately, with more sauce and garlic chips on the side.

Red Snapper Steamed with Ginger and Lemon Grass

Serves 4

This Thai recipe, a simple dish of the freshest fish steamed with a little ginger and shredded scallions, shows the pervasive influence of Chinese cooking. Though the Thai version is still simply prepared and delicately flavored, it gains complexity with a sprinkling of cilantro leaves, a few rounds of sliced chillies, and their ubiquitous fish sauce, to conjure more flavor from the steam-induced pan juices.

We love our Thai steamer made of light-gauge aluminum. It has a full-sized pot, allowing it to keep a good head of steam, and a pair of double-handled steam racks under a dome-shaped lid. You could instead use a large wok with a rack insert, or a large saucepan fitted with a colander. Just make sure that you set the fish on a heat-proof plate that fits easily onto your rack. And use a plate that isn't too shallow—you want to capture all the pan juices released by the steam.

2 plump stalks lemon grass or 1 tablespoon grated lemon zest

2 tablespoons peeled and julienned fresh ginger

2 tablespoons peeled and julienned fresh Siamese ginger (*galanga*, see Note)

2 tablespoons thinly sliced shallots or finely chopped red onion

1/2 teaspoon thinly sliced small Thai or serrano chillies

4 fresh or frozen kaffir lime leaves, stacked and cut crosswise into thin slivers, or

   1 1/2 teaspoons grated lime zest

3 tablespoons Asian fish sauce

3/4 cup loosely packed fresh cilantro leaves

2 pounds red snapper fillets

1. If using the lemon grass, trim the root ends and discard the tough outer leaves. Cut a 6-inch length from the bulb end of each stalk and discard the rest. Lightly crush the bulb end with a mortar and pestle or a rolling pin.

2. In a small mixing bowl, combine the ginger, *galanga*, shallots, chillies, lime leaves, fish sauce, and $1/2$ cup of the cilantro leaves, reserving the rest for a garnish.

3. Scatter about a third of the herb-and-fish sauce mixture over a heat-proof plate large enough to hold the snapper fillets in a single layer, yet small enough to fit inside your steamer. Arrange the fish on top and sprinkle with the remaining herb-and-fish-sauce mixture, plus the lemon grass. Put the plate of fish on the steamer rack and set aside.

4. Fill a steam pot about two-thirds full of water and set over medium-high heat. Bring the water to a rolling boil and fit the rack with the plate of fish over the pot. Cover and steam the fish until it is cooked all the way through and will flake easily, 10 to 15 minutes. Carefully uncover, watching out for the burst of steam. Remove the rack from the steamer. Using towels or pot holders, carefully lift the plate out of the rack. Discard the lemon grass bulbs.

5. Sprinkle the fish with the reserved cilantro leaves. Serve directly from the plate, and include some of the collected juices with each portion.

Note: If you don't have Siamese ginger, double the quantity of regular fresh ginger.

Sea Gypsies, Hill Tribes, Remote Peoples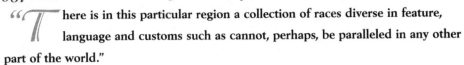

"There is in this particular region a collection of races diverse in feature, language and customs such as cannot, perhaps, be paralleled in any other part of the world."

These words, published in 1899 by an explorer named Sir George Scott, may be even truer today. In addition to its great variety of culinary offerings, Southeast Asia is home to an astounding variety of peoples and has been for at least half a million years. Many tribes depend wholly on nature for survival, and on animistic spirits for protection. They live as though untouched by the last few centuries. Their ways of life may vanish soon, but for now, untold numbers of people in tropical Asia consider themselves Jinghpaw, Yinbaw, Mon, Hmong, Lisu, Pa-O, Taungyo, Karen—or some other tribal identity—rather than citizens of a nation, state, or province.

Off the coast of Burma and Thailand, moving from place to place with the seasons among a sparsely populated string of tropical islands called the Mergui Archipelago, the Moken (often called sea gypsies) speak a language that is quite distinct from others in the region and has no written form. The only modern aspect to their lives is a recent willingness to power their long boats with diesel engines. Just south of their islands, in between the island of Sumatra and the Malay Peninsula, lies the Strait of Malacca. There, in the days of sailing ships, unpredictable winds made the rich merchant vessels running between India and China easy prey for pirates. Tremendous treasures still lie at the ocean's bottom there, evidenced by the Ming vases local fishermen occasionally dredge up in their nets.

Among the tribes living in the highlands of Burma, many people adorn their necks, arms, and legs with massive coils of brass and silver. Most striking of them all are the so-called giraffe women of the Paduang tribe. They are fitted with their first neck ring around the age of five. Before they've reached womanhood, they may wear more than a dozen, altogether weighing around fifty pounds, creating a solid metallic column from collarbone to chin.

More people of Lao tribes live in adjacent Thailand than Laos itself, which bears their name. The Lao believe that a great chieftain in ancient times grew a vine that produced three pumpkins. When they became ripe, the chieftain poked holes in them with a hot iron. People poured forth, darkened by the heat, who moved south and became the Malays. When the chieftain cut more holes with his knife, Laos and other lighter-skinned peoples emerged.

At least half of all the people in Laos live in mountain hinterlands, where they often eat raw meat with their home-brewed rice whiskey. Some are Muslims, descendants of nineteenth-century invaders who stayed on to become middlemen in trade between mountain peoples and rice-growing farmers of the lowlands.

The inland territories of Malaysia are home to several isolated peoples, including nomadic tribes known as the Semang, and seminomadic tribes called the Senoi. They hunt birds, bats, monkeys, and wild boars with bamboo blowpipes longer than their men are tall. According to their beliefs, they are sustained by an earth goddess who reunites with her heaven-dwelling husband whenever there is lightning.

Interior tribes in the Philippines may be descendants of the very first people to inhabit Southeast Asia. Some of them believe that there was once nothing in creation but the sky, the sea, and a bird that had nowhere to land—until it cannily provoked a fight between sky and sea. The sea threw huge waves at the sky, which then hurled great rocks into the sea. That made the first land, the islands of the Philippines.

The Yao people, who live in Vietnam as well as Laos and Thailand, may be the original people of southern China, driven out of their homeland six or seven centuries ago. They are excellent paper makers, a craft that likely traveled with them from China. Like many of the remote tribes of Southeast Asia, they work the land through slash-and-burn agriculture, worship their ancestors, and depend on priests to exorcise evil spirits and ensure good health and full harvests.

If any descendants of Sir George Scott were to visit the Yao or any other remote tribe of Southeast Asia today, they would find people who almost exactly match the photographs and descriptions made of them over a hundred years ago.

Crispy Flounder with Chilli-Peanut Dipping Sauce

Serves 4

*B*ecause flounder is so mild tasting and fine textured, it takes beautifully to pan-frying. The dipping sauce is a homey and wonderful concoction: a bright citrus base sweetened with palm sugar and spiked with bits of hot red chilli and crushed peanuts. It goes well with practically any steamed or grilled fish.

Serve your flounder with plenty of jasmine rice on the side. Spoon a bit of sauce over a portion of fish, and let it seep into the hot rice.

CHILLI-PEANUT DIPPING SAUCE:

3 tablespoons fresh lemon juice

3 tablespoons fresh lime juice

1/4 cup plus 1 tablespoon Asian fish sauce

2 tablespoons palm sugar or light brown sugar

3 tablespoons Tamarind Sauce (page 290) or liquid tamarind concentrate, or
substitute 1 tablespoon fresh lime juice mixed with 1/2 teaspoon Worcestershire
sauce and 1 teaspoon light brown sugar

1 red serrano or small Thai chilli, minced

FLOUNDER:

1/2 cup all-purpose flour

Salt and freshly ground black pepper to taste

4 flounder fillets (about 1/2 pound each)

1/4 cup vegetable oil

1/3 cup unsalted dry-roasted peanuts, crushed

Steamed Jasmine Rice (page 145)

1. To make the sauce, combine all the ingredients in a small serving bowl. Set aside while you fry the flounder.

2. To make the flounder, combine the flour, salt, and pepper in a large shallow bowl and mix well. Dredge the flounder fillets in the flour mixture, shaking off any excess. Heat the oil in a large skillet over medium-high heat. When the oil is hot, cook the fillets, 2 at a time if necessary, until golden brown, about 3 minutes per side. Keep warm in a low oven if necessary.

3. Transfer the crispy flounder to a serving platter. Stir the crushed peanuts into the dipping sauce. Serve the flounder immediately with rice and dipping sauce on the side.

Bangkok-to-Bali Beer-Battered Catfish

Serves 4

Choose thickly cut catfish fillets or a firm, white-fleshed fish, such as red snapper or halibut, for this sure-to-please dish. Hot 'n' Cool Cucumber Relish (page 256) or Tomato *Sambal* (page 93) will accent the Southeast Asian flavors.

1 1/2 pounds thick catfish or other firm white-fleshed fish fillets
1 recipe Bangkok-to-Bali Beer Batter (page 288)
Peanut or vegetable oil for frying

1. In a large mixing bowl, place the fillets in the beer batter.

2. In a large wok or deep, heavy skillet, add enough oil to reach a depth of 1 to 1 1/2 inches. Heat the oil over medium-high heat to 375 degrees F. (To test the oil temperature, dip a wooden spoon in the hot oil. The oil should bubble and sizzle around the bowl of the spoon.)

3. Using tongs, lift each fillet, letting the excess batter drip off, and place in the oil. Fry the fish, in batches if necessary, turning twice to ensure an even golden brown color, about 5 minutes.

4. Drain the fillets on a flattened brown paper bag or on paper towels, then serve immediately.

Bali-Style Marinated Grilled Fish Kebabs

We've paired this Balinese-style citrus-and-spice marinade with sword-fish, but it's just as delicious with fresh tuna or sea scallops.

Fragrant Malay Rice with Mixed Fresh Herbs (page 150) and Cointreau and Palm Sugar–Glazed Pineapple (page 258) both make great accompaniments.

BALI-STYLE SEAFOOD MARINADE:

4 large cloves garlic, minced

1 teaspoon peeled and minced fresh ginger

$^1/_2$ teaspoon turmeric

$^1/_4$ teaspoon cayenne pepper

3 tablespoons sweet dark soy sauce, or substitute 2 teaspoons light soy sauce mixed
with 2 tablespoons pure maple syrup

1 tablespoon Asian fish sauce

$^1/_4$ cup fresh lemon juice

$^1/_4$ cup fresh lime juice

$^1/_2$ teaspoon sugar

KEBABS:

2 pounds swordfish, cut into $1^1/_2$-inch chunks

3 limes, each sliced into six $^1/_2$-inch-thick rounds, or a mix of lemon and lime slices

2 tablespoons minced fresh lemon basil (optional)

Six 10-inch bamboo skewers, soaked in a tray of cold water for 30 minutes or more

1. Combine the marinade ingredients in a large mixing bowl and blend well.
2. To begin the kebabs, toss the swordfish chunks in the marinade, then cover
   with plastic wrap and marinate in the refrigerator for 3 hours.

3. Preheat an outdoor grill, or preheat a grill pan for 3 to 5 minutes over medium-high heat. Brush the grill rack or pan with vegetable oil. Thread the swordfish and lime slices onto the skewers, using 3 citrus slices per skewer to space out the swordfish chunks. Grill 5 to 10 minutes, turning frequently and brushing with any remaining marinade, just until the fish begins to flake when tested with a fork.

4. Transfer the kebabs to a serving platter, sprinkle with the lemon basil, if desired, and serve immediately.

Indonesian-Style Tempeh Curry

Serves 4

Like tofu, tempeh is made from soybeans. You can find it in the refrigerator or frozen foods sections of health food stores, usually in vacuum-sealed, eight-ounce packages. It was created centuries ago on the island of Java, and is used in literally hundreds of Indonesian dishes.

For a vegetarian product, tempeh actually resembles meat quite a lot. It has a firm texture, an earthy aroma that will remind you of mushrooms, and a taste that's slightly nutty. A four-ounce serving contains about 21 grams of protein.

Serve this dish with Steamed Jasmine Rice (page 145) on the side or with your favorite noodles, or with Malaysian-Style Flatbread (page 286).

INDONESIAN SPICE PASTE:

3 small red Thai chillies, chopped

1 medium-size onion, chopped

1 large clove garlic, crushed and chopped

2 teaspoons peeled and chopped fresh ginger

1 teaspoon turmeric

2 teaspoons palm sugar or light brown sugar

TEMPEH CURRY:

1 tablespoon peanut or vegetable oil

One 8-ounce package tempeh, cut into ½-inch cubes

Salt and freshly ground black pepper to taste

One 14-ounce can unsweetened coconut milk

1 to 2 serrano chillies (optional), to your taste, thinly sliced

1. To make the spice paste, grind the ingredients in a mortar to achieve a fairly smooth paste. Or process them in a mini–food processor or blender. Transfer to a small bowl and set aside.

2. To begin the curry, in a large wok or deep skillet, heat the oil over medium heat. Add the tempeh and stir-fry until golden brown, 4 to 6 minutes. Transfer to a plate or bowl, season with salt and pepper, and set aside.

3. Skim the thick cream from the top of the canned coconut milk and pour into a medium-size saucepan, reserving the milk. Set the pan over medium-high heat, stir in the spice paste until blended, and bring to a simmer. Cook, stirring constantly, for 2 minutes. Add the reserved coconut milk and bring the mixture to a boil. Add the cooked tempeh and serrano chillies, if desired, and simmer until the tempeh is heated through, about 1 minute.

4. Serve hot with rice or your favorite kind of noodles, or with flatbread.

Golden Tofu Squares with Sweet-and-Sour Tamarind Sauce and Garlic Chips

*I*n America, we're familiar with using tofu in stir-fries and soups. Another very savory and delicious way of preparing tofu, much loved throughout tropical Asia, is shallow-frying. It's a great method. When you cut tofu into squares and shallow-fry them, they become puffy golden pillows—lightly crisp on the outside, soft and mellow on the inside. And, as the Asians do, you can serve these inviting morsels with any of literally hundreds of sauces.

We've selected a Thai-inspired vegetarian tamarind sauce that's both fruity and savory, and topped the dish with Thai Fried Garlic Chips (page 101), fresh scallions and cilantro. After trying this version, you may want to go further and invent some variations of your own or try these suggestions: Serve Golden Tofu Squares with warm Spicy Peanut Sauce (page 88), adding Hot 'n' Cool Cucumber Relish (page 256) on the side, or serve the tofu with Balinese Dipping Sauce (page 83) and sliced tomatoes or a mixed salad on the side.

This dish has several components, but you can prepare the sauce and garlic chips a day ahead.

SWEET-AND-SOUR TAMARIND SAUCE:

1/2 cup vegetable broth or water

1 tablespoon palm sugar or light brown sugar

2 tablespoons Tamarind Sauce (page 290) or liquid tamarind concentrate

2 teaspoons Thai mushroom soy sauce or light soy sauce

GOLDEN TOFU SQUARES:

One 24-ounce bottle peanut or vegetable oil

One 15-ounce package soft (silken) tofu, drained and cut into 12 pieces about
2 1/4 x 1 1/4 x 1 inch

TOPPINGS:

2 slender scallions (white and tender green parts), angle-cut into thin slices

Thai Fried Garlic Chips (page 101)

1/4 cup chopped fresh cilantro, including the stems

1. To make the sauce, heat the vegetable broth and sugar together in a small saucepan over medium-high heat. Stir until the sugar is dissolved and well blended with the broth and bring to boil. Stir in the tamarind sauce and soy sauce, reduce the heat to maintain a simmer, and cook, stirring a few times, until the sauce begins to thicken, 3 to 5 minutes. Cover and set aside, off the heat.

2. To make the tofu squares, pour the oil into a large, deep skillet and heat over medium-high heat to 360 degrees F. (To test the oil temperature, dip a wooden spoon in the hot oil; it should bubble and sizzle around the bowl of the spoon.) Fry the tofu squares, a few at a time, turning them after about 1 minute on each side, until puffy and golden brown on all sides, about 6 minutes total. Remove with a wire skimmer or slotted spoon and drain on a baker's rack with paper towels placed underneath.

3. Gently rewarm the sauce, if necessary. Transfer the fried tofu to a serving platter and sprinkle with the scallions and garlic chips. Top with the cilantro. Serve hot, with the tamarind sauce on the side.

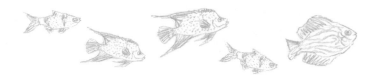

Side Dishes

GRILLED SCALLIONS WITH
THAI CITRUS SPLASH

BANGKOK-TO-BALI BEER-BATTERED
ONION RINGS

FILIPINO-STYLE POTATOES ADOBO

GOLDEN MASHED POTATOES

GRILLED SWEET POTATOES WITH
SPICED COCONUT CREAM

YARD-LONG BEANS THAI'D IN KNOTS

BRAISED BABY BOK CHOY

GARLICKY GREENS

GRILLED MARINATED PORTOBELLO MUSHROOMS
AND VEGETABLE CRUDITÉS WITH
HEAT WAVE DIPPING SAUCE

SAUTÉED OYSTER MUSHROOMS

STEAMED BROCCOLI WITH SOY AND SESAME

STIR-FRIED CAULIFLOWER WITH
GARLIC, GINGER, AND LIME

ASPARAGUS WITH SRI RACHA–SHALLOT
VINAIGRETTE

CHILLI-BUTTERED CORN ON THE COB

HOT 'N' COOL CUCUMBER RELISH

BANGKOK-TO-BALI BANANA CURRY

COINTREAU AND PALM SUGAR-GLAZED PINEAPPLE

The essence of From Bangkok to Bali

in 30 Minutes is to help you get many tempting new flavors to your table in record time with simplicity and ease. This chapter of side dishes will show you some of the quickest and easiest ways possible.

First, you can use these recipes as opportunities to easily try out new flavors on your family and friends. Just add a Bangkok-to-Bali side dish to a family meal or dinner party, alongside more familiar recipes, inviting anyone who would like a home-cooked dish with the flavors and fragrance of the great cuisines of Southeast Asia.

Corn on the cob, that all-American favorite, is also a favorite street snack throughout Southeast Asia. Our version, Chilli-Buttered Corn on the Cob (page 254), showcases one of the many uses for Thai Red Curry Paste (page 292) in everyday dishes. It's the foundation for the chilli butter, slathered over boiled or grilled corn on the cob. Golden Mashed Potatoes (page 242) are absolutely delicious, subtly spiced with garlic, turmeric, and cayenne, then mellowed with soft butter and hot milk so even the most cautious, conservative eaters will want to give them a try. Grilled Sweet Potatoes with Spiced Coconut Cream (page 243) will be a revelation for everyone who is weary of the gooey, overdone, candied sweet potatoes from holiday dinners past. When you're planning a barbecue, and a simple little salad will hardly compete with the tasty morsels of meat and fish

coming off the grill, these savory sweet potatoes will come to the rescue—in minutes.

Speaking of barbecues and salads, you'll want to try the Southeast Asian classic we call Hot 'n' Cool Cucumber Relish (page 256), which is made with crisp, fresh cucumber slices bathed in a tangy sweet-and-sour vinegar dressing and tossed with crushed peanuts and fresh cilantro. It's a traditional accompaniment to grilled meat satés, curries, and fried rice, and equally at home with roast chicken, crab cakes, and fried fish.

Another thing we hope this book conveys is an understanding of how Southeast Asian chefs and home cooks think about putting a meal together. Throughout the countries whose cuisines inspire these recipes, there is an artistic passion for balance and harmony at the table. Cooks and chefs want to present counterbalancing opposites of taste, color, and texture: the crunchy with the soft, for example, or the spicy with the mild, or the hearty with the delicate, as well as vivid colors contrasted with muted ones. Exciting contrasts can exist within an individual dish, and also between the various dishes being served.

These side dishes provide an easy way to achieve balance and contrast at mealtimes, whether you pair them with other Asian dishes or with your Western favorites. They will give you a wide range of provocative flavors, textures, aromas, and visual appeal, adding a measure of artistry to any meal you serve. Cointreau and Palm Sugar–Glazed Pineapple (page 258) makes a succulent combination with roast pork, beef short ribs, or fried rice. Garlicky Greens (page 246) and Steamed Broccoli with Soy and Sesame (page 251) take only minutes to prepare and deliver a health-conscious, flavorful

approach to everyday vegetable dishes. Asparagus with *Sri Racha*–Shallot Vinaigrette (page 253) is crunchy and sharp, while Bangkok-to-Bali Banana Curry (page 257) turns a familiar item from the fruit basket into a lush, homey side dish perfect for everything from grilled or fried fish to pork chops or spicy curries.

Grilled Scallions with Thai Citrus Splash

*T*his is one of our favorite side dishes for a barbecue. It goes with just about anything you might want to grill—chicken, fish, steaks, you name it.

Scallions are featured here, but the accompanying Thai Citrus Splash is delicious on any grilled or steamed vegetables.

3 bunches scallions

THAI CITRUS SPLASH:

5 tablespoons fresh lime juice

1 tablespoon Asian fish sauce

1 tablespoon finely chopped fresh cilantro, including the stems

$1/8$ teaspoon cayenne pepper

1 tablespoon light brown sugar

Peanut or vegetable oil for brushing

Salt and freshly ground black pepper to taste

Cayenne pepper to taste

1. Trim the scallion roots and about one third of their green tops.
2. To make the citrus splash, mix the ingredients together in a small mixing bowl and stir until the sugar is dissolved and blended into the mixture.
3. Preheat an outdoor grill, or preheat a grill pan for 3 to 5 minutes over medium-high heat. Brush the grill rack or pan well with oil.
4. Place the scallions on the rack or pan and season them with salt and pepper. Grill until charred and wilted, 5 to 7 minutes, turning once or twice.
5. Transfer the grilled scallions to a medium-size serving dish. Pour the citrus splash over the grilled scallions, sprinkle with a little cayenne pepper, and serve at once.

Bangkok-to-Bali Beer-Battered Onion Rings

*H*ere's a foolproof way to encourage an enthusiasm for Southeast Asian flavors among the conservative eaters in your family. The light spicing of the Bangkok-to-Bali Beer Batter will add an exotic note to a very familiar dish, and a wide range of dipping sauces and condiments can be introduced at the same time, for example, Tangy Citrus *Sambal* (see page 220), or ketchup mixed with *Sri Racha* Hot Sauce (page 81) to taste.

About 3 1/2 quarts peanut oil for deep-frying

3 large eggs, beaten

3 large yellow onions, sliced 1/4 inch thick and separated into rings

Bangkok-to-Bali Beer Batter (page 288)

1. In a deep, heavy pot, pour the oil to a depth of 3 inches and place over medium heat until it is very hot, about 375 degrees F. (To test the oil temperature, dip a wooden spoon in the hot oil. It should bubble and sizzle around the bowl of the spoon.)
2. Put the beaten eggs in a shallow dish and pour the batter into another one. Put as many onion rings as possible into the dish with the beaten eggs. Using a meat fork or tongs, lift an onion ring out of the eggs and dredge it through the batter, then lift it out and let the excess batter drip off. Carefully drop the onion into the hot oil. Repeat with additional onion rings, taking care not to crowd the pan, and fry until golden brown, turning once, about 3 minutes. Use the fork or a slotted spoon to transfer each fried onion ring to paper towels to drain.
3. Place in a basket and serve immediately.

Filipino-Style Potatoes Adobo

*A*dobo is a traditional, immensely popular dish in the Philippines. It's earthy, sharp, and mellow, all at the same time. Pork, chicken, and shrimp are what you'll usually find in an adobo sauce, but vegetables can also be simmered in its lusty flavors. We love making adobo with potatoes. Instead of stewing the potatoes in the soy and vinegar sauce, we pan-fry them a little in olive oil with the garlic and onions. They take on that home-fried texture and flavor we all love, and hold their shape as they simmer in the sauce. Distilled white vinegar and a little water is a perfect stand-in for the less acidic palm vinegar used in the Philippines.

3 tablespoons olive oil

2 bay leaves

1 large onion, thinly sliced

2 large cloves garlic, crushed and chopped

Salt and freshly ground black pepper to taste

1$\frac{1}{2}$ pounds Yukon Gold or other potatoes, peeled and sliced into $\frac{1}{4}$-inch-thick rounds

$\frac{1}{4}$ cup light soy sauce

$\frac{1}{4}$ cup distilled white vinegar

Pinch of sugar

2 tablespoons water

1. Place a large, heavy skillet over medium-high heat. When it is hot, add the oil. When the oil is hot, add the bay leaves, onion, and garlic, season with salt and pepper, and stir-fry just until the onion is translucent, about 2 minutes. Add the potatoes and cook, stirring often, until they begin to brown, about 5 minutes.

2. Add the soy, vinegar, sugar, and water. Stir to combine. Reduce the heat to low, cover, and simmer 5 minutes, then uncover and stir the potatoes up from the bottom. Cover and cook until the potatoes are soft and tender, but not mushy, 5 to 8 minutes. Serve hot.

Golden Mashed Potatoes

Serves 4

Mashed potatoes are a well-loved comfort food, and they lend themselves to many variations. These are enriched with butter and hot milk in the traditional American fashion, but are also subtly spiked with the pan-Asian flavors of garlic, turmeric, and cayenne. You could substitute paprika if you're serving the mashed potatoes with a spicy entrée. Using Yukon Gold potatoes will save you the time and effort of peeling them—the delicate skins of these potatoes almost disappear when you mash them, and the flesh is particularly creamy and tasty.

6 medium-large Yukon Gold potatoes, left unpeeled, quartered

2 large cloves garlic, peeled

2 tablespoons unsalted butter at room temperature

2/3 cup milk or half-and-half, heated

1/4 teaspoon turmeric

1 or 2 pinches of cayenne pepper or paprika, to your taste

Salt and freshly ground white or black pepper to taste

1. Place the potatoes and garlic in a large saucepan and add enough water to cover by 2 inches. Bring the water to a boil and continue boiling until the potatoes are fork-tender, 9 to 10 minutes. Drain well.

2. Add the butter and hot milk to the pan. Mash the potatoes, then beat with a wooden spoon until the mixture is well blended. Mix in the turmeric and cayenne, season with salt and pepper, and serve immediately.

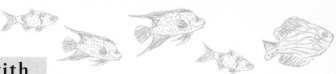

Grilled Sweet Potatoes with Spiced Coconut Cream

*I*f someone you know doesn't like sweet potatoes, these creamy, grill-marked beauties just might change their mind. The sugar melts into the butter, while the coconut cream topping merges with butter, sugar and spices, creating a tasty soup for dipping each bite as you enjoy the light smoky back note from the grill. You can parboil the sweet potatoes ahead of time, if you like.

1 pound small to medium-size sweet potatoes

1 tablespoon unsalted butter, melted

1 tablespoon palm sugar or light brown sugar

One 14-ounce can unsweetened coconut milk, chilled

1 whole star anise or $1/4$ teaspoon ground

$1/4$ teaspoon ground Saigon or regular cinnamon

1. Peel the sweet potatoes and halve lengthwise.
2. Bring a large saucepan of salted water to a boil over high heat. Add the potatoes and continue boiling until they are tender but still firm when pierced with a fork, 8 to 10 minutes. Drain in a colander and cool to room temperature.
3. Preheat an outdoor grill, or preheat a grill pan for 3 to 5 minutes over medium-high heat. Place the sweet potatoes on the grill and cook until nicely browned, 3 to 5 minutes total, turning once with a metal spatula so you have grill marks on both sides.
4. Transfer the sweet potatoes to a serving dish. Brush them with the melted butter and sprinkle with the sugar. Skim $1/2$ cup of the coconut cream from the top of the chilled can of coconut milk and spread it over the sweet potatoes. If using whole star anise, grate it over the top with a nutmeg or cheese grater to taste, or sprinkle the sweet potatoes with the ground star anise. Sprinkle with the cinnamon and serve hot or warm.

Yard-Long Beans Thai'd in Knots

*T*his is a keynote recipe that illustrates how easy it can be to make a culinary trip to Bangkok. It's a simplified version of a classic Thai salad that is traditionally made with lacy-edged winged beans. Here Chinese long beans (also known as yard-long beans) or green beans are substituted, and are equally delicious.

Yard-long beans can be found in Asian markets and in some large supermarkets. They actually are long enough to tie in loose knots.

1¼ pounds Chinese long beans or regular green beans, ends trimmed

3 tablespoons Chilli-Lemon Vinaigrette (page 294)

2 tablespoons Toasted Coconut (page 99), plus extra for serving

2½ tablespoons Crisp-Fried Shallots (page 100), plus extra for serving

1. Blanch the beans in a large pot of boiling salted water until crispy-tender, 3 to 4 minutes. Drain in a colander, refresh under cold running water, and drain again.
2. If using long beans, tie each one into a series of knots, about 1 inch apart. Cut between the knots so that each piece has a knot in the center.
3. Place the beans in a serving bowl. Pour on the vinaigrette and sprinkle with the toasted coconut and shallots. Toss gently to mix well and serve with toasted coconut and shallots on the side.

244

Braised Baby Bok Choy

ok choy is an Asian vegetable that Americans take to quite readily, once they've been introduced. It's much milder than the cabbage that's traditionally served in this country, and it goes well with various sauces and flavorings. Baby bok choy is the most tender, but mature bok choy will also give you delicious results.

2 pounds baby bok choy or mature bok choy
2 tablespoons extra virgin olive oil
^{1}/2 cup chopped red onion
^{1}/2 teaspoon salt
^{1}/2 teaspoon white pepper
2 tablespoons seasoned rice vinegar

1. Trim the base of the bok choy, then chop off the leaves. Cut the base in half lengthwise, then cut the halves crosswise on a diagonal into ^{1}/4-inch-thick strips. Cut the leaves crosswise on a diagonal into 1^1/2-inch-wide strips.
2. Place a large wok or a pot large enough to hold all the bok choy over medium heat. When it is hot, add the olive oil and rotate the wok or pot a bit to coat it evenly. When the oil is hot, add the onion and stir-fry until softened, 2 to 3 minutes. Add the bok choy and season with the salt and pepper. Cover and cook until tender, stirring occasionally, about 10 minutes. Stir in the vinegar and serve hot.

Garlicky Greens

*T*hese greens are simplicity itself, and bring home a good measure of healthfulness and vibrant flavor to boot. It's the kind of everyday dish that you'd find served in a Thai or Vietnamese home. You can use Asian or Western greens—in Thailand or Vietnam it might be water spinach or Chinese broccoli—but we seem to choose spinach every time. It's readily available and pairs well with most anything else you might be making for dinner. Choose perfectly fresh, crisp spinach that's a rich, deep emerald green in color. The other key to great results is a hot pan and lots of garlic.

2 pounds fresh spinach or other greens
3^1/$_2$ tablespoons peanut or vegetable oil
4 large cloves garlic, crushed and finely chopped
Salt and freshly ground black pepper to taste
1^1/$_2$ tablespoons Asian fish sauce

1. Trim and wash the spinach: Even prewashed, leaf-picked spinach needs the odd stem trimmed off and should be rinsed before cooking so some water is left clinging to the leaves. Strip the spinach leaves from their stems. (Discard the stems, or save for soup or vegetable stock.) Place the leaves in a colander and rinse under cold running water. You may need to do this in batches. Or plunge them in a basin filled with cold water, then lift out and drain. Whatever method you use, shake off the excess water and place the leaves in a large bowl, or just heap them on a countertop near the stove.

2. Heat a large wok or stockpot set over medium-high heat. When it is hot, add the oil and rotate the wok or pot a bit to coat it evenly. When the oil is hot, add the garlic and stir-fry just until fragrant and light golden, about 1 minute. Add the spinach, season with salt and pepper, and stir-fry until wilted, about 2 minutes. Add the fish sauce, stir, then cover and cook another 30 to 45 seconds.

3. Transfer the greens to a platter and serve immediately.

Grilled Marinated Portobello Mushrooms and Vegetable Crudités with Heat Wave Dipping Sauce

*H*ere's a dish that will introduce you to the Southeast Asian tradition of leisurely indulgence, a way of dining that involves dunking an array of vegetables and leafy greens into a fiery dip, along with fried fish or grilled meats. You simply dip one thing and then another, sometimes rolling up a few tidbits into a leaf-wrapped package for dunking or eating neatly, sometimes eating a bite without dunking, to clear the palate. This would be a great addition to a Western barbecue feast, a vegetable dish that can take equal billing with whatever tasty meat or fish comes off the grill.

6 large portobello mushrooms (about 1^1/$_2$ pounds), stemmed and caps wiped clean

2 tablespoons Asian fish sauce

^{1}/$_4$ cup plus 2 tablespoons fresh lemon juice

^{1}/$_4$ teaspoon freshly ground black pepper

6 hearts of romaine lettuce leaves

6 radicchio leaves (optional, see Note)

Vegetable oil for the grill

One 15-ounce can baby corn, drained

1 large red bell pepper, seeded and cut into ^{1}/$_2$-inch-wide strips

^{1}/$_2$ cup torn fresh Thai, sweet, or purple basil leaves

Heat Wave Dipping Sauce (page 84)

1. Arrange the mushroom caps in a shallow glass dish in a single layer. In a small mixing bowl, stir together the fish sauce, lemon juice, and black pepper and pour over the mushrooms. Turn the mushroom caps and spoon some marinade over the underside. Marinate for 15 minutes.

2. Arrange the romaine and radicchio in a fan shape at one end of a large serving platter. Set aside.

3. Preheat an outdoor grill, or preheat a grill pan for 3 to 5 minutes over medium-high heat. Brush the grill rack or pan with vegetable oil, and grill the mushrooms just until firm and brown, about 3 minutes on each side.

4. Transfer the mushrooms to a cutting board and let cool slightly. Cut crosswise into $1/2$-inch-thick slices. Heap the grilled mushrooms on the empty end of the platter and surround them with the corn and pepper strips. Shower the basil over the vegetables and serve immediately with the dipping sauce.

Note: If you don't want radicchio leaves, use 12 hearts of romaine instead of 6.

Sautéed Oyster Mushrooms

Serves 4

Where once only button mushrooms could be found, a wide array of cultivated mushrooms is now available in American supermarkets, including oyster mushrooms. They are widely cultivated in Asia, too. Pale gray and flat-topped, they often come with several caps attached to a common base, as they were grown. The whole mushroom "log" can be sliced and cooked.

This recipe exemplifies the Filipino way with vegetables, which are simmered in spiced coconut milk. You would typically encounter this method in a preparation of leafy greens, such as fresh spinach.

We first sauté the mushrooms with olive oil and garlic to bring out their best flavors. Then we stir in and reduce just enough coconut milk to create a light coating, scraping up all the toasty bits of garlic from the bottom of the pan to incorporate them into the sauce. To add a note of anise, both the fragrance and the flavor, we top these soft and mellow mushrooms with Thai basil.

3 tablespoons extra virgin olive oil

2 tablespoons finely chopped garlic

1 1/4 pounds fresh oyster mushrooms, wiped clean and cut crosswise into 1/4-inch-thick slices

Salt and freshly ground black pepper to taste

1/2 teaspoon ground ginger

1/2 teaspoon finely chopped small Thai or serrano chillies

1/2 cup canned unsweetened coconut milk

1/4 cup torn fresh Thai, sweet, or purple basil leaves (optional)

1. Heat the olive oil in a large wok or skillet over high heat. Add the garlic and mushrooms and stir-fry until the mushrooms begin to color, 5 to 7 minutes. Transfer the sautéed mushrooms to a large plate or bowl and season with salt and pepper.

2. Place the ginger, chillies, and coconut milk in the wok and bring to a boil over medium heat. Reduce the heat and simmer for about 3 minutes, scraping up the garlicky bits from the pan and stirring them into the mixture.

3. Transfer the mushrooms and their juices back into the pan and simmer just until heated through, 1 to 2 minutes.

4. Transfer to a serving dish and top with the Thai basil, if desired. Serve immediately.

We'll Always Have Ginger

Fish sauce and palm sugar keep well at room temperature in your kitchen cupboard—always at the ready when a recipe calls. Canned coconut milk keeps seemingly forever. But fresh ginger is seasonal, highly perishable, and too often offered in sorry condition by American supermarkets. This is especially vexing when you need some ginger for a recipe and only can find lightweight, wrinkle-skinned knobs.

Fortunately, there's a great way to keep fresh ginger on hand at all times. Whenever you do find smooth, plump, fresh ginger in your store, buy a sizable piece, perhaps big enough to fill the palm of your hand—whether you need it right away or not. When you get your ginger home, break or cut it into four to six chunks. Place them in a freezer bag, seal it well, and stash your ginger reserve in the freezer.

Whenever you need some fresh ginger, just take a chunk out, peel and grate as much as you need, and then return the unused portion to the freezer before it can thaw out. Substitute an equal amount of grated ginger for the minced fresh ginger your recipe calls for. Your secret stash can carry you through until the next time your market has plump and beautiful specimens, and you can replenish your ginger reserves.

An easy way to peel ginger, whether fresh or frozen, is by scraping off the skin with the edge of a spoon. You want to keep the skin on as long as possible to seal in the ginger's natural moisture.

Steamed Broccoli with Soy and Sesame

A simple dish like steamed broccoli takes on a real Southeast Asian flair with the addition of sweet dark soy sauce. Just that one essential ingredient lifts the dish to a sweet, yet earthy level of flavor. Sweet soy is both sweeter and mellower than the salty light soy sauce we're all familiar with. Molasses and sugar define its personality. It's a wonderful ingredient, worth seeking out in Asian markets.

If you want to keep this strictly vegetarian, simply omit the fish sauce. For added savor and crunch, sprinkle the finished dish with a handful of toasted sesame salt or rice powder.

2 pounds broccoli

2 tablespoons sweet dark soy sauce, or substitute 1$\frac{1}{2}$ teaspoons light soy sauce mixed with 1$\frac{1}{2}$ tablespoons pure maple syrup

4 teaspoons distilled white vinegar

1 teaspoon Asian fish sauce

$\frac{1}{2}$ teaspoon toasted sesame oil

Toasted Sesame Salt (optional, page 99) or Toasted Rice Powder (optional, page 98)

1. Trim the ends of the broccoli stalks. Cut off the florets at the base of their stalks. Pare the tough outer layer of the main stalk down to the moist flesh, then cut crosswise into thin rounds. Cut any oversize florets a little smaller to keep them nearly uniform in size for even cooking. Place all the broccoli pieces in a steamer rack or basket set over 2 inches of boiling water. Cover and steam until crisp-tender, 3 to 5 minutes.

2. Meanwhile, mix the sweet soy, vinegar, fish sauce, and sesame oil together in a small mixing bowl. Drain the broccoli and transfer it to a serving dish. Pour off any water from the plate. Pour the soy dressing over the broccoli and, if desired, scatter the toasted sesame salt or rice powder evenly over the top. Serve hot or at room temperature.

Stir-Fried Cauliflower with Garlic, Ginger, and Lime

Cauliflower dishes tend to be bland in both flavor and appearance, but here the flavors are bright and rich, and the color inviting. The wok-browned florets are showered with garlic chips, ginger, and chilli powder, then tossed with fresh lime juice for a piquant balance of flavors.

3¹/₂ tablespoons sesame oil (not toasted) or vegetable oil

1 large clove garlic, angle-cut into thin slices

1 tablespoon peeled and julienned fresh ginger

1 head cauliflower (about 1¹/₄ pounds), cut into 2¹/₂-inch florets

Salt and white pepper to taste

3 tablespoons fresh lime juice

Pure chilli powder to taste

3 tablespoons chopped fresh cilantro leaves

1. Heat a large wok or skillet over medium-high heat. When it is hot, add the oil and rotate the wok or pan a bit to coat it evenly. When the oil is hot, add the garlic and ginger and stir-fry until light golden brown, 20 to 30 seconds. Transfer to paper towels to drain and set aside.

2. Add the cauliflower to the hot oil in the pan. Season with salt and white pepper and stir-fry until the florets are nicely browned and crisp-tender, 10 to 12 minutes. Remove the pan from the heat and toss the cauliflower with the lime juice.

3. Transfer the cauliflower to a serving bowl and sprinkle with the fried garlic and ginger and the chilli powder. Top with the chopped cilantro and serve.

Asparagus with Sri Racha–Shallot Vinaigrette

We like to cook asparagus in a large sauté pan rather than a steamer. The spears lay flat in the boiling water and you can tell at a glance when they're cooked just right. The cumin-scented *sri racha*–shallot vinaigrette is a lush concoction based on a traditional olive oil and vinegar dressing. *Sri racha* is Thailand's favorite hot sauce—sweet, spicy, and heady with garlic. You'll also want to try this over salads or grilled vegetables.

Select tender, young asparagus whenever they're available.

2 tablespoons finely chopped shallots

1 tablespoon balsamic vinegar

$1^1/_2$ teaspoons aged red wine vinegar

$^1/_4$ teaspoon salt, plus 1 big pinch

1 pound asparagus

$2^1/_2$ tablespoons extra virgin olive oil

1 to $1^1/_2$ teaspoons *Sri Racha* Hot Sauce (page 81) or prepared *sri racha*,
  to your taste

$^3/_4$ teaspoon ground cumin

Freshly ground black pepper to taste

1. Put the shallots into a small mixing bowl with the vinegars and $^1/_4$ teaspoon of the salt. Stir and set aside while you prepare the asparagus.

2. Snap off the bottoms of the asparagus spears and discard. Peel the lower halves with a vegetable peeler.

3. Fill a large, deep skillet about two-thirds full of water. The skillet should be wide enough so the spears can be laid out flat. Add the remaining pinch of salt. Bring the water to boil over high heat, then lay in the asparagus with tongs. The asparagus tips can rise out of the water a bit, but keep the stalk

ends submerged. Return the water to a boil and cook until the asparagus is bright green and crisp-tender, 1 to 1½ minutes for thin spears, or more for larger spears; watch them closely.

4. Lift out the cooked asparagus with tongs and set them on a serving plate. Pour off any water from the plate. Tent the asparagus with aluminum foil and set aside.

5. Whisk the olive oil into the shallot mixture, then add the hot sauce and cumin and whisk until smooth. Uncover the asparagus, dress them with the vinaigrette, season with freshly ground black pepper, and serve warm or at room temperature.

Chilli-Buttered Corn on the Cob

Serves 4

This is a great example of why it's wonderful to have homemade curry paste on hand. Just a single ½-cup portion in your freezer lets you create sophisticated flavors in a hurry, such as the flavorful chilli butter in this recipe.

Any leftover chilli butter can be placed in a small, covered container and refrigerated for up to two weeks, though you'll probably use it up much sooner than that. Try it on grilled cheese sandwiches. Spread it on thick slices of French bread for dunking into soups or chowders. Melt a pat of chilli butter over fish just off the grill.

You can cook the corn in boiling water or grill it for additional flavor. Most people remove both the husks and corn silk before cooking. We prefer to remove only the thicker, looser husk leaves, leaving the corn in a tight sheath of tender leaves with the silk underneath. Cooked this way, either boiled or grilled, the corn is steamed by the moisture from the tender husks, intensifying its flavor. After cooking, the silk comes off easily with the husks.

If possible, buy your corn the same day you plan to cook it so it doesn't have to be refrigerated. The fresher and more tender the corn, the less cooking time it will need, and the more flavorful it will be.

If you use commercially made curry paste for the chilli butter, avoid the canned varieties. They're intensely hot and lack enough herbs and aromatics needed for flavor balance. Even the color is a bit dull. The curry pastes sold in plastic tubs are generally better, though never as good as homemade.

6 tablespoons (3/4 stick) unsalted butter, at room temperature
2 tablespoons Thai Red Curry Paste (page 292) or prepared curry paste
1 teaspoon salt
1 tablespoon fresh lime juice
8 ears sweet white or yellow corn, outer husks removed

1. In a small serving bowl, stir together the butter, curry paste, salt, and lime juice until well combined. Set aside.

2. If you're going to boil the corn, don't salt the water, as that would make the corn tough. Drop the ears, one at a time, into a large pot full of boiling water. Cook the ears about 1 minute.

   If using a grill, decide how intense you want the grill flavor to be. For less intensity, soak the corn in its husks for 1 or 2 hours, so the corn will steam on the grill. For the full grill flavor, do not soak them at all. Preheat an outdoor grill. When it is ready, lay the ears on the rack. Using tongs, turn them 2 or 3 times so they roast evenly as you grill, 8 to 10 minutes total.

3. When the corn is cooked, remove the remaining husks. The silk should come off readily at the same time. Place the corn on a serving platter and serve hot, warm, or at room temperature, with the chilli butter on the side.

Hot 'n' Cool Cucumber Relish

Throughout Thailand this sweet-and-sour relish, spiked with chopped chillies and crunchy with crushed peanuts, is a favorite accompaniment for barbecued chicken and fiery curries. It's also wonderful alongside corn fritters or to complement meat satés. You'll want to try it with everyday dishes such as grilled or fried fish, or turkey burgers.

The dressing can be prepared a day in advance, then chilled in the refrigerator. Wait until serving time to add the relish ingredients, so the cilantro will be fresh and bright, the peanuts crunchy, and the cucumbers crisp.

DRESSING:

3/4 cup distilled white vinegar

1/4 cup water

3/4 cup firmly packed light brown or white sugar

1 teaspoon salt

6 small pickling cucumbers or 1 pound large cucumbers

1 tablespoon finely chopped shallots or red onion

1 teaspoon finely chopped small Thai or serrano chillies

1/4 cup unsalted dry-roasted peanuts, crushed in a mortar or finely chopped

1/3 cup chopped fresh cilantro, including the stems

1. To make the dressing, combine the vinegar, water, sugar, and salt in a small saucepan over medium heat and bring to a boil, stirring to dissolve the sugar and salt. Boil gently 1 to 2 minutes, stirring occasionally. Remove the pan from the heat and let the mixture cool to room temperature. When cooled, transfer the dressing to a covered container and chill in the refrigerator until serving time.

2. Just before serving, peel the cucumbers and cut them in half lengthwise. If using large cucumbers, scrape out the seeds with a spoon. Cut the cucumber halves crosswise into ¼-inch-thick slices.

3. Combine the cucumber slices, shallots, chillies, peanuts, and cilantro in a serving bowl. Pour the chilled vinegar dressing over the relish, mix gently, and serve immediately.

Bangkok-to-Bali Banana Curry

When the natural sweetness of bananas is made savory with the addition of fish sauce and onion, then spiced a bit with curry powder, the result is ambrosial. Try it with roast pork or pork chops or as a mellow counterpoint to spicy Thai curries.

1½ teaspoons peanut or vegetable oil

1 large clove garlic, finely chopped

1 small onion, chopped

1¼ teaspoons curry powder

¼ teaspoon ground ginger

6 large ripe, but not soft, bananas, peeled and coarsely chopped

¼ cup Chicken Stock (page 289) or canned low-sodium chicken broth

1½ teaspoons Asian fish sauce

1. Heat the oil in a large skillet over medium heat. Add the garlic, onion, and curry powder and cook, stirring, for 1 minute. Increase the heat to medium-high and add the ginger, bananas, chicken stock, and fish sauce. Cook, stirring frequently, until the bananas become quite soft, but not mushy, about 5 minutes. The mixture should resemble a rough-textured, thick puree.

2. Transfer the banana curry to a serving bowl and serve warm.

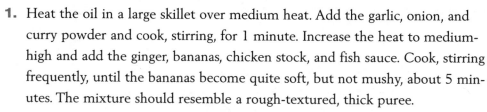

Cointreau and Palm Sugar–Glazed Pineapple

*T*hese grilled pineapple spears are a great sweet-and-savory accompaniment to fiery curries, grilled seafood, or roast pork. We've updated the typical rum-and-sugar baste with palm sugar, which adds a caramel note, and Cointreau, which contributes a more lively citrus spice.

1 firm, ripe pineapple (about 2¹/₂ pounds)

3 tablespoons Cointreau

2 tablespoons palm sugar or light brown sugar

1. Using a large, sharp knife, cut off the top of the pineapple. Trim away the pineapple's base just enough so the fruit can stand upright on the cutting board. Slice away the tough skin and green rind with a series of downward strokes. Remove any remaining traces of skin and rind, then use the tip of the knife to remove any "eyes" still attached to the fruit. Cut the pineapple lengthwise into 6 wedges. Cut the core out of each wedge. Score each wedge into 6 sections by cutting the flesh crosswise down to the rind, leaving each section attached at the base. Arrange the pineapple wedges on a baking sheet.

2. Combine the Cointreau and palm sugar in a small mixing bowl and stir with a wooden spoon until the sugar is dissolved. Pour the mixture over the pineapple wedges and let stand for 30 minutes to marinate.

3. Preheat the broiler. Broil the pineapple about 1 inch from the heat, without turning, until hot and lightly browned, 10 to 12 minutes. Serve warm or at room temperature.

Desserts

COCONUT JUMBLE MACAROONS

JASMINE RICE PUDDING WITH COCONUT CREAM
AND SAIGON CINNAMON

SILKY CARAMEL CUSTARD, FILIPINO STYLE

BANGKOK-TO-BALI KEY LIME PIE

SWEET CHEEKS OF CARAMELIZED MANGO WITH
VANILLA BEAN ICE CREAM

BANGKOK-TO-BALI BAKED APPLES

FRESH PINEAPPLE WITH SUGAR AND SPICE

ORANGE BLOSSOMS

GRILLED FRUIT KEBABS WITH SWEET SYRUP

GINGER-GLAZED GRILLED BANANAS

ICE CREAM SNOWBALLS

SAIGON CINNAMON ICE CREAM

THAI COFFEE GRANITA

GINGERED GRAPEFRUIT SORBET

COCONUT SORBET

SPIRITED PINEAPPLE-LEMON SORBET

Southeast Asians think of dessert quite

differently than we do. First, the region's consistently hot, humid climate has shaped preferences for light, refreshing dishes. And tropical Asia's lush abundance of fruit provides a perfect way to end a meal—with beautifully presented fresh oranges, mangoes, papayas, jackfruit, guava, mangosteen, cheremoya, rambutan, bananas, and pineapple. They are eaten simply, out of hand, or composed into fruit salads laced with spiced syrups, or carved into works of art as edible adornments to table or altar. Since most cooking in this part of the world developed from working over a fire rather than at an oven, baking isn't as well established as a cooking form.

More significantly, people in the Asian tropics love to combine the sweet and the savory in ways that would challenge the palates of most Americans. Therefore, we decided that the best approach for this chapter would be to develop signature Bangkok-to-Bali dishes that combine Asian flavor accents with Western forms. These desserts are delightful and surprising, but with a comfortably familiar feeling. These recipes have been chosen for their flavors and their ability to complement a tropical Asian meal, or even a traditional American one.

Bangkok-to-Bali Baked Apples (page 269), which you can serve warm or cold, are rich with ginger syrup and cinnamon. Our Key lime pie (page 266) pays homage to the fact that these limes, which we tend to associate with the Florida Keys, actually originated in Malaysia.

Despite the differences noted above, Southeast Asians have borrowed many things from traditional Western dessert cookery.

They are delighted by our puddings, custards, sorbets, and ice creams. Silky Caramel Custard, Filipino Style (page 264) is an adaptation of the flan recipes that Spanish traders and colonialists brought to the Asian tropics long ago. Jasmine Rice Pudding with Coconut Cream and Saigon Cinnamon (page 263) utilizes the favorite variety of rice in Southeast Asia, spiking it with plenty of the region's finest cinnamon.

Speaking of that much-loved flavor, Saigon Cinnamon Ice Cream (page 277) will introduce you to a quality of cinnamon that only recently has become available in the United States. Other ice creams and sorbets, all easy to make, also evoke the tropics with their lavish use of coconut, coffee, citrus, and pineapple.

Even though Southeast Asian desserts can be quite different from our own, many recipes in this chapter would be right at home in any of the countries whose cuisines inspired this book. They include Orange Blossoms (page 272), Grilled Fruit Kebabs with Sweet Syrup and Saigon Cinnamon Ice Cream (page 273), Fresh Pineapple with Sugar and Spice (page 270), and the always-pleasing Grilled Bananas (page 274). Despite the divide between how Westerners and Asians view dessert, there is also ample opportunity to merge and adapt, creating a mutual meeting ground, one that you will find is a delicious place to visit.

Coconut Jumble Macaroons

The secret within these chunky little macaroons is the use of unsweetened shredded coconut, found in natural food stores, instead of the less satisfying, sugar-laced coconut that supermarkets generally stock.

Studded with chocolate chunks and macadamia nuts, these no-fuss coconut jumbles are a great treat—especially when served with a rich, dark-roasted coffee, or a Vietnamese- or Thai-spiced brew.

3³/₄ cups unsweetened dried shredded coconut (about 12 ounces)

1 cup sugar

3 large egg whites

1¹/₂ teaspoons pure vanilla extract

¹/₄ cup plus 2 tablespoons semisweet chocolate chips

¹/₄ cup plus 2 tablespoons chopped macadamia nuts

1. Place the oven racks in the center and upper third of the oven. Preheat the oven to 350 degrees F. Line two cookie sheets with parchment paper or well-greased aluminum foil.

2. In a large mixing bowl, combine all the ingredients. Using your hands or a wooden spoon, mix well until the ingredients are thoroughly combined.

3. Drop heaping tablespoons of batter onto the prepared cookie sheets, spacing them about 1 inch apart. Dampen your hands with cold water and shape the cookies into loose haystacks.

4. Bake until golden brown, about 15 minutes, switching the cookie sheets between the top and bottom racks and rotating them 180 degrees halfway through baking.

5. Transfer the cookie sheets to wire racks to cool. Carefully peel the macaroons from the paper and store in an airtight container for up to 3 days.

Jasmine Rice Pudding with Coconut Cream and Saigon Cinnamon

Serves 6

*J*asmine rice, with its fine perfume and nutty flavor, makes a great rice pudding. We like it creamy and slightly runny, flecked with vanilla bean and dusted with Saigon cinnamon.

Folding in chilled coconut cream before serving gives this homey favorite a lush new persona. Chill the can of coconut milk while you prepare the pudding. The cream will be easily spooned from the top at serving time.

³/₄ cup jasmine rice

1¹/₂ cups water

Big pinch of salt

4 cups whole milk

¹/₂ cup sugar

¹/₂ vanilla bean, split lengthwise

One 14-ounce can unsweetened coconut milk, chilled

Ground Saigon or regular cinnamon for serving

1. Place the rice, water, and salt in a large, heavy saucepan. Bring to a simmer over medium-high heat, then reduce the heat to its lowest setting. Cover and simmer until the rice absorbs the water, 12 to 15 minutes.

2. Stir in the milk, sugar, and vanilla bean and cook, uncovered, over medium heat, stirring often as it simmers; adjust the heat as needed, especially near the end of the cooking. The pudding is done when the rice becomes soft and porridge-like, 30 to 35 minutes. Do not overcook or the pudding will become solid rather than creamy.

3. Transfer the pudding to a serving bowl, remove the vanilla bean, and press a film of plastic wrap onto the surface to prevent a skin from forming. The rice pudding can be served warm, at room temperature, or cold.

4. Just before serving, skim the thick coconut cream from the top of the chilled can of coconut milk and mix it into the pudding. Sprinkle with cinnamon to taste and serve.

Silky Caramel Custard, Filipino Style

*I*n Vietnam they make a French-style flan called *flan au caramel* with coconut milk in the custard. Filipinos learned about flan from the Spanish, who invented the dish. But they make it using canned evaporated milk, the dairy staple of the tropics, which actually makes the creamiest, silkiest flan.

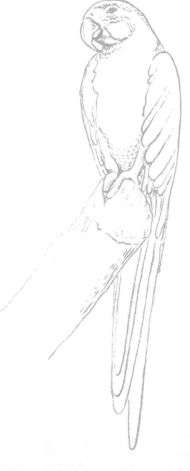

CARAMEL:

3/4 cup sugar

1/4 cup water

CUSTARD:

4 large eggs

1 large egg yolk

3/4 cup sugar

1/8 teaspoon salt

4 1/2 cups canned evaporated milk

2 1/2 teaspoons pure vanilla extract

1. Preheat the oven to 325 degrees F.
2. To make the caramel, combine the sugar and water in a small, heavy saucepan over medium heat and cook, swirling the pan by the handle, until the mixture becomes a clear syrup, 10 to 12 minutes. Do not stir. Reduce the heat to its

lowest setting and continue to cook, swirling the syrup occasionally, until it is golden brown and smells like caramel, 3 to 4 minutes. Immediately pour the caramel into a 2$^1/_2$-quart soufflé dish (see Note). Using a potholder, tilt the dish, swirling the caramel to coat the bottom and sides evenly (it should go about halfway up the sides). Let stand while you make the custard.

3. To begin the custard, in a large mixing bowl, whisk together the whole eggs and egg yolk just until blended. Mix in the sugar and salt and continue stirring until well combined. Set aside.

4. Heat the evaporated milk in a medium-size saucepan over medium heat until steaming hot, but do not allow to boil. Whisk the egg mixture briskly as you gradually add the hot milk. Stir in the vanilla. Pour the custard into the caramel-lined dish. Heat a kettle of water for the custard's hot water bath.

5. Arrange the pan on a roasting rack or cake rack set in a large roasting pan. The soufflé dish should not touch the sides of the pan. Place the pan in the hot oven and immediately pour enough hot water into the bottom of the pan to come halfway to two-thirds up the sides of the soufflé dish. Bake the custard in its water bath until the center is firm, 50 to 75 minutes. When done, it should quiver slightly if shaken, like a gelatin dessert, and a knife inserted in the center should come out clean. Do not disturb the custard while it is baking.

6. Carefully remove the pan from the oven. Using pot holders, remove the soufflé dish from the hot water bath. Press a piece of plastic wrap onto the surface of the custard and let cool for 30 minutes. Then refrigerate for at least 4 hours and up to 2 days.

7. To unmold, remove the plastic wrap and run a knife around the edges, then invert the custard onto a large serving platter. The platter for a large flan should be deep or wide enough to catch all the caramel. Serve cold.

Note: If you don't have a large soufflé dish, you can use an 8-inch-round x 2-inch-deep cake pan and four 4-ounce custard cups. Pour all of the caramel into the cake pan. Fill the pan about $^2/_3$ full of custard and divide the rest of the custard among the cups. Set the pan onto the center of the oven rack and space the cups evenly around it. The cups take 35 to 50 minutes to bake; the pan of custard, 45 to 70 minutes.

Bangkok-to-Bali Key Lime Pie

*L*imes and condensed milk are both widely used throughout tropical Asia, so it seems quite fitting to serve a version of this easy-to-make American favorite after a Southeast Asian meal.

The small, aromatic citrus fruits we call Key limes are actually indigenous to Malaysia. Also called Mexican or West Indian limes, they were brought to the Caribbean by the Spanish. The first groves in the United States were planted in Key West, so Amerians call them Key limes. They're turning up, increasingly, in fresh produce sections of well-stocked supermarkets, but you can also find the juice bottled.

Borden's created condensed milk in the 1850s, mainly for out-of-the-way communities where fresh milk just wasn't available. Since tropical Asia is not a dairy-producing region, condensed and evaporated milks were soon imported there for use in drinks and desserts.

Variations of Key lime pie include meringue toppings and various cookie or nut crusts. Some cooks bake their pies. We like ours the old-fashioned way, on a graham cracker crust, filled with a simple chilled custard and dollops of fresh whipped cream. The lime juice acts much as it does in a ceviche. It "cooks" the custard and eliminates the need for baking. You don't even need egg yolks. As long as the filling is properly chilled, just lime juice and condensed milk create a soft but sliceable pie.

A mortar and pestle is great for turning the graham crackers into crumbs, and so is a hammer.

PIE CRUST:

¹/₂ cup (1 stick) unsalted butter, melted

1³/₄ cups graham cracker crumbs (about 14 crackers)

3 tablespoons sugar

FILLING:

One 14-ounce can sweetened condensed milk

¹/₂ cup Key or regular lime juice (10 to 12 Key limes)

WHIPPED CREAM TOPPING:

1¹/₂ cups heavy cream, chilled

1 tablespoon sugar

¹/₂ teaspoon pure vanilla extract

1. To begin the crust, preheat the oven to 375 degrees F. Butter a 9-inch pie plate with some of the melted butter and set aside. Combine the graham cracker crumbs, sugar, and remaining melted butter in a medium-size mixing bowl. Press the buttered crumbs evenly into the bottom and up the sides of the pie plate to form a crust. Bake until lightly browned, about 8 minutes. Remove the crust from the oven and set on a wire rack to cool to room temperature.

2. Whisk the condensed milk and lime juice together in a medium-size mixing bowl just until combined. Pour the filling into the prepared crust quickly, since the mixture will begin to thicken immediately. Refrigerate the pie for at least 3 hours before serving.

3. Just before serving, put the cold heavy cream, sugar, and vanilla in a well-chilled large mixing bowl. Beat the mixture with a whisk or an electric beater on high speed just until the cream holds soft peaks. Do not overbeat. Decorate the pie with large dollops of the whipped cream and serve immediately.

Sweet Cheeks of Caramelized Mango with Vanilla Bean Ice Cream

*T*he plump rounded sides, or "cheeks," of ripe mangoes take beautifully to a sweet caramel glaze. Here they are gently sautéed, then served warm from the pan, snuggled up to scoops of Vanilla Bean Ice Cream.

The hot pan juices make the best ice cream topping ever—a warm, rich, fruity caramel sauce that hardens on contact with the cold ice cream.

2 large ripe but not soft mangoes
1/4 cup (1/2 stick) unsalted butter
1/4 cup plus 1 tablespoon sugar
1/4 cup plus 1 tablespoon fresh lime juice (about 3 limes)
Vanilla Bean Ice Cream (see page 275) or premium vanilla ice cream

1. Peel the mangoes. Hold a mango on end, stem side up, and cut down one side of the fruit, sliding the blade next to the flat pit, to release one cheek. Repeat on the other side, then cut all the fruit from the two ends. Repeat with the second mango. Julienne the fruit from the ends and set aside. Leave the cheeks whole.

2. Put the butter, sugar, and lime juice in a large nonstick skillet and bring to a boil over medium heat, stirring to melt the sugar. Boil gently until the syrup begins to thicken and caramelize, 2 to 3 minutes.

3. Use a metal spatula to set the mango cheeks in the pan and return the sauce to a boil. Cook the mangoes until they are nicely glazed with the caramelized sauce, 3 to 4 minutes total, turning once and basting them with the sauce as they cook. Remove the pan from the heat.

4. To serve, fill 4 wide, shallow dessert bowls with a scoop or two of vanilla ice cream. Arrange a glazed mango cheek alongside the ice cream and top each portion with the reserved julienned mango. Spoon the caramelized pan juices over each serving and serve immediately.

Bangkok-to-Bali Baked Apples

We're willing to bet that you'll get requests for this sweet snack over and over again. It takes more than our usual 30 minutes, but most of the time the apples are baking in the oven and you're free to do other things—or to just take it easy!

4 large apples, such as Granny Smith, Rome Beauty, McIntosh, Gala, or
Golden Delicious
1¹/₂ teaspoons cold unsalted butter, cut into small pieces
¹/₂ cup Bangkok-to-Bali Sweet Syrup (page 294)
¹/₄ cup dried fruit, such as finely chopped dried mango, raisins, or dried cherries
¹/₄ cup chopped macadamia nuts
2 tablespoons water

1. Preheat the oven to 375 degrees F. Cut the top ³/₄ inch off each of the apples, reserving them for lids. Scoop out the cores with a melon baller.

2. Arrange the apples in an ovenproof dish. Dot them with the butter and pour the syrup into their cavities. Put the tops back on the apples. Sprinkle with the dried fruit and nuts, letting the excess spill into the pan. Add the water to the pan and bake, uncovered, on the center rack of the oven for 30 minutes. Baste the apples with the pan juices and bake another 20 to 25 minutes. They should be tender, but still hold their shapes.

3. Transfer to a dessert platter or bowl and serve warm, with the pan juices spooned on top.

Fresh Pineapple with Sugar and Spice

Serves 4 to 6

North of Bangkok, in the former capital of Ayutthaya, vendors sell this sweet, chilli-accented snack to visitors touring the ancient ruins. It's a perfect treat on a hot summer day, one that can go into an ice chest packed for the beach, to refresh and rejuvenate you after a long swim.

1 large medium-ripe pineapple
Juice of 1 lime
1 teaspoon sugar
1 teaspoon salt
1 to 2 small Thai chillies, to your taste, minced
$1/3$ cup chopped fresh cilantro, including the stems

1. Using a large, sharp knife, trim the pineapple's base just enough to allow the fruit to stand up on a cutting board. Cut off the top. Slice away the tough skin and green rind with a series of downward strokes. Remove any remaining traces of skin and rind, then use the tip of your knife to remove any "eyes" still attached to the fruit. Cut it into quarters lengthwise, through the core. Cut away the core from each quarter, then cut each quarter lengthwise into 1-inch-wide spears.

2. Arrange the pineapple spears on a serving platter like spokes in a wheel. Drizzle them with the lime juice. Mix the sugar, salt, and minced chillies together. Sprinkle the mixture over the pineapple, top with the cilantro, and serve.

Perfect Pineapple

*P*ineapple grows abundantly in the Asian tropics, with many local varieties to choose from, some as big as ten pounds. With such bounty, people in Southeast Asia grow up knowing how to choose the best pineapple. Most Americans need to learn that art.

The hallmarks of a ripe fresh pineapple are much like the qualities you'd want in a sweetheart: a well-shaped body that's neither too firm nor too soft, and gives just a little when gently squeezed. The big difference, of course, is that a pineapple should also have a bright topknot of leafy greens.

You'll notice that the color of the skin is not among these fine points. A golden hue is a pleasing sight, but a greenish fruit can be completely ripe, while a pretty yellow pineapple with no fragrance will simply not be flavorful. Hold the pineapple right up to your nose. You want to discover a sweet smell. Sour notes indicate that a pineapple is on its way downhill, losing flavor as it ferments. If a pineapple is too firm, but it meets all the other tests, just give it a day or two to soften. But once they've been picked, pineapples don't get any sweeter.

A perfect pineapple is cause for celebration, so here's a simple carving technique to present it in style. Using a large, sharp knife, trim just enough of the pineapple's base to let you stand the fruit up on a cutting board. Cut away the skin, slicing from top to bottom. Lay the pineapple on its side to cut off the skin around the top, leaving the leafy topknot in place. Now cut off any skin remaining around the base, then clear away all cuttings and give yourself an unobstructed work surface.

Look at the "eyes" of the pineapple's skin. You'll see that they can be connected in diagonal rows that spiral around the fruit. Starting from the top, cut a narrow channel that begins at one of the eyes and spirals toward an eye below it. Keep cutting in this way, removing the cuttings as you go, until you've cut a spiraling line all the way from the top to the bottom. Return to the top and cut another spiraling groove, parallel to the first. Continue in this way until you've cut away all the eyes. When you're through, the pineapple will stand up straight, topknot held high, with lines twirling around and around its body, a beautiful centerpiece for your table.

To serve the pineapple, simply cut it lengthwise into equal halves from top to bottom, right through the topknot. Lay the halves, curved side down, on a cutting board and cut a V-shaped channel in each to remove the tough core. Then turn the halves over and cut each one lengthwise into thirds, leaving the pieces still connected at the topknot. Holding the three pieces together gently, cut the pineapple halves crosswise into slices of whatever thickness you desire. Slide the two halves, now cut into chunks, onto a serving platter and serve at once.

Orange Blossoms

Serves 4 to 6

This simple, lovely, and refreshing dessert represents a typical post-meal offering you might be presented with in Vietnam or Thailand.

6 navel oranges, peeled
1/2 cup Bangkok-to-Bali Sweet Syrup (page 294)
Sprigs of fresh mint for garnish

Cut the oranges crosswise into 1/3-inch-thick rounds. Arrange these "orange blossoms" on a serving platter. Pour the sweet syrup over them, garnish with the fresh mint, and serve.

Grilled Fruit Kebabs with Sweet Syrup

G rilling fresh fruits intensifies their flavors—it caramelizes the sugars and turns the flesh soft, lush, and warm. These kebabs are irresistible, whether served with Saigon Cinnamon Ice Cream (page 277), Vanilla Bean Ice Cream (see page 275), or a premium brand bought at the market. And the sweet syrup plays off the natural fruit flavors with a haunting medley of exotic spices.

6 firm, ripe peaches, pitted and cut into 8 wedges per peach

5 firm, ripe plums, pitted and cut into 8 wedges per plum

10 firm, ripe apricots, halved and pitted

One 20-ounce can pineapple chunks, in their own juice, drained; or about 1/3 ripe
   pineapple, peeled, cored, cut into 1-inch chunks

Bangkok-to-Bali Sweet Syrup (page 294)

36 eight-inch bamboo skewers, soaked in cold water 30 minutes or more

1. Preheat an outdoor grill, or preheat a grill pan for 3 to 5 minutes over medium-high heat. Brush the grill rack or pan lightly with vegetable oil. Thread 4 assorted pieces of fruit onto each skewer.

2. Grill the kebabs in batches, turning once, until lightly browned and slightly softened, about 5 minutes. Transfer to a platter and serve with the sweet syrup on the side and, if you like, your choice of ice creams.

Ginger-Glazed Grilled Bananas

G rilled bananas make a delicious yet simple finale for an outdoor barbecue. You can also prepare them indoors in a grill pan or a ridged, cast-iron skillet. We love our grilled bananas with Coconut Sorbet (page 280), Saigon Cinnamon Ice Cream (page 277), or just straight from the grill, with an extra drizzle of the delicious, spice-infused syrup.

6 ripe, but still firm, bananas
Ginger Syrup (page 296) or Bangkok-to-Bali Sweet Syrup (page 294)

1. Peel the bananas and cut them in half lengthwise. Cut each half on a diagonal into 3 pieces.
2. Pour the syrup into a large, shallow baking pan and turn the banana pieces gently until all are coated with syrup. (You can hold the bananas in the syrup for an hour or so before grilling.)
3. Preheat an outdoor grill or preheat a grill pan for 3 to 5 minutes over high heat. Arrange the banana pieces crosswise on the grill rack, or place half of the pieces on the grill pan. Grill just until the bananas are marked on the bottom, then turn and grill just until the other side is marked, about 30 seconds for each side.
4. Arrange the bananas on a serving platter and serve with more of the syrup on the side, if there's any left over, and sorbet or ice cream, if you like.

Ice Cream Snowballs

*y*ou'll have a hard time finding anyone who won't love the crunchy bits and creamy mouthfuls of these rich vanilla ice cream balls rolled in toasted coconut. They're great when made with homemade vanilla ice cream.

To scoop a well-rounded ball, it helps to freeze the ice cream in a somewhat shallow square or rectangular food storage container. Then you can take a long pull across the surface to scoop up a neat, round ball.

VANILLA BEAN ICE CREAM:

³/4 cup sugar

3 cups half-and-half

3 vanilla beans

2 large eggs

1 recipe Toasted Coconut (page 99)

1. To begin the ice cream, in a large, heavy saucepan, combine the sugar and half-and-half. Split the vanilla beans lengthwise with a sharp knife. With the tip of a knife, scrape the beans from the pods into the mixture, and then drop in the pods. Stir over high heat until bubbles form at the edge of the pan, 5 to 8 minutes.

2. Meanwhile, in a large mixing bowl, whisk the eggs together until blended and continue whisking as you add the hot cream mixture in a slow stream. Pour the mixture back into the saucepan and cook over medium-low heat, stirring constantly and scraping down the sides and bottom of the pan for an even texture, until slightly thickened and an instant-read thermometer registers about 170 degrees F, 8 to 10 minutes. The custard should coat the back of a spoon. Do not let the mixture boil.

3. Pour the custard through a fine mesh sieve into a bowl. Set aside to cool, stirring occasionally. Chill, covered, with plastic wrap, until very cold, at least 3 hours.

4. Transfer the mixture to an ice-cream maker and freeze according to the manufacturer's instructions. Transfer the ice cream to a rectangular or square food storage container with a tight-fitting lid and put in the freezer until serving time. (If the ice cream is frozen solid, transfer it to the refrigerator for about 30 minutes before serving to allow it to soften slightly before you make the snowballs.)

5. To make the ice cream balls, use a full-size (about $2\frac{1}{2}$-inch-diameter) ice cream scoop, pulling the scoop across the length of the container to create nicely rolled balls. Release the ice cream balls onto a cookie sheet lined with wax paper and place it in the freezer until the ice cream balls are quite firm.

6. To make the snowballs, spread out the toasted coconut on a plate. Put an ice cream ball on the plate and roll it around, gently pressing the coconut flakes into its sides, until it has a nice, crispy coating. Repeat for all of the ice cream balls and serve immediately. If you're not serving all the snowballs at once, place some in a roomy covered container and refreeze for later.

Saigon Cinnamon Ice Cream

S aigon cinnamon, a high-quality cinnamon with a rich taste and fragrance, is now available in the United States. It has a sweet little zing and a brighter flavor than that of lesser grades of cinnamon found on most supermarket shelves. This ice cream is absolutely delicious on its own, and even more so when served with all-American desserts such as apple pie and peach cobbler.

You can speed up the recipe by quickly chilling the custard after you have mixed in the vanilla and cinnamon. Simply nest the bowl inside a larger one filled with ice and water. Stir often until the custard is cold, about 15 minutes.

3/4 cup sugar

3 cups half-and-half

2 large eggs

2 teaspoons pure vanilla extract

2 teaspoons ground Saigon or regular cinnamon

1. In a medium-size heavy saucepan, combine the sugar and half-and-half and stir over high heat until bubbles form at the edge of the pan, 5 to 8 minutes.

2. In a large mixing bowl, whisk the eggs until blended. Add the hot cream mixture in a slow stream, whisking constantly. Pour the mixture back into the saucepan and cook over medium-low heat, stirring constantly and scraping the sides and bottom of the pan for an even texture, until slightly thickened, 8 to 10 minutes. (It will register about 170 degrees F on an instant-read thermometer.) The custard should coat the back of a spoon. Do not let the mixture boil.

3. Pour the custard through a fine mesh sieve into a bowl. Add the vanilla and whisk in the cinnamon. Set the custard aside to cool, stirring occasionally. Chill, covered with plastic wrap, until very cold, at least 3 hours.

4. Transfer to an ice-cream maker and freeze according to the manufacturer's instructions. Serve when the ice cream is just frozen and still soft and smooth, or transfer to an airtight container and put the ice cream in the freezer to harden.

Thai Coffee Granita

Most attempts to enliven coffee's flavor with additives actually detract from the classic brew. But Thailand has truly managed to improve coffee's rich, natural taste. The secret is an unusual blend of corn, chicory, and sesame seeds. Brewed strong and dark, Thai-spiced coffee lends this granita a smooth, haunting flavor.

If you're not near a Thai market, you can substitute three cups of strong, freshly brewed coffee made from espresso or other dark-roast beans.

4 cups water
$^3/_4$ cup Thai ground coffee
$^1/_3$ cup plus 1 tablespoon sugar
1 cup cold heavy cream
$^1/_2$ teaspoon pure vanilla extract

1. Bring the water to boil in a large pot. Whisk in the coffee. Return the mixture to boil and remove from the heat. Cover and let stand for 10 minutes.
2. Pour the mixture through a fine mesh strainer, then through a coffee filter, to remove all sediment.
3. Measure 3 cups of the strained coffee into a medium-size mixing bowl. Add $^1/_3$ cup of the sugar and stir until it is dissolved. Let cool to room temperature. Pour the cooled coffee into two ice cube trays and freeze it.
4. Meanwhile, combine the cream, vanilla, and remaining tablespoon of the sugar in a chilled bowl and whip the cream until it holds soft peaks.
5. When the coffee is completely frozen, unmold the cubes and place them in a food processor fitted with a metal blade. Pulse just until coarsely ground. Spoon the granita into chilled wine goblets or sherbet glasses. Top with dollops of the fresh whipped cream and serve at once.

Gingered Grapefruit Sorbet

Makes 1 1/2 pints

*T*his sorbet could be made with pomelo, the pudgy, sweetly perfumed ancestor of the grapefruit. Occasionally you'll find pomelo in specialty markets here in the United States, but you can simply use juicy, sweet, pink grapefruits. This sumptuous, elegant blend of simple ingredients, highlighted by the grapefruit's tanginess and the candied ginger's sweet bite, makes a great finale for any meal.

1 cup water

1/2 cup plus 2 tablespoons sugar

1 tablespoon finely chopped crystallized ginger, plus 1 tablespoon (optional) for
   sprinkling on sorbet

1 1/2 cups strained pink grapefruit juice (about 2 medium-size grapefruits)

1 teaspoon fresh lime juice

1/8 teaspoon pure vanilla extract

1. Combine the water and sugar in a medium-size saucepan and bring to a boil, stirring occasionally. Continue to boil for 5 minutes.

2. Remove the pan from the heat and stir in 1 tablespoon of the crystallized ginger. Let cool to room temperature.

3. Stir in the grapefruit juice, lime juice, and vanilla. Cover with plastic wrap and chill until cold.

4. Transfer the mixture to an ice cream maker and freeze according to the manufacturer's instructions. Serve when the sorbet is just frozen and still soft and smooth, or transfer to an airtight container and put the sorbet in the freezer to harden.

5. Scoop the sorbet into dessert bowls and sprinkle with the remaining 1 tablespoon of crystallized ginger, if desired.

Coconut Sorbet

*T*his has some of the creamy richness of ice cream, thanks to the coconut milk, and yet it is a true sorbet because it has no cream or eggs. Vietnamese-style coconut sorbets often contain lime juice to balance the richness. We've added both lime and orange juice, and the zest of both fruits as well, for a pleasing roundness of flavor.

1 cup water
3/4 cup sugar
1 lime
1 orange
One 14-ounce can unsweetened coconut milk

1. Place the water and sugar in a medium-size saucepan and bring to a boil over medium-high heat, stirring until the sugar is well dissolved. Reduce the heat to medium-low and gently simmer for 5 minutes. Set aside to cool.
2. Grate the lime and oranges zests into a small bowl, then juice the lime and the orange, removing any seeds. Add the zest and juices to the cooled syrup, then mix in the coconut milk, cover with plastic wrap, and chill until cold.
3. Keep an eye on the mixture and transfer it to an ice-cream maker before the coconut cream rises to the top and hardens. Freeze according to the manufacturer's instructions. Serve when the sorbet is just frozen and still soft and smooth, or transfer to an airtight container and put the sorbet in the freezer to harden.

Spirited Pineapple-Lemon Sorbet

*H*ere's a sorbet that is lovely, tangy, and sweet, with an underlying hint of vodka. A perfect finish to almost any meal.

1 cup water

1/2 cup sugar

Grated zest of 1 lemon

2/3 cup pineapple juice

1/3 cup fresh lime juice (about 4 limes)

1/4 cup Absolut Citron Vodka

2 tablespoons finely chopped fresh or canned pineapple

1. Combine the water and sugar in a medium-size saucepan and bring to a boil over medium-high heat, stirring until the sugar is dissolved. Reduce the heat to medium-low and gently simmer for 5 minutes. Set aside to cool.

2. Combine the lemon zest, pineapple juice, lime juice, vodka, and chopped pineapple in a medium-size mixing bowl. Stir in the sugar syrup. Cover with plastic wrap and refrigerate until cold.

3. Freeze the mixture in an ice cream maker according to the manufacturer's instructions. Serve when the sorbet is just frozen and still soft and smooth, or transfer to an airtight container and put the sorbet in the freezer to harden.

Basics

These recipes will become very familiar

friends to you. They give you foundations on which to build beautiful meals, as well as tricks to keep up your sleeve for when you want to make something quickly that tastes as satisfying as a meal that took hours to prepare.

Most of the recipes in this chapter are absolutely traditional, while others are quite modern, showing an East-West intermarriage of culinary styles. Of those traditional recipes, a few—including Chicken Stock (page 289), Shrimp Chips (page 285), Thai Red Curry Paste (page 292), and Thai Green Curry Paste (page 291)—could simply be bought off the shelves of an Asian or American market. But in each case, we've given you the simplest way to produce the most flavor. When you make them at home from scratch, the results are going to be infinitely more pleasing. And with these great elements at hand, whenever it's necessary or just convenient to make a meal quickly, you'll be able to create rich and complex flavors almost instantly.

You may be pleasantly surprised to encounter a versatile, homemade flatbread recipe (page 286) in this chapter—perfect for quick wraps and roll-ups. In the many regions where you find a Muslim population, it's just as truly Asian as rice.

Speaking of wraps, it may take practice to master the delicate and pretty Egg Nets (page 287) you'll learn about in this chapter, but they're a great example of the Southeast Asian magic that turns a little extra effort into a great deal of added delight.

Some of the modern recipes will give you a way to introduce new tastes to your family and guests, alongside flavors they already

love. For example, our Bangkok-to-Bali Beer Batter (page 288) imparts a subtle Asian note to favorites like deep-fried shrimp, onion rings, and catfish. And those familiar dishes are great foils for the Asian sauces and condiments (pages 74–104) you'll want to try. Likewise, Bangkok-to-Bali Sweet Syrup (page 294) has many traditional and contemporary uses, and it brings a new flavor, star anise, to your table alongside the well-loved flavor of vanilla.

The Southeast Asian way of making salads creates lively balances of sweetness, tartness, and spiciness. Chilli-Lemon Vinaigrette (page 294) will introduce you to the healthful, oil-free kind of salad dressing people of tropical Asia use, and will give you a ready-made balance of flavors that can beautifully accent many dishes, even one as simple as sliced tomatoes, or a platter of grilled vegetables at your next barbecue.

Shrimp Chips

*H*ere's a quick favorite of Asian cooks—crispy, featherweight puffs made from tapioca, ground shrimp, and egg whites. They're served with drinks, with hors d'oeuvres, and as a "scoop" for eating salads. The chips are available in precooked form at Asian markets, but most Asian cooks prefer buying them in dehydrated form to keep on hand and fry just in time to serve them.

Before cooking, they resemble small rounds or large rectangles of dehydrated potato chips. Also labeled "prawn crackers" or *krupuks*, they swell to triple their size when they hit the hot oil. Freshly cooked shrimp chips may get a little soggy when kept in a container. If so, just open the lid and let them "breathe" a while. They'll become crisp once more.

Vegetable oil for frying

1¹/₂ cups small round dried shrimp chips (4 ounces)

1. Heat about 1¹/₂ inches of vegetable oil in a large wok or deep, heavy skillet set over high heat. Adjust the heat under the oil to maintain an even temperature of 350 degrees F. (To test the oil temperature, dip a wooden spoon in the hot oil. The oil should bubble and sizzle around the bowl of the spoon.) Add 3 or 4 rounds to the oil at a time, or 1 rectangular chip, if using the larger size. Using a slotted spoon, keep the chips immersed in the hot oil so they puff up and cook evenly, first on one side, then the other, about 10 to 12 seconds per side.

2. Remove the chips with a slotted spoon and set them on a flattened brown paper bag or paper towels to drain. When all the chips are cooked, serve immediately, or let them cool a bit, then store in zipper-top plastic bags at room temperature until serving time. Shrimp chips will keep for up to 4 days if kept sealed in an airtight container.

Malaysian-Style Flatbread

Known as *roti* throughout Southeast Asia, these round, slightly puffy grilled flatbreads are often served instead of rice, especially in countries where there is a Muslim influence. Thai people will often use *roti* instead of rice to eat their traditional curries. In Malaysia and Singapore, *roti* are used to scoop up both wet and dry curries. You can also eat *roti* as a sweet snack—just add a quarter cup of freshly grated or dried shredded coconut to the batter.

We enjoy making *roti* together. One of us flattens the little balls of the dough into rounds while the other pan-fries them. *Roti* for two!

1 cup unbleached all-purpose flour

1 teaspoon sugar

1 large egg, lightly beaten

3 to 4 tablespoons whole milk, as needed

1/4 cup (1/2 stick) unsalted butter, melted

1. Mix the flour and sugar together in a medium-size mixing bowl. Add the egg and mix well, then add the milk, 1 tablespoon at a time, kneading with your fingers to make a soft dough. Gather the dough into a ball and knead until it is smooth, about 2 minutes.

2. Divide the dough into 10 balls. On a floured board, roll out each ball to make a thin, round pancake 6 to 8 inches in diameter.

3. Heat a grill pan or heavy skillet over medium-low heat. Add about 1 teaspoon of the melted butter, just enough to grease the surface of the pan. When sizzling hot, fry the *roti* one at a time, about 1 minute on each side. The liquid within the dough will turn to steam, creating little bubbles as the *roti* cooks. Those areas will turn darker brown, while the rest of the flatbread should be a light golden brown. Repeat with the remaining dough and butter.

4. As the *roti* cook, you can place them in a low-heat oven or wrap them in aluminum foil to keep warm. Serve warm with any curry-style dish.

Egg Nets

These lacy nets of gently fried egg can be used to delicately wrap a variety of savory fillings. In the royal traditions of Thai palace cooking, they are paired with the filling from Stir-Fried Pork, Shrimp, and Coconut in Lettuce Leaves with Crushed Peanuts (page 68). Whatever savory filling you choose, your guests will love seeing it peek invitingly through the filigreed strands of egg.

As with pancakes, you may need to make one or two of these nets before the results are just right. With just a little practice, your egg nets will become fine and delicate.

6 large eggs, beaten
3 tablespoons water
Vegetable oil to brush the pan

1. Beat the eggs and water together in a pie plate or other shallow dish until blended.

2. Brush a 5-inch crêpe pan or nonstick frying pan with a little vegetable oil and set over medium-high heat until hot (sprinkle with a few drops of water; they should dance across the surface of the pan). Place your fingers flat in the egg mixture, then carefully wave your hand back and forth across the width of the pan, 5 to 6 inches above its surface, with unhurried, even strokes. Dip your fingers back into the egg mixture, then wave your hand across the pan again, this time crisscrossing the first set of strands. Repeat this method until you have three or four layers that form a lacy netting. Cook until the egg is set and lightly golden. It should be just cooked through, 2 to 3 minutes.

3. Use a metal spatula and gently loosen the net around the edges, then peel it from the pan and set it aside on a cookie sheet and lay a sheet of aluminum on top. Repeat to make about 18 egg nets in all. Now and then brush the pan with oil. Stack the finished nets on the cookie sheet between layers of aluminum foil.

4. Make a filling of your choice. Put 1 heaping tablespoon of the filling in the center of an egg net. (The amount of filling can vary, depending on the size of the net.) If using Stir-Fried Pork, Shrimp, and Coconut, top with a few bean sprouts and a small sprig of fresh cilantro. Fold in at the sides and place the bundle, seam side down, on a serving platter. Fill the rest of the egg nets and serve warm or at room temperature.

Bangkok-to-Bali Beer Batter

Makes about 2 cups

This multipurpose batter is unbelievably simple to make and delivers a fluffy yet crispy coating. The chilli powders and coriander give a subtle lift without overwhelming the good, simple, fried flavor. Although you'll discover many more uses of your own, there are recipes elsewhere in the book for beer-battered catfish (page 229), shrimp (page 63), and onion rings (page 240).

1 cup unbleached all-purpose flour

1 cup Thai or other full-bodied beer

1 teaspoon salt

$1/4$ teaspoon pure chilli powder

$1/2$ teaspoon cayenne pepper

$1/2$ teaspoon ground coriander

Place all the ingredients in a large mixing bowl and whisk or beat until smooth. For extra-crispy texture, let the batter stand for 30 minutes before use.

Chicken Stock

*T*his takes more than 30 minutes because it needs to simmer slowly. But the active time for the cook is not long at all, and the resulting aroma, plus the great usefulness of homemade chicken stock, make this one kitchen task that's tremendously rewarding. Chicken stock is a versatile comfort food that greatly improves homemade soups. Asian cooks keep a pot of it on hand to flavor stir-fries, noodles, and curries.

Though they are more expensive these days, chicken wings make a delicious stock, but chicken backs, necks, feet, or other meaty bones are good, too. Ask your butcher to save you the bones from the chicken breasts they debone. They make the most delicate stock of all.

3 pounds chicken wings or other chicken parts or bones

8 cups water

1 small onion, halved

3 cloves garlic, lightly crushed

1 small handful fresh cilantro sprigs, stems and all

1. Combine all the ingredients in a large stock pot and bring to a rolling boil over medium heat. For the next 8 to 10 minutes, skim off and discard any foam that collects on the surface.

2. Reduce the heat to low and let simmer, partly covered, for 1 hour.

3. Turn off the heat, uncover the pot, and let the stock cool. Pour through a fine mesh strainer into a smaller pot or heat-proof bowl. Discard all the solids and dregs. Cover and chill.

4. Before using, remove the fat that is now sitting on top of the stock. Chicken stock will keep for 1 week in a covered container in the refrigerator, and for 1 to 2 months in the freezer.

Tamarind Sauce

While we love the convenience of liquid tamarind concentrate, we make fresh tamarind sauce at home for a deeper flavor. This is the quickest method we know.

Tamarind pulp is sold in bricks in Asian and Indian groceries. Making the sauce from scratch can be a long and messy affair because those bricks of dried pulp must be soaked, strained, pressed, and strained again. Fortunately, we once saw a recipe by the great expert on Indian food, Madhur Jaffrey, which called for briefly simmering the pulp rather than soaking it. We found that by cutting the cooking time to a minimum and making a relatively small amount, the process became quite easy.

To keep fresh tamarind sauce on hand, see our method for making tamarind cubes on page 38.

One 1-pound brick wet, seedless tamarind pulp
2 cups water

1. Break off $1/2$ pound of tamarind from the brick and pull it apart with your hands into small pieces. Put the remainder in an airtight container and refrigerate.
2. Combine the tamarind and water in a medium-size saucepan. Bring to a boil over medium-high heat, then reduce the heat and let the mixture simmer for 10 minutes, stirring occasionally.
3. Place a large fine-mesh strainer over a medium-size glass or stainless-steel bowl. Pour the tamarind mixture through the strainer. Push down on the pulp with a wooden spoon to extract as much sauce as you can. Scrape off the puree clinging to the strainer and drop into the bowl. (Discard the fibrous pulp inside the strainer.) You should have about 2 cups of puree. Thin with a little warm water, about $1/3$ cup, for a more sauce-like consistency. You can store tamarind sauce in the refrigerator in a tightly sealed jar for 1 to 2 days, or freeze it (see page 38).

Thai Green Curry Paste

Green Thai curry paste is made with fresh chillies, rather than the sun-dried chillies used in making a red curry paste. Even though this curry paste is traditionally made searing hot, green curries are among the most sophisticated dishes—thanks to the Thai genius for complex, balanced flavors and their use of aromatic herbs and spices, such as fresh lemon grass and wild lime.

You can create a first-rate homemade curry paste whether or not you have the more exotic ingredients. Lemon and lime zest are good substitutes for fresh lemon grass and Kaffir lime peel, and anchovy paste precludes the need for dried shrimp paste.

Green curry paste is versatile. You can use it in chicken, beef, pork, and duck dishes and with all manner of fresh vegetables, fish, and shellfish. We like to make the curry paste with a combination of *phrik khee nu* (the small Thai chillies) and serranos, to create layers of varying heat and flavor. For a fiercely hot curry, use all *phrik khee nu*. For a moderately spiced green curry, just use serranos.

1 tablespoon coriander seeds

1 teaspoon cumin seeds

10 black peppercorns

1 teaspoon coarse salt

1 plump stalk lemon grass or 2 teaspoons grated lemon zest

1/2 cup finely chopped cilantro stems (from 1 bunch fresh cilantro)

1/2 cup sliced serrano chillies (about 8 large)

1 tablespoon sliced small green Thai chillies (about 8), or more to taste

2 1/2 tablespoons chopped garlic

2/3 cup chopped shallots

1/4 cup peeled and finely chopped fresh Siamese ginger (*galanga*) or regular ginger

1 tablespoon minced fresh kaffir or regular lime zest

1 teaspoon anchovy paste

1. Dry-roast the coriander and cumin seeds in a small skillet over medium-low heat until aromatic, about 3 minutes, shaking the pan often to avoid burning the spices. Transfer the roasted spices to a mortar or spice mill. Add the peppercorns and salt and grind the mixture to a coarse powder. Set aside.

2. If using fresh lemon grass, trim the root end and discard the tough outer leaves. Cut a 4-inch length from the bulb end, slice crosswise into thin rounds, and then mince.

3. Combine the minced lemon grass or lemon zest, cilantro stems, chillies, garlic, shallots, ginger, and lime zest in a food processor and process until a moist paste begins to form, stopping now and then to scrape down the sides of the bowl. Add the anchovy paste and the ground spices and process to a fairly smooth paste.

Freshly made curry paste can be refrigerated in a covered container for up to 2 weeks and in the freezer for up to 2 months.

Thai Red Curry Paste

Makes about 1 cup

Dried red chillies are the central ingredient of a red curry paste. They are soaked long enough to become soft, then mixed with herbs and spices. We like to use a mixture of large and small dried red chillies, depending on availability.

Red curries are paired with most meats and seafood and the paste itself has multiple uses. It's a key ingredient in Spicy Peanut Sauce (page 88), for example. Your creative instincts will probably suggest many other uses. Here's one worth trying: Spread a little bit of red curry paste, thinned with olive oil, on a big porterhouse steak before it hits the grill.

4 large dried red chillies, such as New Mexico or guajillo
1/2 cup small dried red chillies, such as chile de arbol or Japanese chilli

1 tablespoon coriander seeds

1 teaspoon cumin seeds

10 black peppercorns

1 teaspoon coarse salt

1 plump stalk lemon grass or 2 teaspoons grated lemon zest

1 tablespoon chopped garlic

1/2 cup chopped shallots or red onion

3 tablespoons peeled and finely chopped fresh Siamese ginger
    (*galanga*) or regular ginger

1 1/2 teaspoons minced fresh kaffir or regular lime zest

1 teaspoon anchovy paste

1. Stem the chillies and shake out and discard most of the seeds. Cut the chillies into 1-inch pieces with kitchen shears or a sharp knife. (Some cooks wear gloves while working with hot peppers. We simply wash our hands very well with soap afterwards.) Put them in a medium-size mixing bowl, add warm water to cover, and soak for 20 minutes.

2. Dry-roast the coriander and cumin seeds in a small skillet over medium-low heat until aromatic, about 3 minutes, shaking the pan often to avoid burning the spices. Transfer the roasted spices to a mortar or spice mill. Add the peppercorns and salt and grind the mixture to a coarse powder. Set aside.

3. If using fresh lemon grass, trim the root end and discard the tough outer leaves. Cut a 4-inch length from the bulb end, slice crosswise into thin rounds, and then mince.

4. Combine the minced lemon grass or lemon zest, garlic, shallots, ginger, and lime zest in a food processor and process until the ingredients are broken down and well mixed. Drain the chillies and add them to the food processor. Process until a moist paste begins to form, stopping now and then to scrape down the sides of the bowl. Add the anchovy paste and ground spices and process to a fairly smooth paste.

    Freshly made curry paste can be refrigerated in a covered container for up to 2 weeks and frozen for up to 2 months.

Chilli-Lemon Vinaigrette

*H*ere's a tangy and bright dressing made from just four ingredients. It's wonderful for salads and steamed or grilled vegetables. You can also mix it with a bit of mayonnaise for a delicious sandwich spread.

1/4 cup fresh lemon juice

1 tablespoon Asian fish sauce

1 1/2 teaspoons palm sugar or light brown sugar

1 tablespoon Thai roasted chilli paste (*nam phrik pao*), or substitute 1 teaspoon Chinese chilli-garlic sauce mixed with 1/2 teaspoon light brown sugar

1. In a small mixing bowl, whisk or stir the ingredients together until the sugar is dissolved and the vinaigrette is well blended.
2. Toss with your choice of salad greens or grilled or steamed vegetables and serve.

Bangkok-to-Bali Sweet Syrup

*I*ndian and Arab traders in the Strait of Malacca introduced Malaysians and Indonesians to many sweet spices such as nutmeg, cloves, cardamom, and cinnamon. Here, those spices infuse a syrup designed to win you over as much with its dreamy aroma as its tempting taste. It's positively ambrosial! Everyone swoons over the flavor this tropical concoction imparts to salads, drinks, desserts, and fruit.

In Thai kitchens they might augment this recipe with a pinch of salt—half a teaspoon or less. In Vietnam, they might add ginger preserved in sweet syrup.

¹/₃ cup fresh lemon juice

Grated zest of 1 lime

1 star anise

1 cinnamon stick, broken in half

6 cardamom pods, lightly crushed

1 vanilla bean

1¹/₃ cups water

1 cup sugar

1. Place the lemon juice, lime zest, star anise, cinnamon, and cardamom in a small bowl.
2. With a small sharp knife, cut the vanilla bean pod in half lengthwise. Scrape out the beans and add them to the bowl, along with the pod halves.
3. Place the water and sugar in a medium-size saucepan and bring to a boil over medium heat, stirring occasionally to dissolve the sugar.
4. Add the spice mixture to the saucepan. Reduce the heat to low and gently simmer, stirring occasionally, until the mixture has thickened slightly, 12 to 15 minutes.
5. Remove the pan from the heat. Strain the syrup through a fine-mesh strainer into a bowl and set aside to cool. Pour the cooled syrup into a container with a tight-fitting lid, cover, and chill in the refrigerator until ready to use. It will keep for up to 2 weeks.

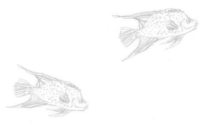

Sugar Syrup

Sugar syrup, also called simple syrup, is a simmered blend of water and sugar. It has the advantage of sweetening drinks smoothly and instantly. Thais use it for iced tea and coffee or to make simple desserts such as orange segments in a bowl of crushed ice, bathed in sugar syrup.

1 cup sugar
1 cup water

Combine the sugar and water in a small saucepan and bring to a boil over high heat. Reduce the heat to low and gently simmer until the sugar dissolves and the liquid thickens, about 5 minutes. Set aside to cool. The syrup can be used immediately, or stored for an indefinite amount of time in the refrigerator in a covered container.

Ginger Syrup

Makes 1 cup

We concocted this for the Malay Tiger cocktail (page 42), but it has lots of other tasty applications as well. You can mix it with your morning orange juice, spoon it over fruit salads, or blend it into fruit smoothies. And if your nightcap of choice is a nice glass of milk, a little ginger syrup adds to the comfort level.

1 cup sugar
1 cup water
2/3 cup coarsely chopped unpeeled fresh ginger

1. Place the sugar, water, and ginger in a medium-size saucepan and bring to boil over medium heat, stirring occasionally to dissolve the sugar. Reduce the heat to low and simmer, stirring occasionally, until the mixture has thickened and the syrup tastes strongly of ginger, 15 to 20 minutes.

2. Remove the pan from the heat. Strain the syrup through a fine mesh strainer into a bowl and set aside to cool. Pour the cooled syrup into a container with a tight-fitting lid, cover, and chill in the refrigerator until ready to use. Ginger syrup will keep for about 2 weeks in the refrigerator.

Rose Syrup

Makes about 1 cup

In tropical Asia, cold drinks are often made from sweet syrups. The Indonesians love to blend rose and tamarind syrups with coconut milk or water and crushed ice. We use Rose Syrup in our Burmese-style drink, the Rangoon Rose Cooler (page 34). It is also wonderful over fruit sorbets, Coconut Sorbet (page 280), or Vanilla Bean Ice Cream (page 275).

The palm sugar adds a complementary, vanilla-like flavor to the rosewater in this syrup. Sometimes called rose flower water, rosewater is found in the ethnic section of most supermarkets and comes in 3-ounce bottles.

^{1}/$_3$ cup palm sugar or light brown sugar
1 cup water
3^1/$_2$ tablespoons rosewater

Combine the sugar and water in a small saucepan and bring to a boil over high heat. Reduce the heat to low and gently simmer until the sugar dissolves and the liquid thickens, about 5 minutes. Set aside to cool. Then stir in the rosewater. The syrup can be used immediately or stored indefinitely, tightly covered, in the refrigerator.

Sources

A Taste of Thai
527 University Avenue
San Diego, CA 92103
(619) 291-7525
www.atasteofthai.com

A wide range of staples, such as coconut milk, jasmine rice, rice stick noodles, fish sauces, curry pastes, chilli sauces, saté sauce.

The Chile Shop
109 East Water Street
Santa Fe, NM 87501
(505) 983-6080
www.thechileshop.com

Dried chillies and spices, including New Mexico–grown whole chillies and several native varieties of pure chilli powder, mild to extra hot.

Ethnic Grocer.Com
www.ethnicgrocer.com

Asian staples such as liquid tamarind concentrate from Thailand by Garden Queen.

Four Winds Growers
P.O. Box 3538
Fremont, CA 94539
(510) 656-2591
www.fourwindsgrowers.com

Dwarf kaffir lime trees.

Melissa's—World Variety Produce
P.O. Box 21127
Los Angeles, CA 90021
(800) 588-0851
www.melissas.com

Fresh exotics such as Key limes, green mangoes, baby corn, and yard-long beans. Fresh and dried chillies.

McCormick & Co.
211 Schilling Circle
Hunt Valley, MD 21031
(800) 6332-5847
www.mccormick.com

Gourmet Collection Saigon cinnamon.

Nichols Garden Nursery
1190 Old Salem Road NE
Albany, OR 97321
(800) 422-3985
www.nicholsgardennursery.com

Premium Vietnamese ground cinnamon. Seeds for Asian basils and baby corn. Herb plants, such as Vietnamese coriander.

The Oriental Pantry
423 Great Road (Route 2A)
Acton, MA 01720
(800) 828-0368
www.orientalpantry.com

Fresh chillies and kaffir lime leaves. Staples, including jasmine rice, sticky rice, *kecap manis*, and Vietnamese rice papers. Cookware.

Pacific Rim Gourmet
i-Clipse, Inc.
4905 Morena Boulevard, Suite 1313
San Diego, CA 92117
(800) 618-7575
www.pacificrim-gourmet.com

Staples, such as *sambal oelek*, star anise, rice
stick noodles, and seedless tamarind paste.
Herb seed, such as Thai basil. Cookware.

Pendery's
1221 Manufacturing Street
Dallas, TX 75207
(800) 533-1870
www.penderys.com

Dried chillies and pure chilli powders,
including New Mexico, and other spices.

Penzeys Spices
19300 West Janacek Court
Brookfield, WI 53008
(800) 741-7787
www.penzeys.com

Dried chillies, Chinese five-spice powder,
star anise, Vietnamese cinnamon.

Rishi Tea
820 East Chambers Street
Milwaukee, WI 53212
(414) 372-3214
www.rishitea.com

Rare and organic teas, such as Jasmine Pearl.

Seeds of Change
320 9 Richards Lane
Santa Fe, NM 87301
(888) 762-7333
www.seedsofchange.com

Organic seeds for Asian basils, serrano
chillies, bok choy, and baby corn.

**The Spice Merchant/Oriental
Cooking Secrets**
P.O. Box 524
Jackson, WY 83001
(307) 733-7811
www.orientalcookingsecrets.com

Asian staples, such as Vietnamese rice
papers, Thai tea, shrimp chips, light soy
sauce, palm sugar. Cookware.

The Thai Grocer
1430 North Bosworth Avenue, Floor 1
Chicago, IL 60622
(773) 988-8424
www.thaigrocer.com

Fresh ingredients. Staples, including Thai
roasted chilli paste, canned lychees, pickled
garlic, green peppercorns in brine, shrimp
chips, Thai coffees and teas. Two-tiered Thai
steam pots.

Vann's Spices
6105 Oakleaf Avenue
Baltimore, MD 21215
(800) 583-1693
www.vannsspices.com

High-quality spices, such as Saigon cinnamon
and Chinese five-spice powder.

Index